An Introduction to
Zen Training

Omori Sogen Rotaishi at his Kaido ceremony, October 1975. This was the ceremony that indicated recognition by the Rinzai Archbishops and Abbots of Japan that he is the direct dharma successor of the Tenryu-ji line of Rinzai Zen.

An Introduction to ZEN TRAINING

A translation of *Sanzen Nyumon*

Omori Sogen

Introduction by Trevor Leggett

Translated by Dogen Hosokawa
Roy Yoshimoto

TUTTLE PUBLISHING
•Boston •Rutland, Vermont • Tokyo

This edition published in paperback by Tuttle Publishing, an imprint of Periplus Editions (HK) Ltd., with editorial offices at 153 Milk Street, Boston, Massachusetts 02109.

Originally published in hardcover by Kegan Paul International in 1996.

Library of Congress Cataloguing-in-Publication Data
Omori, Sogen, 1904-
    [Sanzen nyumon. English]
    An introduction to Zen training : a translation of Sanzen nyumon / Omori Sogen;
    introduction by Trevor Leggett; translated by Dogen Hosokawa, Roy Yoshimoto.
        p. cm.
    "Originally published in hardcover by Kegan Paul International in 1996"--Copyright page.
    Includes index.
    ISBN 0-8048-3247-1 (pbk.)
    1. Meditation--Zen Buddhism. I. Leggett, Trevor. II. Hosokawa, Dogen. III.
    Yoshimoto, Roy Kenichi. IV. Title.

BQ9288.O4713 2001
294.3'4435--dc21   20011046464

Distributed by

North America, Latin America, and Europe
Tuttle Publishing
364 Innovation Drive
North Clarendon, VT 05759-9436
Tel: (802) 773-8930
Fax: (802) 773-6993
Email: info@tuttlepublishing.com
Web site: www.tuttlepublishing.com

Japan
Tuttle Publishing
Yaekari Building, 3F
5-4-12 Osaki, Shinagawa-ku
Tokyo 141-0032
Tel: (03) 5437-0171
Fax: (03) 5437-0755
Email: tuttle-sales@gol.com

Asia Pacific
Berkeley Books Pte. Ltd.
130 Joo Seng Road
#06-01/03 Olivine Building
Singapore 368357
Tel: (65) 6280-3320
Fax: (65) 6280-6290
Email: inquiries@periplus.com.sg

Indonesia
PT Java Books Indonesia
JI. Kelpa Gading Kirana
Blok A14 No. 17
Jakarta 14240 Indonesia
Tel: (62-21) 451-5351
Fax: (62-21) 453-4987
Email: cs@javabooks.co.id

07 06 05 04   7 6 5 4 3
Printed in Singapore

Designed by Ann S. Rose

Table of Contents

Acknowledgments

Finding *Sanzen Nyumon* ready to appear in English leaves us grateful to the many people who made it possible. The work of Tenshin Tanouye Rotaishi, Archbishop of Daihonzan Chozen-ji and dharma successor to Omori Rotaishi, has been foremost as he steadfastly insisted that the *kiai* or energy/spirit of Omori Rotaishi's words be of primary significance in the translation. We are grateful as well to Yoshie Omori for permission to translate her late husband's work from Japanese.

Trevor Leggett has been writing for almost forty years about the relationship between Zen and *budo* or martial arts and we have long relied upon his work in the teaching at Daihonzan Chozen-ji. We are honored that he consented to write a personal introduction to Omori Rotaishi and his text. Many years ago Jackson Morisawa first drew the figures that illustrate the principles of posture and breathing outlined in Chapter 3 and they have served us well as aids to teaching *zazen*.

Arthur Koga, Director of the Institute of Zen Studies, led the final push to get the manuscript into print. In this effort, he was assisted by Gordon Greene, Teri Kaneshiro, Kristine Khoo, Sandra Kunimoto, Beverly Mukai, Cheryl Okazaki, and Betty Whitmore. Neal Kunimura, a long-term supporter of our publishing program, provided the well-equipped setting in which Gregg Kam worked long hours to make the manuscript press-ready. Our thanks as well go to the numerous Dojo members who offered financial support over the last year of work.

Dogen Hosokawa Roshi, Abbot, Daihonzan Chozen-ji
Roy Yoshimoto

Omori Roshi's calligraphy carved in wood, "Daihonzan Chozen-ji," placed at the entrance to Daihonzan Chozen-ji/International Zen Dojo in Honolulu, Hawaii. The temple and accompanying lay organization were founded by Omori Roshi in 1972 as "a place of Zen training where persons of any race, creed, or religion who are determined to live in accordance with Buddha Nature may fulfill this need through intensive endeavor...." The name that Omori Roshi gave the temple, "Chozen-ji" means "to transcend the form of Zen." In October 1979, Omori Roshi established Chozen-ji as a *daihonzan*, the main temple and headquarters of a new line of Rinzai Zen, with Tanouye Tenshin Roshi as Abbot.

Canon

Zen is to transcend life and death (all dualism), to truly realize that the entire universe is the "True Human Body" through the discipline of "mind and body in oneness." Miyamoto Niten (Musashi) called it *Iwo no mi** (body of a huge boulder—going through life rolling and turning like a huge boulder); Yagyu Sekishusai named it *Marobashi no michi** (a bridge round like a ball—being in accord with the myriad changes of life). Besides this actual realization, there is nothing else.

Zen without the accompanying physical experience is nothing but empty discussion. Martial ways without truly realizing the "Mind" is nothing but beastly behavior. We agree to undertake all of this as the essence of our training.

All our students, strive diligently! Gentlemen of the Rinzai Honzan (Main Temple) in Japan, open your eyes to this and together let us send it out to the world.

Archbishop Omori Sogen Rotaishi,
Dated 1 October 1979

Note (*): For these phrases, Omori Rotaishi used old Japanese. The modern pronunciations would be *Iwao no mi* and *Marubashi no michi* respectively.

Painting of Bodhidharma by Omori Sogen

Foreword to the English Edition

The facing page shows a painting of Bodhidharma by Omori Sogen. The four characters on the left are *kaku-nen-mu-sho*, "Emptiness, no Holiness," the answer that Bodhidharma gave to the Emperor Wu of China when asked, "What is the first principle of Buddhist doctrine?" Omori Rotaishi frequently painted Bodhidharma, and the subject is particularly appropriate to this book.

Bodhidharma is the monk who traveled from India to China early in the 6th century. When he realized that the Emperor of China did not understand his answer, he entered the Shaolin Temple where he meditated for nine years. In the end, he successfully transmitted Zen to Hui-ke, known to us now as the Second Chinese Patriarch of Zen.

Omori Rotaishi was one of this century's foremost Japanese Zen Masters, calligraphers, and swordsmen. And of significance to us here in the West, he was the founder of Daihonzan Chozen-ji, the first *daihonzan* or headquarters temple to be established under canon law outside Japan. Chozen-ji and the accompanying lay organization, International Zen Dojo, were founded as "a place of Zen training where persons of any race, creed or religion who are determined to live in accordance with Buddha Nature may fulfill this need through intensive endeavor." Omori Rotaishi wrote this book thirty years ago because in Japan at that time, there was little available in print to describe the basic training principles of Rinzai Zen. We have found the same to be true today outside of Japan and have worked to bring out this translation.

We are honored that Trevor Leggett wrote the Introduction to this text, writing from his many years of knowing Omori Rotaishi in Japan. Like D. T. Suzuki, Mr. Leggett is one of an older generation who were able to grasp the essence of Japanese culture. He is unique in that, through his long years of severe training in *judo*, he understands the culture especially through his body and it is this solid understanding that Omori Rotaishi writes about here.

Tenshin Tanouye Rotaishi
Archbishop, Daihonzan Chozen-ji

The large temple bell at Daihonzan Chozen-ji, Honolulu. The bell, cast in 1966 at the famous Kyoto foundry of Takahashi Imono Kojo, is known as the Peace Bell as symbolized by the two doves placed at the top of the bell. The inscription reads:

Pray for the Eternal Peace of the World and for the
Everlasting Friendship between Honolulu and Kyoto,
1st January 1966, Gizo Takayama, Mayor of Kyoto, Japan.

Introduction

This is a translation of a well-known Zen training manual by a well-known modern master (*roshi*), Omori Sogen. The book is essentially practical. Omori Roshi repeatedly points out that injunctions and declarations, however exalting, without right practice are thinner than paper. In this book there are a few directions on practice, ones that usually are left for oral instruction, but there is no point in commenting on the practices. The book speaks for itself and comment is a dilution.

The reader who knows of the Buddhist No-self doctrine must be prepared for references to the True Self. Zen does not encourage philosophy, but it often uses such terms of the Mind-Only school of Buddhism, with which Japanese readers will have at least a bowing acquaintance. If its main thrust has to be summed up briefly for Westerners, it could be, "The True Self is the ultimate subject. The basis for all our illusions is the act regarding the objectifications of our own mind as a world independent of that mind which is really its source and substance."

A feature of the book is its freedom from the narrowness which tends to appear in many traditions—Eastern or Western, religious or secular—under the slogan of "In or Out, All or Nothing." Omori was a keen fencer, and first encountered this narrowness there. Yamaoka Tesshu had been a great fencing master of the nineteenth century. When his teacher found that Tesshu was also becoming interested in Zen and in calligraphy, he warned him against splitting his aim, saying "You will miss all the targets." But Tesshu persisted and became a famous master in all three fields. In the twentieth century, Omori was similarly warned by his fencing teacher, but he too went ahead and became famous in the same three fields.

He has shown an equally wide vision in the religious field. Father Kadowaki, a Japanese Jesuit, completed Zen training under Omori Roshi without needing to abandon his faith. Father Kadowaki went on to write a remarkable book, *Zen and the Bible*, which for many Christians has vivified their faith. When Omori first read the Bible and came to the passage in Exodus where Moses asks the voice in the burning bush, "Who shall I say has sent me?" he thought to himself, "Now we shall hear the name of God, something we have not yet heard." But the voice says, "I AM WHAT I AM; say I AM has sent me." Omori Roshi told me he was very impressed—it is pure Zen.

When Zen came from China, there were some changes as it mixed with a certain amount of Japanese culture and history. The Chinese monasteries, for instance, were mostly on mountains, remote from cities. The big Japanese monasteries are still called *honzan*, "mountain," though mostly they are found near or in a city. We can see from some of the incidents in this book that the Chinese pupils were not given systematic instruction, whereas in Japan there were strict schedules. The interviews with the Chinese masters were in public, whereas in Japan, the master and pupil face each other alone. Unlike in China, the warrior rated high on the scale of Japanese society. Many warriors were men of culture, poets and artists, with their work often illuminated by their Zen training. Musashi's carvings, for example, are now national treasures.

Some incidents that Omori uses to make his points can be surprising. Consider his story of Tesshu and the rats—such powers were practiced by warriors engaged in life-and-death contests, but accounts can always be brushed aside. They are attained by severe austerities—Tesshu did not lie down to sleep for years—but they are not the object of Zen as Omori Roshi makes clear. Why then are they mentioned? Because those who practice may experience something remarkable as a passing side effect of their training. If they have never been told of such experiences, they may become excited when it appears and disappointed when it goes. But if they have been told that such things are known, and not wanted, in Zen, they do not get disturbed.

Western-educated people often tend to look at the one-pointed conviction displayed in Zen stories with some reservations, fearing that conviction may be irrational fanaticism. This may be a disadvantage in confronting some of the crises which Zen deliberately produces. The West does not have the doctrine that one-pointedness in a pure mind produces infallible inspiration.

Where the Westerner may have an advantage is in his ability to stand alone, or at least in his ability to try to do so. Many Japanese shrink from the ringing declarations of George Bernard Shaw's St. Joan, "Yes, I am alone on earth . . . My loneliness shall be my strength" or from the final words of Henrik Ibsen's *Enemy of the People*, "Yes, I am alone. And because I am alone, I am the strongest man on earth!" Some Japanese think such a man is like a mere dot on a big piece of paper, but Omori Roshi was not afraid to be alone—"one against a million" as he says. Alone, he was not alone; the True Self was at one with them. But, as the saying goes, this was one man in a million.

I remember an interview at one of the biggest Japanese Zen training temples, an interview which was to decide whether I could enter for a short time. After I had passed a preliminary test (sitting alone in a huge hall for two hours before dawn, secretly watched to see whether I moved), the old master of novices said to me, "In Zen, you stand alone." Then he became silent. I thought, "Of course you stand alone," and waited for him to go on. After two or three minutes he did so. I later found that there was usually a reaction to these words, and he had been waiting for one from me. It was his big gun, so to speak, but this time the target was not there. (It was, for other guns later.)

The self-reliance based on individualism may, however, be accompanied by a disadvantage: the feeling of "I am good as you are, so my judgment is as good as yours." This triple-ringed egoism is a great barrier in Zen.

Omori Roshi explains his points carefully, so far as they can be explained at all in words. But he also expects students to see a point. His own clothes were simple but always clean and neat. When some hippies argued that this was not "natural," Omori said nothing but pointed to a nearby cat, busy cleaning and smoothing its fur.

I used to see Omori Roshi when I visited Japan every two or three years. He had a gentle voice and manner, but my Judo experience could recognize the long severe training that lay behind that. He made no attempt to impress any more than a rock or a willow does, but he was impressive. He never looked out of place. When he came to meet me in his simple priest's robes, he did not look out of place standing on the railway platform. In a garden, he did not look like a human visitor; he looked part of the garden.

Trevor Leggett
London, October 1995

Omori Sogen Rotaishi

Preface

It is said that Zen, though all the while professing that the essence of Zen cannot be captured by words and letters, abounds with literature. This may be so. Even Shakyamuni,[1] teaching the eighty-four thousand Buddhist doctrines continuously for forty-nine years, taught "say not one word." Likewise in our Zen sect, although we boast of having no words or phrases, we cannot help the profuse amount of literature because it expresses compassion or what we call "grandmotherly concern."

When I look for suitable books for prospective students of Zen meditation, however, most of the books I find seem to be inadequate. It is very hard to find any that I could recommend to meet their needs, primarily because there are very few books on zazen[2] written by competent practitioners. As far as I know, I wonder if there are any better books on zazen than *Zazen no Shokei*[3] by Kawajiri Hogin, a lay Zen Master of the Rinzai Sect of Zen Buddhism, and *Sanzen no Hiketsu*[4] by Zen Master Harada Sogaku of the Soto Sect of Zen Buddhism. Of these two books, the former is excellent, being concise and meeting every need of the student. However, it was originally published in the Meiji Era, and, to my great regret, it is very difficult to obtain nowadays.

For these reasons, I have come to write this book after hearing repeated requests even though it looks like this may be another addition to the useless Zen literature. In fact I am embarrassed that it will hardly bear comparison with either of the two books mentioned above. However, this book can be read as a record of my Zen training—an accumulation of my experiences, ranging from my earlier days, when I threw myself into the severe discipline of Seki Seisetsu[5] at Tenryu-ji as a lay student of Zen, to the later days spent as a training monk under the guidance of Seki Bukuo.[6]

However, not to be overly confident, I will be more than satisfied if this book can be used as a reference to prevent beginning students from going in the wrong direction.

Omori Sogen, Author
Early Spring 1964

View from the entrance of Daihonzan Chozen-ji, Honolulu. The Budo Dojo and Kyudo Dojo are on the left.

CHAPTER 1

Why Do Zazen

To Know Our True Self

We live day after day, year after year, sleeping and waking, crying and laughing, gaining and losing, slipping and falling. Why in the world do we live like this? Or, who is causing us to live this way? I think there are many people who go straight to their graves, consumed by their careers, without ever taking time to ask such questions. There are, however, many others who become so obsessed with such doubts and questions that they find it difficult to work. While some might say that such reflection is a pastime of the idle, we might also say that our essential difference from other animals is found in our drive to consider such problems.

If we were living in Europe during the Middle Ages, when people were regarded as servants, or even slaves, of God, we might be able to solve all of our problems simply by convincing ourselves that God's will is responsible for all the phenomena and events of our lives. Today, however, most people are no longer satisfied by that approach. Even school children would start laughing if they heard us say that our tears and laughter, wins and losses, were caused by a God in Heaven. They would say that these things are our own doing. No doubt the majority of adults are even more likely to think that we ourselves are creators, and that gods and Buddhas are products of our own minds.

For now, set aside the question whether such a way of thinking is right or wrong. When we ask, "What is the Self?," we find that we do not know our True Self. Most of us look at ourselves as limited in time and space to what we Japanese call the "fifty-year life span and five-foot body." Such a view is fine, of course, if people could live their entire lives in peace, without problems and without questioning. But, for most people, this peace never exists. Despite all the changes in practice and doctrine, this is the reason that religion has not completely disappeared from the surface of the earth.

We often compare the state of our minds to that of our stomachs. When we are in good health, we forget that our stomachs even exist. But, as soon as we have a stomachache, we are continually conscious of the pain there. This happens because we don't pay attention to our bodies until we become ill. Only then, for the first time, we become conscious of the part that is ailing. In the same way, as long as we live in peace and good health, we are not even conscious of our own selves. Nor is there a need to be conscious.

However, in the course of our long lives, we experience grief and pleasure, joy and sorrow, ups and downs. At times, we may shrink back from the pain of living and despair at the uncertainties of life. There may be times when we are discouraged by the limits of our strength and feel the need to

ponder such questions as, "What is life?," "What is the truth of human existence?," or "What is the Self?" Feeling uncertain about our own existence—
the "fifty-year life span and the five-foot body"—we begin to despair. It is there
and then that religion comes to our rescue as a prescription to restore us to
health.

For thousands of years scholars have been discussing religion.
Although they differ in the details, generally they seem to agree that the
essence of religion is becoming one with infinity while living in this finite
world and finding eternity in every moment of this changing life. When we feel
insecure about our existence and find no solace in our small selves, we are
driven by an unbearable feeling to become one with the "Eternal" and united
with the "Absolute."

With regards to the methods of attaining the essence of religion, there
are generally two types as described by Imazu Kogaku:[1] the meditation type
and the prayer type. The prayer type of religions are characterized by the idea
that the Whole (God) exists outside the one who prays. In the meditation type,
the individual is regarded as primarily identical with the Whole (God). This
distinction is easy to understand.

In the prayer type of religion, it is natural that theology and philosophy must be regarded as indispensable subjects of study in order to prove the
existence of God and to describe God's relations with human beings. On the
other hand, in the meditation type of religion, the study of theology and philosophy is not essential.

In Zen meditation, for instance, students are expected to be individually awakened to their primal oneness with Buddha (the Whole) through the
actual experience of *samadhi*.[2] Students need a teacher to guide them in the
proper practice of meditation, to interpret the experience of that state of being,
and to show them the proper discipline in the affairs of daily life. For these reasons, records of the lives and teachings of Zen masters are highly valued.

I do not think it necessary to deal with prayer-type religions here, but
I would like to write further about the meditation type of religion. For example, the founder of Rinzai Zen, Rinzai Gigen (Lin-chi I-hsuan)[3] often said, "On
your lump of red flesh is a true person without rank who is always going in
and out of the face of every one of you." The "lump of red flesh" refers to the
body; the "true person without rank" refers to all categories of men and
women—rich and poor, young and old. To put it another way, it refers to the
true person who cannot be limited by the categorization or measurement of
the everyday world. We may say that the true person pertains to the Whole just
as the body pertains to the individual. In other words, Rinzai is saying, "All of

you, look carefully at the individual that is your body. Isn't the Whole that is unlimited by anything also found there?" Recognizing that an individual is by nature the Whole is what Imazu means by the meditation type of religion.

In this way, the Whole is not any God, Buddha or Absolute Being apart from the Self. It is the individual that is fused to the Whole. Here we can know that the individual is that which is fused to the Whole, and the Whole is that which is fused to the individual. In this sense, when we learn that this lump of red flesh, this five-foot bag of dung, is really infinite and eternal, unlimited by anything, we are liberated from our limited viewpoints. What we call the source of human personality—the True Self—is said to be this kind of eternal existence, yet it does not exist outside the living body. The realization of this fact is the essence of the meditation type of religion. At the same time, it is the way of human self-realization in Rinzai Zen.

In Zen we often use the phrases, "to die the Great Death" and "to be reborn to the True Self." I think these words truly express the character of Zen. "To die the Great Death" is to root out ideas and beliefs we commonly accept, such as having a "self," and to negate the small self or the ego. "To be reborn to the True Self" is to affirm the Whole and our true selves without ego. To phrase this in terms of one sect of Buddhism,[4] it may be called the exalted life of the Absolute Buddha. Therefore, in Zen one awakens to one's True Self and takes firm hold of it. To give life to one's True Self sufficiently in all the affairs of daily life and to practice living as a human being while purifying the entire world is perhaps the most complete way of saying it.

If this is Zen, it should be clear what problems Zen addresses in the modern world. "Human alienation," "loss of self," "human development," and "restoration of autonomy" are now popular phrases. In fact, we may say that there has never been a time when Zen has been needed as much as today when solutions to these problems are so urgently needed.

Now, Here and I

Let us accept that there are two types of religious methods: the prayer type and the meditation type. I will discuss the meditation type and how it can help us to seek the unlimited within the limited and to touch the eternal in the moment.

In the T'ang Dynasty of China, there lived a Zen man named Kyosho Dofu (Ching-ch'ing Tao-fu.)[5] In his youth, he trained diligently under Zen Master Gensha Shibi (Hsuan-sha Shih-pei)[6] but for some reason, Zen realization always seemed to be beyond his grasp. One day, seeking guidance, Kyosho spoke to his teacher about this. At that moment, Gensha heard the murmuring of the mountain stream and asked,

> "Do you hear that sound?"
> "Yes, I hear it," Kyosho replied immediately.
> "You should enter Zen from there," instructed Gensha.

Is limitless Zen in the murmuring of the mountain stream? Or is it that at the moment Gensha heard the rushing sound of the water, he touched the eternal? Rinzai often said, "Right here . . . before your eyes . . . the one who is listening to this lecture." In other words, "Right now at this very moment, who is the one listening to this lecture?" Can we say that this is the infinite eternal Buddha? If we think of it in a shallow fashion, I am afraid it would only mean living on the impulse of the moment the way dogs and cats do. Therefore, I must add the following explanation, though it may be redundant.

It is often said that truth is something that is universally valid. To put it simply, it is something which can be applied anytime, anywhere, and to anyone. For instance, fire is hot no matter what time it is. Fire was hot thousands of years ago as surely as fire will be hot hundreds of years from now. Of course fire is hot today. Furthermore, fire is hot in America, and it is hot in Russia as well as in Japan. Fire is hot no matter where it is. Moreover, fire is hot to you, to me, and it will burn anyone who touches it. In this way it is true that fire is hot anytime, anywhere, and to anyone. Therefore, the fact that fire is hot is recognized as an indisputable truth.

Let us see just where that fire which is hot anytime, anywhere, and to anyone exists. Can you see that it is nowhere except in theory and has nothing more than an abstract existence? It is not the real fire which will burn your hand if you touch it. Similarly, that which does not have universal validity anytime, anywhere, and for everyone is no more than a partial and arbitrary view of things; what is universally valid in itself is abstract and conceptual and cannot be real and concrete.

The reality that would satisfy the thirst deep within our minds and hearts is not found in abstraction. We are not ghosts. How could anything abstract which is valid anytime, anywhere, and for everyone become a religious objective which would actually relieve our thirst?

If Rinzai's "right now, before your eyes, the one who is listening to this lecture" does not become the concrete "now, here, I," it will not have an active life in reality. On the other hand, if it is merely "now, here, I," it is no different from the impulsive way of living only for the moment in the world of dogs and cats, or even earthworms and maggots. There is not one speck of human dignity or freedom of personality in that. The eternity of "anytime" shines in this moment "now" while the unlimitedness of "anyplace" is manifested in the limits of "here." When the universality of "anyone" dances out in the individual "I," for the first time you have the world of Zen.

It may be said that Zen uncovers the form of one's True Self in the experience of oneness in this physical body. In terms of time, there is eternal life without birth and death. In terms of space, there is infinite light with no limit in space. I think this is what Priest Gensha taught his young disciple Kyosho when he expressed the anguish of his inability to gain a foothold in Zen.

Budo Dojo, Daihonzan Chozen-ji, Honolulu. The calligraphy is by Omori Sogen Rotaishi. The swords to the right of the *Butsudan* are used for training in the martial arts.

Omori Roshi's *enso* engraved in marble, Daihonzan Chozen-ji. The circle does not represent anything in the conventional sense of the word but it can be said to mean "absolute."

CHAPTER 2

The Aim of Zazen

For some years now, interest in Eastern culture, especially in Zen Buddhism, has been increasing among people in Europe and America. Not only are Westerners reading books on Zen, but the number of those who actually attempt to sit in meditation has grown as well. If we consider that the founding patriarch of Zen, Bodhidharma,[1] was called a "blue-eyed barbarian monk" and that Shakyamuni Buddha also belonged to the Aryan race, it could be said that Zen meditation originated in the West. Even in Japan, as talk of human development becomes more widespread, the number of young men and women who do zazen is rapidly increasing.

As Zen teachers we are truly grateful for this trend, both within Japan and in the West. But once we examine people's reasons for sitting, we find that they are extremely varied and sometimes not necessarily sound. Therefore, our joy over the trend cannot be unqualified. It cannot be said that all of those who knock at the gate of Zen for the first time aspire to understand the essential meaning of Zen.

When we read newspaper and magazine articles about the health benefits of putting strength in the lower belly while sitting, or statements like "zazen is good for your health," we may expect that many readers who are sick and weak will immediately take up zazen as a way to good health. Also, as the world becomes increasingly chaotic and confused, anyone can easily become spiritually tired and prone to neurosis. Therefore, surely there must be many who sit in meditation as a kind of mental therapy.

When I reflect upon my own experiences, they are now so vague that I cannot recall what my purpose was when I first began Zen training. I do recall that in grade school I read a story about a man named Oki Teisuke. It said in one passage that Teisuke had the wits scared out of him when a strange young man doing zazen "in icy silence" suddenly shouted at him. After being told that this spiritual forcefulness was fostered by Zen training, Teisuke himself began to train. I remember not knowing the word "Zen" so I would often look it up in dictionaries and ask people its meaning. But I still did not understand it, and it always remained in back of my mind. Years later that may have been what led me into Zen.

Certainly Zen teachers of long ago heard of students using Zen for good health and spiritual renewal or heard of students training in Zen because they were fascinated by the power of scaring the wits out of someone with one shout. But they must have wept at the thought of Zen being used this way.

Deciding clearly why you study Zen is an important question, one that will determine whether you succeed in Zen training or go astray. This is the main reason why Zen teachers have always insisted upon this point. The traditional instruction is, "If one does not have true resolve to attain enlightenment, all of one's efforts will be in vain." That is true in any learning, not only in Zen. Just as you focus on a target before you aim an arrow, if you focus your mind and decisively determine the direction in which you are going, you are already halfway there. This means that "for what purpose . . . ?" is a question of great importance.

In the first section of the classic text *Zazen-gi* it is said:

> Bodhisattvas who study *prajna*-wisdom[2] must first have deep compassion for all beings and a deep longing to save all of them. They must practice *samadhi* meditation with great care. Refusing to practice zazen only for their own emancipation, they must promise to ferry these sentient beings over to the other shore.[3]

From a different perspective, though, we must recognize that lecturing about the significance of resolve and focus will probably be in vain when dealing with those who know nothing of Zen. No matter what your purpose when you begin your training, it is the teacher's responsibility to guide you onto the proper path. For example, if a person starts off doing zazen for health purposes but then is able to receive proper guidance from a teacher, gradually that person will advance along the way, will start to see into his true nature, and may finally attain enlightenment.

TYPES OF ZAZEN

According to Harada Sogaku Roshi, there are two or three hundred kinds of Zen.[4] Even in Shakyamuni's day there were said to be 96 kinds of Ways, each cultivating a samadhi similar to that of Zen. Therefore, it could be said that there were 96 different types of Zen within early Buddhism.

But Ways for the cultivation of samadhi are found not only in Buddhism. In one type of Confucianism, particularly Sung Confucianism, "quiet sitting" was practiced. In the Western tradition, Protinus, Eckhart, and even Jesus are said to have engaged in a kind of "quiet sitting." Their meditation may have been similar to zazen. In the Shinto rite of pacifying divine spirits there is something called "sinking the freely-moving spirit into the center of the body." Some people say this is a kind of Zen.

In addition, in those performing arts and martial arts that are concerned with the integration of mind and body, acts are carried out—at least to a small degree—with mind and body in oneness. The realm of samadhi is in all of them regardless of small differences between them. Nanin Roshi[5] is said to have commented while watching an acrobat ride a ball in Asakusa, "If he became one with the universe with a spin of the ball, that would be splendid Zen." This means that there should be a connection even between acrobatics and Zen. Thus to put it in extreme terms, it is logical to say that there are as many kinds of Zen as there are human beings.

There are various ways of classifying types of Zen but the most representative is considered to be the five types discussed by the 9th century Chinese Zen Master Keiho Shumitsu (Kuei-feng Tsung-mi.)[6]

Zen Outside the Way (*Gedo Zen*)
Common Zen (*Bompu Zen*)
Small Vehicle Zen (*Shojo Zen*)
Great Vehicle Zen (*Daijo Zen*)
Supreme Vehicle Zen (*Saijojo Zen*)

To Master Shumitsu, our self-nature—"the original mind," "one's True Self," or "the root of one's personality"—has exactly the same nature as Buddha. It is something that originally was universal and not limited by anything; thus it makes no distinction between sacred and profane. However, just as there are different starting points for climbing Mt. Fuji, there are shallow as well as profound starting points for Zen training. Because of this diversity there is no escape from the development of several types of Zen.

Gedo Zen (Zen Outside the Way), the first type listed, is best considered as a Way apart from the principles of Buddhism. In terms of substance it means seeing the Way or truth outside of yourself. Shumitsu defined Gedo Zen as religious discipline following teachings based on a perspective outside of Buddhism.

The phrase "perspective outside" is somewhat difficult to understand, but it probably means to determine superiority or inferiority by a measure that is separate from the Dharma,[7] to rejoice in the good and to detest the bad. Because the ego is the yardstick by which superiority and inferiority is measured, training in Gedo Zen means that the ego remains at the center of the act of accepting or rejecting. Consequently, no matter how far you train, you cannot leave the world of dualism.

The second type of Zen is Bompu Zen (Common Zen). According to Shumitsu, it entails "correctly understanding cause and effect though still training with the dualism of joy and loathing." In general, though expounding a belief that good causes bring good effects and bad causes bring bad effects, it is a type of training which does not embody any penetrating truth. Those who practice Zen to cure an illness or for the sake of their health should probably look at this type of Zen. In general, though, Gedo Zen and Bompu Zen are called "Zen in the midst of delusion."

The third type, Shojo Zen (Small Vehicle Zen), is training in which you are enlightened to the one-sided truth that the ego is empty and has no real substance. It describes training in which you think about the existence of truth or Buddha and then become trapped by your thoughts. There are various interpretations of Shojo Zen, but here I think it would suffice to simply interpret it as believing in the truth of Dharma but lacking in the altruistic spirit of sharing your understanding of Buddhist Truth with others. You are too intent on your own gain and think only of your desire for the perfection of your own personality.

As for the fourth kind of Zen, Daijo Zen (Great Vehicle Zen), Master Shumitsu called it training in which you are enlightened by the realization that the ego and the Dharma are both empty. It is training with the realization that subject and object, ego and the surrounding environment are all void. Training in Daijo Zen is like carrying many people on a large ship from this shore of delusion to the other shore of enlightenment, simultaneously emancipating oneself while rescuing others, and praying for the perfection of personality with self and others in oneness.

The fifth kind of Zen, Saijojo Zen (Supreme Vehicle Zen), can also be called *Nyorai Shojo Zen*. Master Shumitsu said that it is training through which one has a sudden realization that one's mind is originally pure, that from the beginning there is no suffering which arises from our attachment to desire. We are naturally provided with uncorrupted wisdom. This mind is Buddha and in the end nothing else. "Uncorrupted" is the condition in which our attachments to desires and passions are severed and we are enlightened to the fact that the mind we are born with is originally pure and unsoiled without one speck of desire. It is something absolute, the same as Buddha. In short, it may be said that Saijojo Zen consists of experiencing the Absolute, realizing the Absolute, and acting out the Absolute in our daily affairs.

In later periods, this kind of Zen became known as Patriarchal Zen. It was also characterized by the phrases "special transmission of the teachings outside the scriptures" and "no dependence on words."

While Master Shumitsu's classification of Zen may be understandable on the whole, it can be difficult to understand the distinction between Great Vehicle Zen and Supreme Vehicle Zen. It is natural that they should appear to be different if we choose to regard them as different, but on the other hand we may say that they are different in name only.

According to Zen Master Daikaku, "Zen is Buddha's inner mind."[8] He said, "If we train in the Dharma with one mind (an absolute non-discriminating mind), how much merit would that be when compared with training in the 10,000 acts of 10,000 goodnesses?" Furthermore, "Even if we train by performing the 10,000 acts, we cannot attain satori[9] without knowing the Dharma mind, just as it stands to reason that we cannot become Buddha without achieving satori." In other words, training based on the truth that "sentient beings are originally Buddhas" and deciding once and for all that "this very body is Buddha" is Supreme Vehicle Zen of the Correct Transmission of the Patriarchs or Patriarchal Zen.

Accordingly, if we put it in extreme terms, all types of Zen other than Patriarchal Zen are inauthentic. However, in a positive sense, it may be said that Zen Outside the Way (Gedo Zen), Common Zen (Bompu Zen), Zen of the Mouth and Head (Koto Zen), Literary Zen (Moji Zen), Zen for Health (Kenko Zen), Zen for Medical Treatment (Ryoyo Zen), and all the rest exist within the realm of Patriarchal Zen.

MISTAKEN AIMS

So many types of Zen have evolved because the talent and ability of students vary. There is a saying, "A cow drinks water and gives milk; a snake drinks water and gives poison." Although originally all water tastes the same, it becomes different when a cow drinks it and when a snake drinks it. Depending on your goal or motivation for training, Zen also changes, becoming Patriarchal Zen for some or Zen Outside the Way for others.

There is an amusing story about a man who was given a rare sword. He showed it to the priest at his family temple because he could not read the inscription on it. The priest read it as "Hahei Gyoan," which means "When the waves of the mind are calm, discipline is easy." But when he showed it to a scholar of Chinese he was told that it said "Nami tairaka ni shite yuku koto yasushi," meaning "When the waves are flat, traveling is easy." Finally he took it to a sword merchant who told him that the characters inscribed were those of a man named Naminohira Yukiyasu.[10]

Although none of them were mistaken—they all gave a possible reading of the inscription—no one was strictly in keeping with the intended meaning of the inscription. When people with only a shallow experience define Zen simply as a way to promote health or a way for human development, it is an embarrassment for Zen even though Zen has these aspects.

It is said that Zen exists in all the activities of daily living, such as doing, dwelling, sitting, and lying down, but here I am limiting its usage particularly to mean zazen. What should the aim of zazen be?

I have already said that Zen is the shortcut to knowing one's True Self. For human beings—limited in time and space to a fifty-year life span and a five-foot body—the aim of Zen is to touch the infinite life and the absolute world, to comprehend that such is one's True Self. To Shakyamuni, all sentient beings have the same essential nature as Tathagata.[11] However, they are not able to realize it because they see things upside down in delusion. But when we break through that delusion, the illusion caused by selfish desires and doubt, and come into contact with the Absolute for a fraction of a second, we realize our original True Self. This experience is called *satori* or *kensho*.[12] In short, this is awakening to one's True Self. It may be said that the aim of Zen is to have that kind of experience.

If we train in the correct manner, with the aim of awakening to one's True Self, will we ever stray off the right path and commit serious mistakes? Yes, it happens quite often. That is why students are traditionally cautioned to choose the right teacher.

I think the greatest mistake that those who practice Zen make is to think such phenomena as "self," "nothingness," and "emptiness" have a fixed existence. It is not only beginners who have delusions about such things. This is a characteristic of Western thought in particular and it is also a strong tendency in those who are engaged in modern scholarship.

A traditional story told about the early training of Zen Master Baso Doitsu (Ma-tsu Tao-i)[13] illustrates this mistake:

In his youth, Baso did zazen diligently every day. Seeing this, Priest Nangaku Ejo (Nan-yueh Huai-jang)[14] asked Baso, "What do you expect to accomplish by doing zazen?" Baso answered, "I sit because I wish to become a Buddha." He had forgotten that zazen itself is Buddhahood and probably was trying to become a Buddha through zazen. To demonstrate his mistake, the priest began to polish a roof tile vigorously while Baso was doing zazen. Baso became puzzled and asked, "What are you doing?" "I'm thinking of turning this into a mirror," replied Ejo. "Will a roof tile become a mirror if you polish it?" asked Baso. Priest Ejo glared at him and answered, "Can you become a Buddha by doing zazen?" Priest Ejo added, "If your carriage stops moving when you are on the road, do you hit the carriage, or do you strike the rump of the ox that is pulling it?" Baso did not know how to answer.[15]

There is a world of difference in the interpretation of this dialogue depending on whether we think it occurred before Baso attained satori or after he already was enlightened. Dogen Zenji[16] cited this story in a section of his *Shobo-genzo*, giving lavish praise to Baso's level of Zen realization. If we interpret the story as Dogen Zenji did, the meaning of it changes completely. For now, however, I will follow the traditional interpretation of it as a story of Baso's immature youth, in keeping with the surface meaning of the words.

From Ejo's viewpoint, he is warning Baso that thinking that the form of Buddha lies outside zazen and searching for it by means of zazen is misdirected, like wildly striking the cart instead of whipping the ox when the oxcart stops moving. Ejo continued his admonition:

> You students, are you trying to learn zazen or are you trying to learn sitting Buddhahood? If you are learning zazen, Zen is not sitting and lying down. If you are learning sitting Buddhahood, Buddha is not a fixed form. According to the teaching of non-attachment or non-settling down, you should not adopt this or reject that. You students, if you try to become a sitting Buddha you kill the Buddha, and if you become attached to sitting you will not reach that principle.[17]

If we interpret this literally it probably means the following:

> You students! Are you trying to learn zazen or are you trying to become a Buddha? If you are trying to learn zazen, you must not be taken up by the form called "sitting" because Zen is something beyond sitting and lying down. Again, if you say you are trying to become a Buddha, you cannot become a captive to the one set form called "sitting" because Buddha is something absolute.

Since that which is called "teaching the Dharma or the true principle" is not something which has substance, we cannot formally make distinctions between accepting or rejecting what is good and what is bad. If you students consciously try to become a Buddha you will grow more distant from Buddhahood. You cannot become a Buddha unless you kill the Buddha which is dualistically conceived as an object. Also, if you have been attached to the form of sitting, no matter how long you train you will not be enlightened to your True Self. This is probably what Ejo meant.

When you do zazen with the intention of seeking a Buddha with form or think of your true self as having a fixed existence, it is just like trying to turn a roof tile into a mirror by polishing it. I am afraid that as your samadhi power grows stronger, the more you will stink of Zen. This is because you forget to cut your ego and only paint more and more layers on it.

The next thing to be discussed is the misunderstanding that doing zazen is the same as entering the psychological condition called "no-thought" (*munen muso*). Two scientists at Tokyo University, Dr. Hirai Tomio and Dr. Kasamatsu, have made great progress in showing that the brain waves of Zen monks in samadhi resemble those of people in very light sleep.[18] Once the results of those experiments were published, many intellectuals suddenly became interested in Zen.

Such interest was heartfelt but most of these people seemed to decide that any practice that calms one's spirit must be similar to the practice of "no-thought" Zen. Of course that is not a bad thing; it is very welcome. Certainly the calming effect has been scientifically demonstrated by the measurement of brain waves and thus cannot be denied. I do not have the slightest intention of perversely contradicting them by saying that Zen excites rather than calms the spirit. However, if Zen is only for calming the spirit, would it not be more expedient to take tranquilizers or drink alcohol and pleasantly fall asleep than to sit for a long time enduring the pain in your legs?

These people simply misunderstood "no-thought." They are overlooking what Kanbe Tadao asked concerning zazen: "Doesn't a state of consciousness exist in Zen meditation which doesn't exist in the mere passivity and ecstasy found in Yoga?"[19] In Zen we think that state of consciousness is where the secret of samadhi concentration lies; zazen is not merely a discipline to lead us into the state of "no-thought."

This "no-thought" group paints on layer after layer of illusion as they try to become Emptiness or Nothingness, only strengthening their ego-centered viewpoint in the process. As a result they fall into the practice of the so-called "Zazen lacking dynamism" as described by Suzuki Shosan.[20] These people sit in meditation like a lifeless stone *Jizo*[21] in the mountains.

If we practice this type of zazen, perhaps to cure an illness or become healthy, it is not unlikely that we will end up frightened at even the sound of a rat's footsteps. This is all because our aim of zazen is mistaken. Suzuki Shosan is known to have once said to people training under him:

> You seem to practice "Empty Shell Zazen" and think that not thinking of anything is "no-thought, no-mind." You even start to feel good sitting vacantly. But if you do that kind of zazen you'll

lose your vigorous energy and become sick or go crazy. True "no-thought, no-mind" zazen is just one thing—to have a dauntless mind.[22]

At another time he said, "Since you cannot do real zazen no matter how much I teach you, I think I'll show you from now on how to use the vigorous energy you have when you are angry."

Even someone as great as Zen Master Hakuin[23] appears to have mistakenly thought that an empty state of mind was satori during the early years of his training. According to accounts of his life, he made a pilgrimage to Mt. Ii in Shinshu to see Dokyo Etan.[24] Seeing Hakuin's rampant pride, Dokyo grabbed his nose and said, "What's this? See how well it can be gotten hold of." At this Hakuin broke into a cold sweat and fell flat on the ground. There was also a period when Dokyo would abusively shout, "You dead Zen monk in a grave!" every time he saw Hakuin.

Even the famous Daito Kokushi[25] wrote in verse, "For more than thirty years, I, too, lived in the cave of foxes (the state of self-deception); no wonder people still remain deceived." Looking at this verse, even if the depth was different from Hakuin, Master Daito seemed to have found the realm of no-thought congenial for thirty years.

If we study Buddhist doctrines and write them out for ourselves, we may be able to keep from becoming inert. I think even I could write a few introductory articles in order to keep students from developing bad habits. But is there not a more direct way?

In the distinguished book *Zazen no Shokei* by the lay Zen Master Kawajiri Hogin, he writes, "Because zazen is training to realize the One Mind of yourself, it is a mistake to set up an aim outside of yourself . . . Not setting up an aim is the true aim."[26]

Ultimately, I think that the best way to avoid bad habits in Zen is to not set up your aim outside yourself but to return to yourself and examine the very place you yourself are standing. In order to do that without pursuing the past which has already gone by or facing the future which has yet to come, I think it best to examine whether or not you are confronting the absolute present which cuts off such notions as "before" and "after." The present moment has been compared to the geometrical one-dimensional point which eludes our attempt to grasp it. Can we appreciate the experience of that moment as it happens before any intellectual judgment or discrimination sets in?

It has been said that the word *majime* (seriousness, straightforwardness, honesty, and truthfulness) is derived from the phrase *ma o shimeru* (to close up the space-time in between).[27] If you move unconsciously—without any room for thoughts to enter between thought and conduct—that is always being in the present. There is a Zen expression, "We are always aware of the Threefold World (past, present, and future existences), the Past and Present, and the Beginning and End." It is necessary for us to examine ourselves to see whether or not we are in that state.

Next, having already discussed the oneness of thought and action, let us take up the same problem from a spatial point of view. This time I want to suggest that we examine ourselves to see if we are in *majime*, the state of mind and body in oneness—so well integrated that there is no room for even a single thought to enter. Further, you should see whether or not self and other—that is, self and strangers, self and family, self and society—are unified in the place called "here." In this place Self and object fuse and become one body in an experience known in Zen as "the boundless realm of time and space where not even the width of a hair separates self and other." If you reflect over what you experience when you are walking along a street or using chopsticks you will probably agree with what I have written.

There is a story about a man named Heishiro of Ihara that is traditionally told on the fifth night of the *rohatsu sesshin*.[28] Heishiro, watching bubbles of foam floating in a pool below a waterfall, observed that they all differed, some traveling one foot, some two or three feet, others even twelve to eighteen feet, but all eventually disappeared. He sensed in these bubbles the transience of life and was suddenly attacked by an uneasiness he could not stand. That night he entered the bathroom alone and did zazen in his own way.

At first he was almost overwhelmed by delusive thoughts attacking him as if they were a swarm of bees from a disturbed beehive. He was full of anxiety but he clenched both fists, opened both eyes wide and shouted, "Damn shit!" He struggled against delusive thoughts and illusions but, after a while, he no longer remembered anything. Upon hearing the cry of sparrows he came to himself. The day had already dawned.[29] This is a good example of completely transcending time and space.

There is a similar case that actually happened recently. One evening a housewife took a short break from her work and did zazen in an upstairs room of her house. She thought only five or six minutes had passed when she heard noises downstairs. She went to look and found that it was already the next morning and her family was busily getting breakfast ready.

This kind of experience is not limited to those who do zazen. It is an experience available to anyone to a greater or lesser degree when you do anything to your utmost, even in your daily life. At the very least, if you always check to see whether self and other objects are separated or joined and see where you yourself are standing you will also know whether the direction of your Zen training is correct or mistaken.

WHAT IS ZAZEN?

So far I have been using the term "Zen" in some instances and "zazen" in others without making a clear distinction between them. I have even inter-changed their meanings at times, but here I would like to explain the word *zazen* more formally. When I speak about zazen, what comes to mind first is the following passage from the *Dan-gyo*, a record of the life and sayings of the Sixth Patriarch of Zen Buddhism, Eno Daikan (Hui-neng Ta-chien):[30]

> Za (sitting) means to not give rise to thoughts (no dualism) under any circumstance. Zen (meditation) means to see your original nature and not become confused.

If we interpret this passage in the orthodox way, "sitting" cannot be said to be only the body sitting vacantly. However, to use a somewhat extreme example, if one does not entertain idle thoughts and fantasies while sleeping, this too can be rightly called "sitting." If we speak of the original meaning in the broadest sense of the term, that is what Eno probably meant.

Be that as it may, I am going to use a more common interpretation of "sitting." In the *Kanchu Jubu Roku* there is a useful commentary on "sitting" written by Machimoto Donku:

> Sitting is one of the four dignified postures: walking, standing, sit-ting, and lying down. Zen is one of the six stages of spiritual per-fection: dedication, commandments, perseverance, progress, med-itation, and wisdom. Zen is clearly known as *dhyana*, a Sanskrit word for meditation. In Chinese it is translated as *ching-lu*, mean-ing quiet contemplation. It means to become stable and then quiet, to become peaceful after becoming quiet, and finally to con-template carefully. For this reason the former four dignified pos-tures and the six stages of spiritual perfection all arise from quiet contemplation.
>
> In Zen Buddhism, Zen combines the above six stages of perfec-tion. In order to train in Zen it is proper to sit in meditation

according to prescribed form. Therefore, sitting is regarded as correct for Zen training. For walking there is the method of *kinhin* or walking meditation. For standing there is the dignified manner of refinement in speaking and being silent in daily life. For lying down there is the way of reclining like a lion. These serve as variations of meditation.

Therefore, it is said that in Zen Buddhism one of the four dignified postures is meditation. Thus there is a start and a finish in things, and a beginning and an end in matters; and if one knows where front and rear are one is near the Way. Students, please quietly contemplate this very carefully.[31]

It is not a bad idea to look at sitting in this way, as one of the four dignified postures. I believe it is a good way for beginners to understand it. That is, you should look at sitting as a purely physical method of regulating one's body. Then, Zen may be regarded from a spiritual perspective as a way of regulating the mind. The unification of mind resulting from it is concentration and the workings of concentration is wisdom.

Let me explain that relationship in more detail. This way of looking at sitting may be criticized as being too analytical, but it is probably the easiest way for beginners and especially for people of today to accept sitting. That is, they can understand the gradually deepening forms of sitting, meditation, concentration and wisdom. In this sense, sitting means to adjust the body and sit with a correct posture; I will explain the details of sitting later.

Next, I will discuss the term *zen*. The word *zen-na* came into Japanese as a transliteration of the Sanskrit word dhyana; that is, zen-na reproduces the sound of dhyana. In China, *ch'an-na* or *shan-na* was the transliteration of dhyana. When the meaning of dhyana was translated, it became *ching-lu* in Chinese and *joryo* in Japanese.

Joryo literally means "quietly contemplating" or "to quiet one's contemplating," but these phrases are slightly different from what zen really means. Even though there is such a word as joryo, it is not used as a translation of dhyana; instead the word zen has been used. This is not only to respect the meaning of the original word, but to show that there may be no suitable translation. However, if the word zen means the unification of the mind or the process of its unification, and if we understand that joryo is not just quieting our thoughts but is quieting those thoughts that fly about wildly like horses and monkeys and that spin so much that we do not know what direction they are going, it will not be too far off the mark.

If we analyze the character for zen, we find that it combines the radical *shi* (to show) with the character *tan* (single). That is to say, the character for zen means "to show singleness of mind." Some people contend that this means the complete integration of subject and object whenever they meet. This interpretation is interesting in content, but it is not necessarily substantiated by anything in the literature of Zen.

Concentration is the stable condition of a unified mind when there has been Zen training. This condition is called samadhi in Sanskrit or *sammai* in Japanese. It has been translated into Chinese in many ways. For instance, there are such words as *teng-ch'ih*, *cheng-ting*, *cheng-shou* and *pu-shou*. It is said there are many phrases built upon this "concentration" such as "concentration without thoughts" and "concentration with self and universe extinct," but any further explanation of "concentration" will only lead to confusion about its original meaning. Therefore, "concentration" may simply be interpreted as the stabilization of our confused and excited thoughts and imaginings. In other words, it may be regarded as a completely concentrated state of mind.

The Chinese phrase cheng-shou means "to accept correctly." It refers to our perception of white as white and red as red, perception of colors as they truly are. It is also translated as "holding equally," meaning that you hold the form just as it is. And yet, if the perceiver and the perceived, or if the possessor and the possessed, are dual and relative, they are no longer capable of perceiving things correctly in accord with the meaning of "accepting correctly" or "holding equally."

When we are confronted with something white, we become completely white; when we see something red, we become completely united as if red is self and self is red. This is when we are said to be in samadhi. To become completely the other means for us to be one with them. It is to give life to them by means of dedicating all of ourselves to them. Therefore, it is as if two mirrors reflect each other without any specific images reflected between them. In such a state there is no sign of perceiving and being perceived. Hence, it is called "no receiving." If we come to think of it this way, if we differentiate between Zen and samadhi, samadhi is what we attain when we train in Zen. Combining the two gives us Zen concentration (*zenjyo* in Japanese).

Jyo literally means "settled" and refers to the concentrated state of mind. It corresponds to shi, meaning "detained" or "fixed" and is used in the Tendai Sect of Buddhism. However, the mere concentration of a mind fixed in a particular state is nothing other than the tranquil, immovable, and blighted Zen known as "submerged under poisonous sea-water." Unless there is something full of life moving in immovability, it is not true immovability. In the teaching of the Tendai Sect of Buddhism this living quality is called *kan* (true intuitive seeing or perception). It refers to the perception of the world from the viewpoint of samadhi or jyo and the unified state of mind corresponding to shi.

When perceiving phenomena of this world through kan, we realize that the common way of viewing the world, prior to entering this state of concentration, was mistaken. As described by the phrase "*tendo muso*" (upside-down illusory thoughts) in the *Hannya Shingyo*,[32] in our common way of seeing we only see what is real in reverse. In this sense, we may say that kan is the renunciation of the viewpoint held before there was proper concentration and a recognition of the world from the viewpoint of satori.

The act of correctly seeing this world from this state of concentration (jyo) and the world of samadhi is called "wisdom." In other words, wisdom is the act of perceiving things of this world as they truly are. The Tendai term *shikan* (perception in concentration) corresponds to the term *jyo-e* (wisdom attained in concentration of mind) used in Zen. Just as in the phrase *jyo-e enmyo* (full and clear perception in the wisdom of concentration), jyo (concentration) necessarily gives birth to e (wisdom) and e (wisdom) must be based on jyo (concentration). Otherwise, no matter how clear our perception, it is nothing but worldly knowledge and discriminating knowledge and can never be called wisdom. Further, to have concentration without wisdom is to idly come to a standstill in an empty world. Therefore, this concentration cannot be called true samadhi.

I have now analytically explained the terms "sitting," "zen," "concentration," and "wisdom." What we must note carefully now are the following words attributed to the Zen Master Eno:

> It is only by entering into samadhi that I can discuss seeing one's true self-nature (kensho) without also talking about self-liberation.[33]

Hearing this, Priest Inshu asked Eno, "Why don't you discuss self-liberation when you enter samadhi?" His teacher replied, "To discuss by discriminating is dualistic teaching and not Buddhist teaching," meaning there is no samadhi nor self-liberation outside of seeing one's true self-nature. It is not that the cause known as "entering into samadhi" is followed by the result known as "seeing one's true self-nature." Seeing one's true self-nature in itself is samadhi, and samadhi in itself is seeing one's true self-nature.

Eno also said, "Seeing one's true self-nature yet not being disturbed is called Zen." From this point of view, both samadhi and self-liberation are due to the nature of the "seeing" of seeing one's true self-nature.

Many years after the time of Eno, Master Dogen wrote, "Learning the Way of Buddhism means studying one's own self."[34] Studying one's own self is to master the Self, which finally means the same thing as seeing one's own self-nature.

Eno also said, "When all things are illumined by wisdom and there is neither grasping nor throwing away, then you can see your own nature and gain the Buddha Way." This touches on the nature of seeing one's true self-nature (kensho). Seeing all things illumined in the operation of profound *prajna*-wisdom, we come to know that the mountain rises, the river flows, the myriad things each are as they truly are. Then and there the world of awakened perception is opened. In the words of Rinzai, it is the world in which "anywhere one becomes a master, everything is true." In such a world, there is no delusion one must cast away, and no enlightenment one must acquire. Willows are green and flowers are red—perfect as they are. Dogs are saved by their barking and cats are freed by their meowing. This is what Eno means by the Way of seeing one's true self-nature and attaining Buddhahood.

Master Dogen wrote, "To study the Self is to forget the Self." It is only when the self is transcended in accordance with these words that the True Self which is said to be true at any time and in any place, reveals itself. When True Self manifests in daily life, this is called Zen.

THE FOUR RELATIONSHIPS BETWEEN SITTING AND ZEN

It is noted in Zen Master Iida Toin's book *Sanzen Manroku*[35] that there are "four ways of viewing zazen." I do not know whether that is an original opinion by Toin, but something similar to Toin's first three ways is found in a recently translated book by a scholar named Hu Shih.[36] In his explanation of the Zen method in ancient China, Hu Shih quotes the following passage from the *Shugyodoji-gyo* (Yogacarya-bhumi Sutra)

> The discipline consists of three kinds: the first is said to be the body exercising the Way without the mind attendant on it; the second is said to be the mind investigating the Way without the body accompanying it; the third is said to be conducting oneself according to the Way with both mind and body realizing it.

Hu Shih continues,

> Even though one sits in the full-lotus position and becomes immovable like a mountain, one's mind is lost and scattered— this is the second kind. The third kind is where the body sits correctly and the mind is not dissolute—inwardly its roots are all quieted and outwardly it does not run wildly about after all kinds of karmic influences.

I do not know whether or not there are classifications other than Zen Master Toin's which divide zazen into four kinds. Although I do not know what the similarities and differences might be, I think it will be very interesting to base my own classification on that four-part division.

The first is for those who sit but do not practice Zen. It corresponds to the first category used by Hu Shih. This kind of sitting follows the prescribed form of the full-lotus or half-lotus position, but it is still not well-integrated sitting. This is an experience many of us had when we first learned zazen, probably because the instruction we received was not good.

When we went to a class for zazen, senior students taught us how to cross our legs and position our hands—the form, but they did not teach us anything about the content—the way of getting into the state of samadhi. Consequently, I thought for quite a long time that if I sat according to the set form I would somehow be graced with satori by Heaven. But even if I *had* been taught how to be well integrated, in the beginning I still would have been likely to remain separate from objects, seeing myself and other things as two. But I simply did not know anything about that. Perhaps it is just that it is very difficult for anyone to understand what the truly integrated realm is. Master Toin states,

> Evil passions, earthly desires, carnal lust, taken all together, are due to two conditions: low vital energy and scattered wits.[37]

In short, even though we sit with the form of Bodhidharma, if the essence of our sitting is like that described by Hakuin—"The mind is as confused as the defeated warriors of the Heike Clan at the battles of Yashima and Dannoura"[38]—our sitting will be confused and without concentration. These are the attributes of one who sits without practicing Zen.

Unless the mind is simultaneously concentrated and unified with vigorous energy and dynamism, we cannot claim to be practicing Zen, no matter how long we may sit with our legs crossed. In the Soto Sect of Zen Buddhism, use of the term "*shikantaza*"[39] does not by any means suggest that it is acceptable to let your mind wander so long as you sit with your legs crossed. Far from it; shikan means that the sitter must be totally integrated with sitting itself and sit in a commanding manner.

Though we do not see many these days, there are those who believe that they are not disciplining themselves unless they sit at any cost or as we say, "like frogs." They certainly belong to the group of people who sit without practicing Zen. This is one of the types of sitting that Hakuin disliked the most. Without doing anything from morning until night, they merely sit like stone Jizo in the mountains. Hakuin scolded them severely, saying that they would be better off gambling.

The empty and tranquil nap-taking Zen, angrily scorned by the Zen teachers of old as the "ghost's cave at the foot of the black mountain," also belongs to this category. It is necessary for us to be extremely careful not to fall into the bad habit of sitting without practicing Zen.

The second group of undesirable students of Zen are those who practice Zen without sitting. I think those who are known in the world as scholars of Zen Buddhism belong to this category, corresponding to the second one mentioned by Hu Shih.

Master Toin wrote:

There are those who repeat the phrase, "Walking is also Zen, sitting is also Zen; Zen is speaking, being silent, moving, resting." Or they ask, "Why should Zen be restricted to sitting and lying down?" This group also misunderstands the words of the ancients.[40]

Generally speaking, the true meaning of the phrase, "Walking is also Zen, sitting is also Zen; Zen is speaking, being silent, moving, resting," is that self and object are mutually integrated to such an extent as to become completely unified. After transcending integration, no matter what the surroundings, you are in a deep samadhi in which you do not lose your calm and immovable Zen concentration.

While it is not a mistake to say that a wave of your hand or a kick of your leg are all expressions of Zen, such a visceral understanding comes to those who have thoroughly seen their own true self-nature. For novices, it is a distant future ideal they can reach only with severe training. In principle, there is no denying that clearing one's throat or lifting a single finger are the workings and doings of Buddhahood, but in reality, unless we become so integrated with things in themselves that it is no longer possible to search for our own self, it is neither the workings of Buddha nor the doings of Buddha. Then we can be active in that realm of integration after having forged our integration sufficiently in zazen, no doubt our walking will also be Zen and our sitting will also be Zen. However eloquent we may be, unless we sit at least for the time it takes one stick of incense to burn we are studying Zen without sitting.

Hida Harumitsu, the founder of a discipline called "The Correct Method of Centering Oneself in Training," once had a sitting competition with Master Toin. According to Hida, Master Toin sat with ease at first in the full-lotus position, then gradually raised the upper part of his body. At the very instant that Hida thought, "Ah, right there!," Master Toin's upper body suddenly stopped moving. His center of gravity had settled right in the center of the pyramid formed by the posture of his legs and torso. With his compassionate eyes, calm expression, dignified appearance, and stately posture, he was immovable. There were no vulnerable openings, only the great spirit reflected in his posture of full emptiness. After all, it goes without saying that as long as the term zazen is used, it must be substantiated by such a way of actual sitting before it may truly be called Zen.

We often have visitors, some of whom evidently have read widely on Zen Buddhism, who like to discuss difficult theoretical problems. Judging from their words, they seem to be great Zen men, but most of them have not sat enough for their vital buttocks to be familiar with their zazen cushions.

It is bad for those who are learning Zen to become like those who study Zen but do not sit. After all, you must have the discipline to sit every day. Ashikaga Takauji[41] had an evil reputation as a traitor, but it is said that he sat zazen for some time every night and never failed to engage in this daily practice even when he became intoxicated. I think this should be a lesson to students of Zen.

The third category pertains to those who sit and practice Zen at the same time. According to Master Toin, these are people who do not have to force themselves to do zazen but who naturally come to sit. This is Hu Shih's third category, the true zazen in which attachments fall away from mind and body.

We are likely to think, "I practice zazen," but when that happens, zazen and self are two, and one's existence with Heaven and Earth is no longer absolute. It is not that we do zazen, but it must be that zazen does zazen. We should enter that state of true integration—even one time is enough—for without the experience of completely forgetting our self, this may be difficult to understand. Even if we count our breaths according to the breath-counting method, in the beginning, no matter what, we tend to be conscious of ourselves counting. Because our self which is counting is separated from the numbers being counted it cannot be said to be the true breath-counting method.

In the tradition of the *Mugai-ryu* (a school of swordsmanship) there is a phrase, "Mind and hands become one, like remembering and forgetting in oneness." It refers to the experience in which the mind forgets the hands, and the hands forget the mind and both become totally one. For example, when one faces an enemy, in the time it takes to think, "This is where to attack," one's hands are already in motion and cutting. In that interval there is no opening to insert even a strand of hair. Or when you cut your opponent, it is simultaneous with your mind moving to decide to do that. This kind of state where one's self and one's sword are joined in oneness is what is called mind and hands becoming one. Sitting and practicing Zen at the same time is the same condition. This is the Great Sitting where one's existence between Heaven and Earth is absolute, with no Self outside of sitting and no sitting outside of Self.

For a person who sits and practices Zen at the same time, according to Master Toin, it goes without saying that they could do the second type, practicing Zen without sitting, but it is not an easy thing. A noble man does not court danger. You who are just beginning your training, first practice sitting thoroughly and sit all you can. As for what lies beyond that, leave it alone until it naturally emerges from yourself.

The fourth category is for those who neither sit nor practice Zen. They are ignored by Master Toin who writes, "It is hard to save those who do not have the right conditions" and "their favor is limited." Accordingly, I, too, will not discuss this fourth group for the time being. The people who read this book are likely to be interested in starting Zen discipline, and so I think it is all right to be totally unconcerned with the category of people who do not sit and do not practice Zen.

Beginners especially should beware of the bad habit of sitting without practicing Zen. I wish the reader to be most careful not to sit in the ways which are not in keeping with the true practice of Zen. To seek for some target outside of oneself is not the true meaning of zazen.

To sit in order to cure neurosis or to develop *hara*[42] so as not to be frightened by things is really up to each person and probably is not bad. Whether such people will be guided from there to training according to the true way of Zen discipline depends on the ability of the instructor. But, if we recall the original aim of zazen, it is correct to say that zazen has no purpose other than zazen.

Zen Master Dogen said that to transmit Dharma means to transmit zazen. Explaining that Dharma is identical to zazen, he writes, "Ever since days of old, only a few people have known that the purpose of zazen is zazen."[43] He means that zazen is not the means of attaining any goal other than zazen and also that zazen is not the way of learning Zen. He goes on to say, "Zazen is something which makes us want to sit in zazen." It is hard for beginners to understand this, but it is an important point to remember.

Ceramic vase (height 120 cm.), hand-built in the ceramics studio at Daihonzan Chozen-ji by Myoshin Teruya Roshi. In this photograph, the piece has just completed its bisque firing; firing was later finished in a four-chamber wood-burning kiln on the grounds. Teruya Roshi was given her artist name of Bunsho by Omori Rotaishi around 1980. (Permanent collection of Daihonzan Chozen-ji)

Statue of the Buddhist deity, Fudo-myo-o (Skt. Acala-vidya-raja), placed by the wood-burning ceramics kiln at Daihonzan Chozen-ji. As described by the famous Takuan Soho:

> [Fuo-myo-o] is represented holding a sword in his right hand and a rope in his left. He is baring his teeth and his eyes glare penetratingly. He stands ferociously to destroy the evil spirits or demons who try to harm or hinder the Buddha's teachings . . . His body embodies Immovable Wisdom and is made for all sentient beings to see. The simple-minded, out of awe, will refrain from hindering the Buddhist teachings. The people who are approaching enlightenment realize that Fudo-myo-o symbolizes Immovable Wisdom as the destroyer of delusions. (Tenshin Tanouye Roshi, trans. *Fudochi Shimmyo Roku*, Daihonzan Chozen-ji, Honolulu, 1989.)

CHAPTER 3

How to Sit in Zen Meditation

PREPARATION BEFORE SITTING

The reader's preliminary knowledge of zazen may still be inadequate, but since I could never write exhaustively about that background, I will now begin to discuss the actual practice of zazen.

Specialists use the term "sitting" for zazen. From that starting point, I would like to interpret the term and develop my explanation. If zazen is sitting, what condition does sitting refer to? If we look up the word *suwaru* (to sit), it is defined as "to be settled and unmoving; well suited."[1]

However, the word suwaru does not only refer to the human act of sitting. The word has many other usages such as saying that a ceramic vase "sits" well or that a man's hara "sits" or that a chop "sits" when stamping an ink seal. All of these refer to a stable, non-wavering, and well-ordered condition, suggesting the state of things as they were originally meant to be. I think it follows that if the same word is applied to humans, it is used for the condition in which mind and body are balanced, harmony is maintained, and there is no movement or disturbance. It also suggests putting one's mind and body in that state.

Bodhidharma said, "Detach yourself from various things in the external world and inwardly your mind will not be agitated. By using your mind like a wall you should gain entrance into the Way." If we interpret these difficult words literally, they mean we should be detached from the external world and not be taken up by it. We should compose our mind by using it like a castle wall and not let disturbances come inside. In short, Bodhidharma alludes to the condition of sitting.

When we refer to the classic text *Zazen-gi* regarding the method of sitting, we find the following written about the essential technique of zazen, "Once the posture has been stabilized and the breath regulated, push forth the lower abdomen; one thinks not of good or evil." In short, the book explains how to regulate and stabilize our posture, breath, and thoughts.

I would like to explain the three aspects of sitting in the following order: (1) seating the body; (2) regulating the breath; (3) stabilizing the mind. Before I begin, however, I would like to briefly discuss the preliminary precautions to take in order to settle the mind and body for sitting. In *Zazen-gi*, it states,

> First awaken your compassionate mind with a deep longing to save all sentient beings. You must practice samadhi meditation with great care, and promise to ferry these sentient beings over to

the other shore, refusing to practice zazen only for your own emancipation.[2]

In other words, our sitting must be based on the compassionate desire to save all sentient beings by means of calming the mind. Our sitting must not be like the Small Vehicle Theravada Way where individuals run to Buddhism only for their own comfort. Rather, we must arouse the Great Bodhisattva Mind in ourselves to vow to save all sentient beings. Dogen is very strict about this point, going so far as to say,

> If the right faith arises in your mind, you should train in Zen. If it does not arise, you should wait for awhile and reflect upon the fact that the Buddha Dharma did not become part of you long ago.[3]

This is extremely important to keep in mind. Zen trainees, no matter who they are, must cultivate the "Right View"[4] that underlies the deep longing to save all sentient beings. However, in actuality it is very difficult to realize. Unless one's discipline has progressed a great deal, the Great Compassion (the vow to save all sentient beings) will not arise of its own accord. Therefore, if you think you do not have that Great Compassion after reflecting upon your present mental attitude, there is no need to be honest to a fault and develop an inferiority complex. Don't lose your nerve and hold back from Zen discipline. Like the teachers of old, we can also sincerely wish to save all sentient beings and can spur ourselves to strive on.

Next, I will describe the physical preparation for zazen as outlined in *Zazen-gi*: "When one takes meals, eat neither too much nor too little; when one sleeps, it should be neither too brief nor too long." Japanese as a whole tend to eat with much more emphasis on quantity rather than quality of food. Traditionally, especially in Zen monasteries, people seem to have taken pride in this emphasis.

No one would object to the statement that the human body is maintained by food. Accordingly, it is indisputable that the strength or weakness of our bodies and our state of health depends on that substance which maintains it. That is why eating correctly is stressed. That being the case, it is necessary to carefully research what food is best for us as Japanese and what food is most suitable for our individual physical constitution. I think this problem of food is an important topic which requires far-reaching investigation. In *Zazen-gi*, only the problem of quantity of food is addressed. However, the problem of quality should also be seriously considered. Since there seem to be any number of suitable reference works on this point being published, I will refrain from writing further on this problem and simply draw your attention to it.

Master Tendai (T'ien-t'ai)[5] wrote about the harmony of eating, sleeping, the body, the breath, and the mind as the harmony of five matters. As for the regulation of food, he writes,

> If you eat too much, your *ki* (intrinsic energy) will strain your body, blood circulation will be stagnated, your mind will be clouded, and your sitting will be made unstable. On the other hand, if you eat too little, you will become fatigued in both mind and body and lose spiritual energy.

If you listen to people who say that small meals are good, you may ignore your own physical strength and eat too little. That can cause you to lose the strength and endurance needed to sit in meditation. I think this is what many people have experienced. Other than that, foods which are unclean, indigestible, or poor in quality disturb the mind and body. This is the reason why the five kinds of spicy foods including leeks and garlic have traditionally been forbidden in Zen monasteries; they are said to disturb the mind and body. One must eat prudently in other words.

The next problem to be considered is sleep. Master Tendai cautions against too little sleep: "Sleep is food for your eyes. You should not restrict your sleep so much that the amount goes against what is commonly accepted." It is said that Napoleon slept for only four hours a day, but clearly nobody will become another Napoleon by restricting his sleep to four hours a day. An acquaintance of mine, a man of inexhaustible energy, sleeps only two hours a day but he only does bad things.

This, however, does not mean that it is better to sleep longer than necessary. According to Tendai, indulging ourselves by sleeping as much as we want will deprive us of the key to enlightenment, darken our minds, and conceal in the depths of our mind the sensitivity to advance toward goodness. Oversleeping should also be guarded against as the cause for both mental and physical lassitude. When Zen concentration ripens, you will come to have the experience of not feeling tired, even with little sleep.

Only after having developed the ability to regulate food and sleep are we ready to sit. According to *Zazen-gi*, "When one wishes to begin zazen, one places a thick cushion in a quiet place, wears a robe and belt rather loosely, and puts all things about oneself in good order. Then one sits with legs crossed in the lotus position." The words are very simple, but they explain the key elements of sitting.

There probably is no one who would purposely listen to comedy on the radio or watch a drama on television while sitting. You should choose as a quiet and peaceful a room as possible. The reason why I use the word "should" is that when we speak of a quiet place to people in cities, we must realize that not everyone has the freedom to choose that kind of room. Under unavoidable circumstances it is all right to sit in an apartment where neighbors play loud music. You can endure unfavorable surroundings if you maintain the conviction that training in the midst of activity is far superior to training in quiet. While the noise of subways and trains may be tolerable, it is better not to sit where you are exposed to strong winds, direct sunlight, or harsh conditions.

You should choose as large a *zabuton* (cushion) as possible to sit on, wide enough so that your knees do not extend beyond the edges. If you can afford it, a fairly thick one is desirable. If thick ones are not available, use two or three thin ones, placing them one on top of the other; this is by no means extravagant (Figure 1). On top of the zabuton place small cushions called *zafu* which are laid under the one's buttocks. If zabu are not available, you can use zabuton folded in two in their place to sit on, but if possible it would be convenient to make zabu measuring about 8 or 9 inches in breadth, about 1 foot in length, and about 2-1/2 inches in thickness.

In *Zazen-gi* it says, "wear one's robe and belt loosely." Trousers are difficult to wear loosely and are not suitable for the long duration of *sesshin*[6]

Figure 1 Placement of Cushion in Sitting

Zafu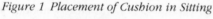

Zabuton

Figure 2 Stabilizing the Body

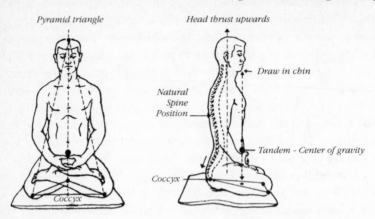

Pyramid triangle

Head thrust upwards

Draw in chin

Natural
Spine
Position

Tandem - Center of gravity

Coccyx

Coccyx

which lasts for five days or one week. Still we must be careful not to look slovenly, and must maintain a dignified appearance and sit in a commanding manner.

ADJUSTING THE BODY

Once the zabuton are ready, we can sit but there are three important elements to bear in mind. They are adjusting the body, the breath, and the mind. First I will begin by explaining how to adjust the body; this is called adjusting the form of sitting.

The form of a well-set and stable body is that of a three-sided pyramid with a base formed by the lines connecting the two knees resting on the zabuton and the coccyx (Figure 2). The diagonal lines extending from the two knees and the coccyx to the top of the head define the three sides of the pyramid that complete the form. This seated form is what is traditionally called the full-lotus position. It can be seen in the seated form of many Buddha images and statues.

Even in *tanza* (the formal posture for sitting on the floor in Japan) with our knees spread apart at least 50 degrees, the body's center of gravity corresponds with the center of the triangle formed at the base of the body. Physiologically speaking, the center falls around the perineum, so you may also think of it that way. Even those who are not accustomed to tanza can sit in that posture for 30 or 40 minutes. (But it is easier to use the half-lotus position when it comes to sitting for long hours in a set position at such times as sesshin in Buddhist monasteries.)

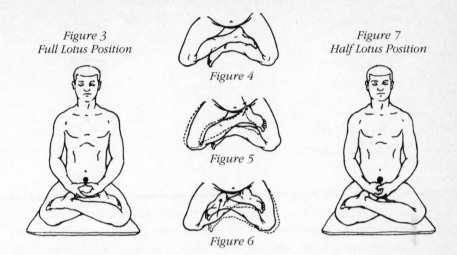

Figure 3
Full Lotus Position

Figure 4

Figure 5

Figure 6

Figure 7
Half Lotus Position

To practice the standard method of sitting in the full-lotus position (Figure 3), place the zabu or a regular zabuton folded in two on the zabuton, then lightly rest your buttocks on it and cross your legs in front of you (Figure 4). Next, put your right foot on your left thigh with the heel just about touching your lower abdomen (Figure 5). After that pull your left foot up to the base of your right thigh (Figure 6). Depending on a person's physical constitution, however, there are those who cannot fold both legs that way and others who can fold them but who cannot bear the pain. In those cases it is all right to rest just one foot on one thigh. That is called the half-lotus position (Figure 7).

The position with only the right foot placed on the left thigh is called *kissho-za*, while that with just the left foot placed on the right thigh is named *goma-za*. In contrast with these terms, the full-lotus position with both legs folded is called *kongo-za*. The kissho-za is known as the Buddha method of sitting while the goma-za is called the trainee's way of sitting. Beginners, however, should not be fussy about these terms and simply use left or right foot alternately.

As for the two hands, in the first position shown (Figure 8), the left hand is placed palm up so that it rests on the palm of the right hand. The inner sides of the tips of both thumbs touch, creating an ellipse. Viewed from above, the thumbs must be in line with the middle fingers. The more common position is the bottom one. Grasp the first joint of the left thumb between the web of the thumb and the index finger of the right hand. Form a loose fist with the right hand and enclose it with the left (Figure 9).

Next, straighten your spine. To do that, first tilt your upper body forward about 45 degrees so that your buttocks push back on the zabu. Then

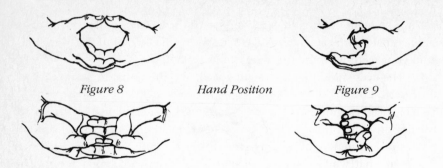

Figure 8   Hand Position   Figure 9

bring your upper body back to an upright position by feeling as though you were thrusting the top of your head towards heaven. This action will straighten the spine into a natural position. In other words, put strength in the area slightly above your coccyx, push the lower abdomen slightly forward as if you were straightening your hips, raise your upper body so that it becomes perpendicular, draw in your chin, and sit as if a coin dropped from the top of your head down through your body would fall out through your anus. By doing this your center of gravity will fall to the middle of the triangle formed at the base of your body (Figure 2). One word of caution: you must be very careful not to put strength in your stomach area.

Next, sway your body side to side like a pendulum, first with a large motion, then gradually decreasing until you come to a stop in the center. In *Zazen-gi* it says, "In order to find a balanced sitting posture for the body, the body should not lean to either side, not forward nor backward. The bones of the hips, back and skull rest atop one another like a *stupa*."[7] In other words you should straighten your body, adjust your sitting posture and sit upright like a pagoda or a tombstone. However, the passage continues by saying, "the body should not be so upright that someone else would feel uneasy seeing it." It must not become a forced posture with one's head thrown back and which does not allow easy breathing.

Zazen-gi continues, "Keep ears and shoulders, nose and navel in line with one another. The tongue should touch the upper jaw. Both lips and teeth should be closed." If we draw in the chin and straighten the back of the neck firmly the ears and shoulders will naturally fall in the same vertical line. Also in that posture, if we push the lower abdomen forward so that the hipbone stands up straight, the line connecting the nose and the belly button will become perpendicular.

If you really put *kiai* (spiritual energy) into your sitting, your lips and teeth will take the correct position naturally without your having to think about it. The main point is to gently bite with the molars so that the teeth are in light contact with each other together and touch the roof of the mouth just behind your teeth with the tip of the tongue.

The eyes should look straight ahead, and the visual field should span 180 degrees. Lower the eyes to a fixed position on the floor approximately three feet ahead (Figure 10). The eyes should be half-closed, neither seeing nor not seeing anything. In essence, it is not looking and not not looking, or looking and not looking. While it may seem easier to unite your spirit with your eyes closed, that would become detached zazen and not living zazen. This warning is also found in *Zazen-gi*, particularly in the words of Zen Master Entsu: "He scolded those who practiced zazen with their eyes closed, calling them ghosts in a black mountain cave." Even when we look at pictures of Bodhidharma we find his eyes are wide open—there is not a single picture showing him with closed eyes.

Zazen-gi also teaches that students must not fall asleep during zazen. It seems as though we were being encouraged to keep our eyes open in order not to fall asleep but this is not the point at all. One has to think that there is a significant reason from the standpoint of experience for keeping one's eyes open. If we remain quiet with our eyes closed like stagnant water, we will never be useful to society. The concentration power of zazen, enabling you to walk through a place as busy as downtown Tokyo as if you were walking alone through an uninhabited desert, springs from a deep principle cultivated only in the practice of samadhi with one's eyes open. It is this point that only a person of attainment would know. You must never make light of opening or shutting your eyes.

The foregoing discussion was limited to what is immediately necessary for sitting, but the significance of improving the sitting of the body or

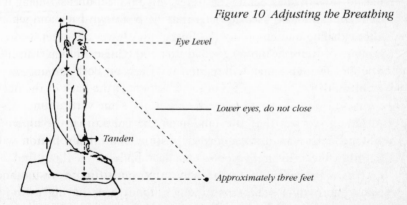

Figure 10 Adjusting the Breathing

Eye Level

Lower eyes, do not close

Tanden

Approximately three feet

correcting the posture is really something much greater. Although it is somewhat long, let me quote a passage written by Sato Tsuji.

> The Way for human beings is based on the act of correcting the form of one's posture to that which it is meant to be. Why? Because human beings have a concrete life span and the body and mind originally are not two.
>
> In this way—raising one's *koshi* (lower back) upright, straightening the body, and still keeping the natural curvature of the spine—one's correct posture fundamentally comes into being. The arms and legs are limbs and since limbs are branches of the body, the principal form of the body should be thought of like the form of Daruma.[8] Because the weight of the major parts of the body settles to the base of the torso (unlike four-legged animals), the center of gravity of human beings must shift to the koshi. This is probably why the written character for koshi is made up of the character for "flesh" and the character for "vital part."
>
> When we say the koshi stands upright we are referring to the tensing of the muscles in the lower trunk of the body. If tension is put into the muscles of the lower body, naturally the point of strength in the lower abdomen must appear as the center of that tension. This center has been known since ancient times in the East as *saika tanden*.[9]
>
> Although it is traditionally said that the saika tanden is two and a half or three inches below the navel, this kind of external measurement cannot be used to determine its position. If one laughs after exhaling and emptying the lungs, one's lower abdomen will tighten. Also, try swallowing saliva after emptying the lungs. Then too, the lower abdomen will tighten and the center of that tension is the tanden.
>
> Although we say that the tanden is the central seat formed when a person maintains correct posture, the tanden is not a definite object. Even if you dissect a dead body you will not find it. This is probably the reason why it has not been understood by Western-style scholarship which tends toward objective recognition.

To make the tanden the center of power is to concentrate strength in the lower abdomen. However, because the strength of the lower abdomen is an expression of the concentration of the entire body, one cannot simply concentrate strength in the lower abdomen as a part of the body cut off and separated from the whole body. The essence is to maintain consolidation of the whole body by having the strength fill the lower abdomen naturally.[10]

The act of correcting the posture in this way may be thought of as fundamental to all the Ways of human beings.

In answer to the question as to how to correct our posture, it is simply as Sato says: keep the koshi upright and maintain the stability of our center of gravity. All things on earth are pulled by gravity towards earth's center. That is, all things are stabilized and maintained in balance by gravitation. Pulled by the earth's gravity, the body resists by using the stability of the koshi as the center. In other words, while following nature in reverse we become its master and subjectively correct our posture. This is the true dignity of the human body.

I have seen it written that, "The method of zazen requires that you first correct your sitting form when taking your seat, for if the sitting form is correct the mind will accord to it."[11] But if the mind is truly correct, the body and posture should also be correct.

In Zen monasteries, when the beginning monks are unable to endure the pain of sesshin, they become bent in the koshi and sit limply. When this is noticed, however, they are showered with abuse. "What do you mean by sitting like kneaded cow dung?!" Senior students use such strong language to spur on their students because they know from long experience how much effect correction of the sitting form actually has on spiritual activity.

Therefore, for those who are going to start practicing zazen, correcting one's sitting form and sitting with the correct posture are important aims which should not be forgotten even in one's dreams. Furthermore, it should be remembered that correction of the sitting posture is the aim of the discipline called Shin Gakudo. Dogen describes this training as meaning, "the Way of learning with the body."[12] It is the Way of learning by means of the lump of red flesh. The body comes out of the Way and what is derived from the Way is also the body. Correcting one's posture is the same thing as learning the Way by means of the body, that is, turning the whole universe into one's own body. It is expressed by Zen Master Dogen as *jin juppo kai* (the whole universe embracing everything) which must consist of training to create a true human body. The significance of the sitting of the body is truly great.

I will list in simple fashion the main points discussed above to be certain they are not missed.

1) Raise the koshi upright, and feel as though you are pushing the lower abdomen forward.
2) Do not put strength or tension in the shoulders and stomach area.
3) Straighten the back of the neck and pull in the chin.

ADJUSTING THE BREATH

The second important point about sitting is the adjustment of breathing. It is written in *Zazen-gi*: "Once the body's form is stabilized, adjust the breathing." In Dogen's manual used in Soto Zen training, the same point is explained as, "When you breathe quietly through your nose, harmonize the body, and take a deep breath."[13] A deep breath is expressed here by the phrase *"kanki issoku shi."* I do not know if *kanki* is a concrete technique of adjusting the breath. The sentence itself is oversimplified and I do not clearly understand it. *Kan* is defined in the dictionary as "to open the mouth wide and inhale air." It pertains to taking a deep breath with the mouth wide open as if yawning. It is the same as deep inhalation. In other words, it means that after the form of the body is adjusted, and one is well seated, we should breathe deeply.

There are many methods of deep breathing but the following method is the one I use. I exhale long with my mouth open as if trying to connect the air around me with my lower abdomen. Without using my throat or chest, I keep exhaling a long fine stream of air using the contracting power of my lower abdomen and try to empty the bottom of my chest (Figure 11). It will take about thirty seconds for the bad or stale air from the chest to be exhaled. However, the wonder of it is that in one breath, I attain a mental state which is detached from my former state of mind and circumstance.

After exhaling all of my air, I relax my lower abdomen. Due to atmospheric pressure, air naturally enters my nose; I inhale naturally until the air fills the area from my chest to my abdomen. After I finish inhaling, I pause for a very brief moment. With my lower abdomen extended slightly forward (while contracting the anus), I gently push my breath into my lower abdomen and squeeze it lightly there with a scooping feeling. At this point in the breathing cycle it is

Figure 11 Adjusting the Breathing

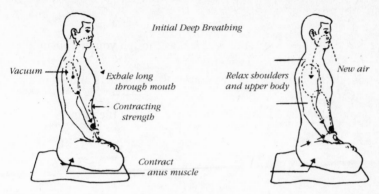

very important not to use a lot of force or to strain oneself. The key point is to keep the anus closed. Then before it becomes uncomfortable, I begin to exhale the air in the manner described earlier.

If we repeat this type of breathing four to ten times, besides completely freeing ourselves from our attachment to our surroundings, we will feel warm even in the winter for such a way of breathing improves blood circulation. Not only that, it is a good way to enter the samadhi condition.

When this type of deep breathing has ended, we should close our mouth, breathe through our nose and use our diaphragm and stomach pressure to do lower abdominal breathing.

It is said that there are four types of phenomenon in breathing. The first is "whistling" (*fu*), the second is "wheezing" (*zen*), the third is "air" (*ki*) and the fourth is "breath" (*soku*). The first three are out of harmony with the proper way of breathing. The last, "breath," alone is harmonized with proper breathing. "Whistling" means "the breath that makes a sound when going in and out of the nose." It describes the whistling kind of breath in which noises are made with the nose. "Wheezing" is the breath that "makes no noise but stops at intervals and has difficulty in going through the wind-pipe." This kind of asthmatic breathing is also undesirable. Another kind of breathing is called "air" (ki). It makes no noise and does not stop at intervals, but it is not a refined breath. It is also not good to breath in this rough manner.[14]

The foregoing are all inappropriate for sitting. It is said, "When you breathe in a whistling manner your mind becomes disturbed. When your breath is wheezing your mind becomes depressed. When your breathing becomes agitated your mind becomes exhausted."

Soku is the most suitable kind of breathing for those of us who sit in

Figure 12 Breathing in Meditation

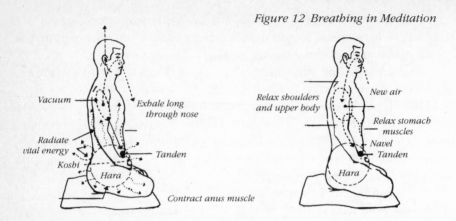

meditation. What kind of breathing is it? It is described as the breath coming in and going out without any break, as if existent and yet non-existent. This description of soku is not complete, but I am sure it corresponds to the lower abdominal breathing (tanden-soku) discussed earlier.

This way of breathing consists of putting strength in the area above the coccyx. Firmly straighten one's hips, push them forward, and close the anus. Keep the mouth closed and quietly breathe smooth, long breaths through the nose using the diaphragm and abdominal pressure. Actually, the inhaled air comes into the lungs alone but if we inhale, quietly relaxing the muscles around the pit of the stomach, we feel as if the inhaled air reaches below the navel. Moreover, when we exhale, we feel as if the air were being pulled out of the area below the navel (Figure 12).

In inhaling and exhaling as well, we should try to concentrate our energy rather than our strength in the lower abdomen. Likewise, do not put strength in the solar plexus. Instead, make that area concave.

The ordinary person's rate of breathing is said to be 18 times per minute. As for those of us who breathe with the tanden, the frequency of our breathing ranges from two or three to five or six times per minute. In the beginning it cannot be done without conscious effort. But as we get used to it we will be able to do it automatically, naturally, and unconsciously. What is called breath coming in and out "without any break as if existent and yet non-existent" refers to the well-regulated manner of breathing, in which "the mind naturally becomes calm and the heart becomes joyful" and "for the first time our minds will be at peace." Thus does Tendai[15] highly praise the effects of soku breathing.

If the body is properly stabilized by breathing correctly, mind and body will be harmonized accordingly, becoming like the shimmer of heated air "as if existent and yet non-existent."

Correction and adjustment of breathing is the key point common to all ways of art and culture, not only to Zen. There are such expressions as "to be in one breath," meaning to be in complete accord, and "to have swallowed the breath of someone else," meaning to understand what someone else means to do. While these expressions concerning breath and breathing are valued by students and masters of the arts, there seem to be few who actually engage in the adjustment of their respiration.

According to Takeuchi Daishin,[16] an authority on the practice of *shikan*, the word *ikiru* (to live) and the word *ikisuru* (to breathe) can be interpreted as identical in meaning. He goes on to comment that the common meaning of these words is not restricted to the ancient Japanese alone. Classical Greek scholars also thought the supernatural spiritual energy of the universe enters the bodies of living creatures by means of breathing, and that the lives of living creatures are controlled by means of the spiritual energy in their bodies. This energy is called "*pneuma*" in Greek. For example, Aristotle also thought that there is something special and non-material in the phenomenal lives of living creatures; he called it "*psyche*." It is said that both "pneuma" and "psyche" originally meant breath. In Takeuchi's opinion, the word "spirit" is derived from the Latin word "*spiro*" (to breathe). My point is that respiration intermediates between the conditions of mind and body, adjusting and harmonizing them.

More than ten years ago I read a work written by an American named Helen Durham who wrote that we should breathe so as to be strong, so as to be beautiful, so as to stand in the correct posture, so as to speak well, and above all, so as to be healthy. She points out that, although we have been accustomed to the use of only the upper parts of our lungs in breathing, it is critical to breathe deeply by using the lower parts of the lungs in order to have strength, beauty and health.[17]

When it first began, swordsmanship was nothing more than *Satsujin-ken* (the sword to kill people). Gradually, however, it was refined to the point where it could be called *Katsujin-ken* (the sword that gives life). Out of this grew *Kendo*[18] or the Way of Swordsmanship.

As I have written in *Ken to Zen*,[19] the transformation of swordsmanship came out of training in the correct use of the breath. When we look at this origin, we cannot help realizing how important it is to adjust our breathing in order to harmonize and stabilize our bodies and minds. In Zen, too, the adjustment of breathing is regarded as very important, for it is essential for the development of the samadhi condition.

We find the following comment in a book by Zen Master Yamamoto Genpo:[20]

> My teacher, a Zen Master named Suimoken, could ring the temple bell from about nine feet away just by exhaling forcefully. He lived to a very great age in the Ryutan-ji (temple) in the district of Iyo.

Yagyu Toshinaga, the fourteenth master of the Shinkage-ryu (a famous school of swordsmanship), interviewed Zen Master Gohoken Mutei at the Kokeizan Dojo in Mino around the third year of Taisho (1914). As Yagyu described the Zen master's breathing,

> One evening my teacher took a long breath to show me how to breathe properly in connection with my studies. He was wearing a light linen robe as it was very hot in the summertime. His clavicles and curved ribs in the uppermost part of his chest were visible through the robe. To my great surprise, they did not move at all when he breathed.

Finally, I should tell the story of how Zen Master Ryoen of Tenryu-ji dealt with the destructive old rats in his temple. After first matching his rate of breathing with the rats, he stopped his breath for about five minutes and the rats all fainted. He is said to have remarked later, "If you cannot do anything like this, you are not worthy of the name of a Zen monk."

From all of these stories, we should recognize how inseparably related the power of Zen and the way of breathing are to each other.

Adjusting the Mind

Adjusting the mind means concentrating and unifying the mind. In other words, it is the same as entering into the state of samadhi. The concrete methods of adjusting the mind are called *susoku-kan* and *koan kufu*[21] in Japanese.

The characters for writing susoku-kan may be literally interpreted as "the Way of (finding) true perception by means of counting the frequency of breaths." In my opinion, it was originally the method of shikan used in the

Tendai Sect of Buddhism. In his Japanese translation of *Hsiao Chih-kuan* (Shoshikan),[22] Ito Nobujiro describes the "six wonderous entrances" to Nirvana: counting, following, retaining, perceiving, returning, and purifying. As excessive explanations of all six ways to enter into Nirvana may only confuse the reader, I am going to restrict myself to the interpretation of *shusu* (mastering the way of counting the frequency of breathing).

According to the *Shoshikan*, shusu means that we should regulate our breathing—not allowing it to be too shallow, too rough, or too smooth—by counting the breaths calmly from one to ten. In this way the mind becomes concentrated. Then we should repeat counting all over again starting from one. If we repeat counting in this way a number of times with all of our effort, our disturbed minds will come to be concentrated and unified naturally.

There are three ways of counting the frequency of our respiration: count the cycles of inhalation and exhalation, count just the frequency of inhalation, or count just the frequency of exhalation. From my own experience, the best way to enter into the state of samadhi seems to consist principally in counting the frequency of exhalation.

As I exhale, I count, saying to myself, "Hito . . ." with second syllable pronounced long as if I were chasing the exhaled air with my mind's eye. Then I add the short sound "*tsu*," the last syllable of *hitotsu* ("one" in Japanese), as I inhale after the long exhalation. Of course, I do not count the frequency of my respiration aloud, for my mouth is closed during meditation. But I count to myself in silence as mentioned above. At first, we have to practice breathing consciously while breathing lightly and slowly in the direction of the tanden, but as we keep on practicing, the duration of our breathing will naturally increase.

We are told to concentrate our minds on counting the frequency of our breathing to keep the mind from being disturbed. Therefore, it is important to concentrate on counting each breath and also to become one with the frequency of each breath. One of my disciples once told me that by earnestly disciplining himself in susoku he came to comprehend the true meanings of such Zen phrases as, "the cutting of the duality between before and after," "the continuation of non-continuation," and "the absolute present." Thus, the counting of the frequency of our breathing should not be undervalued.

My late teacher, Seisetsu Roshi, used to say that even when *kufu* (training) with koan we might resort to susoku-kan.

As for kufu, many people misunderstand and think that kufu is a sort of means, conceptualized in their minds, by which the koan presented by the teacher are solved as if they were mathematics problems or quizzes. This is a gross error. In *Zengaku Jiten*[23] the word kufu is said to have been originally applied to the masters of various arts who tried hard to give full play to their ingenuity in making things. Master Muso[24] writes in his *Muchu Mondo* that kufu is the Japanese pronunciation of the Chinese word "*kung-fu*" which has the secular meaning corresponding to that of the Japanese word *itoma*, which embraces all kinds of doings or activities. The tilling of the field is the kufu of the farmer, and the furnishing of houses is the kufu of the cabinetmaker. The Buddhist discipline experienced by men of the Way in terms of these secular meanings of the word is called kufu. Master Muso further writes,

> In kufu you dress yourself and eat your meals; in kufu you see, hear and know things; in kufu you do, dwell, sit, and lie down. In kufu you express your joy, anger, sorrow and pleasure. If you live in this way, you will be called men doing everything in kufu. Such kufu is indeed kufu without kufu, that is alertness without alertness. Those who are aware of this fact turn both memory and forgetfulness into kufu. Waking and sleeping should not be separate in kufu. . . .

The Zen disciple Kawajiri Hogin also writes,

> This word kufu is represented by the Chinese characters read kung-fu, which mean a man of physical work in the literal sense of the word. Therefore, kufu alludes to the earnest way each artisan applies himself to the art of his own choice. For instance, a carpenter engaged in hewing with his adze would hurt his own leg if his hand slipped and failed to do his work properly. He cannot afford to turn his attention from his work even for a moment. Likewise, if a fireman even slightly overstepped the plank of the scaffold in walking on it, he would fall to the ground. He must be alert all the time. This state of alertness is called kufu.[25]

At any rate, the true significance of kufu without doubt consists in being fully absorbed into the koan itself. For instance, in the case of the koan of "*Mu*," we should try to be one with it as we inhale and exhale properly, saying to ourselves, "mu."[26] This is exactly what we do when we count the frequency of our respiration in susoku-kan. It is the right way of solving the koan of "Mu." In time, we will become used to this way of solving the koan of "Mu," and even when we are asleep, we will concentrate on the koan in accord with our respiration. Thus, we will naturally be prompted to become one with all things both inside and outside ourselves.

There is another important thing I would like to note regardless of what sort of koan we must solve. Susoku means counting the frequency of breathing. In order to avoid the disintegration of our respiration and the counting of its frequency in susoku, it is essential to stress the concentration of the mind on the counting rather than on the respiration as such, and to feel as if we were breathing in accordance with the counting of its frequency. For instance, we say to ourselves, "Hito-tsu [Jpn. "one"]." In our effort to solve the koan problems as well, it is important to take care to adjust our breathing to our koan as we inhale and exhale properly, saying to ourselves, "Mu." This method is what is called "nentei."

In order to understand the level of intensity that a student uses to solve the koan presented by his teacher, recall the story of Princess Kiyo, the heroine of a traditional Japanese drama. It is said that the princess was chasing after her beloved monk Anchin when she came upon the River Kidaka. The river was flooded because of heavy rains over the last several days and no ferry boats dared the trip into the rough current. Without hesitation, Princess Kiyo transformed herself into a snake and threw herself into the water, saying, "I will never stop swimming even if I become a devil or a snake!" (Notice the unflagging will of the princess.)

As for the monk Anchin fleeing from the princess, when he came to the temple he hid within a great temple bell resting on the ground. Sensing this, the princess who had turned into a snake wound herself around the bell, melting it with the heat of her passion and, in the end, becoming one with Anchin.

The unbridled will of Princess Kiyo's spirit exactly demonstrates the nature of nentei. Driven by such a spirit to consume everything in this universe including ourselves, we are expected to engage in nentei and to solve the koan.

I have briefly discussed the adjustment of the body, the breath, and the mind separately just for my own convenience. However, these three things should not be discussed separately. They should be well harmonized into one, as the various aspects of zazen are. Rather, only when the three are realized as one will it be possible to sit well, that is, to succeed in stabilizing and tranquilizing body and mind at the same time.

Logically speaking, we might say that body and mind should be integrated into one through the medium of respiration. But any one of these three things are inseparably related to the other two. If the body is corrected, mind and breath will be reasonably correct in themselves. It is no use correcting mind and respiration when the body is neglected and the posture incorrect.

A philosopher of the Sung Dynasty of China named Shushi (Chu Hsi)[27] is said to have had a crooked neck in his youth. His teacher always told him, "You cannot master the Way if your neck is bent." However, it was difficult for him to straighten his neck. It took him seven long years. And, it is said that when his bent neck became straight at last, everything he did and said was in accord with the Way. The correction of the improper form of his body itself represented the spiritual discipline which rectified his conduct. Conversely, by correcting the mind, our posture and breathing will also become proper.

The Zen Master Suzuki Shosan, the advocate of Nio Zen, always emphasized the proper attitude filled with alertness, the ability to act spontaneously at the right moment. How can we actually attain such an attitude filled with dynamic energy and dignity? Even if we imitate it with strained perseverance, we will not be able to sustain such an attitude even for thirty minutes.

Master Torei[28] in his *Shumon Mujinto Ron* teaches, "If we wish to attain the Buddha Way, we must by all means have great faith." I am sure we believe that "we are originally endowed with the spiritual nature and inexhaustible Wisdom of many Buddhas." Yet, unless this faith remains stable and immovable enough not to be agitated in any way, our bodies will never be filled with true energy. In other words, if our great faith is well established and stabilized, our bodies will become well balanced. Then our posture and breath will become stable and will be in harmony.

When a cat is going to catch a rat, or when a spider is going to jump at prey caught in its web, the predator takes an alert posture such that it can kill its prey at one blow without fail. It strikes such an attitude instinctively. But I wonder if it is not the irrepressible expression of its desperate desire to catch its prey at any cost. More so in the case of the great man who is constant in his faith and "filled with the sense of the right opportunity for self-realization"—how can he refrain from revealing himself as a Buddha?

Our body then is no longer a mere physical body but the body of Buddha and the True Body of the individual. It embodies and concretely expresses the spiritual nature and inexhaustible wisdom of various Buddhas. It is as if the body is the whole universe.

In the first chapter of the *Mumonkan*, Master Mumon Ekai (Wu-men Hui-k'ai)[29] writes a commentary as follows, "Awaken your three hundred and sixty bones and eighty-four thousand pores into one great body of inquiry and concentrate yourself into this mu (void)." I think the three hundred and sixty bones and eighty-four thousand pores are probably the constituents of the human body as conceived by people in early China. Namely, they represent the whole body of the human being. That is to say, we should be aware of individuality, which is the same as nothingness, expressing it in every cell of our bodies. He continues, "Repeat mu (void) with all the spiritual power you possess." This means that we should put our bodies and minds into mu, concentrating all our power as if it could make a hole through our buttocks and zazen cushions, and even burst through to the other side of the world.

The same can be said about susoku. We should count our breaths, "One, two . . . ." with all our might, as if trying to penetrate the earth. If we do not do this, the mind will never be brought into harmonious unity with breath and body.

Thus, the integration of the body, breath, and mind is nothing other than what we mean by *suwaru* (to sit). After all, we may safely say that the word suwaru is the harmony of mind, breathing, and body when we are in a very balanced and stable condition.

ILLUSTRATIONS OF THE UNIFICATION OF MIND, BREATH, AND BODY

Thus far I have been a little too theoretical and so I would like to include a story or two about Zen men of old. In the T'ang Dynasty of China there was a monk named Shiba Zuda (Ssu-ma T'ou-t'o) whose knowledge ranged from geography to the *I Ching*. When Shiba left the Province of Hu-nan to visit the well known Zen Master Hyakujo Ekai (Pai-chang Huai-hai)[30] who lived in the Prefecture of Nan-ch'ang in the Province of Chiang-hsi, he asked Hyakujo, "In Hunan there is a great mountain called Mount Ta Wei. I wonder if any of your pupils are willing to live on this mountain."

Master Hyakujo volunteered himself saying, "Don't ask the others. Instead, how about me?"

Shiba, however, shook his head in refusal and said, "No, that won't do. The place is not meant for someone like you."

"Why not?"

"Because you look like a bony lone wolf, a man of lofty character who remains aloof from others. You will not fit such a rich and fertile place. Man and environment must match each other. Therefore, if you live there, even though it is such a fertile and rich mountain, not even a thousand disciples will come."

"I see. Well, then, choose a promising one from among my disciples here, please."

"Please let me see them."

At that time Kakushuza (Chiao Shou-tso), head monk of Hua-lin, was the most advanced disciple of Master Hyakujo. Thus, it was natural that Kakushuza would be summoned ahead of the other monks.

Shiba said to the head monk, "I want you to walk five or six steps and clear your throat."

Shiba watched Kakushuza intently as he did what he had been told, said to Master Hyakujo, "Regretfully, this monk is not acceptable. He has failed."

Master Hyakujo's disciples were tested in this way one by one in the order of their rank in the monastery. But they all were disqualified until it finally came to the turn of Reiyu (Ling-yu) whose title in the monastery was *tenzo* (cook monk). Like all the other monks, Reiyu walked a few steps and cleared his throat. As soon as he did so Shiba made a decision on the spot.

"This monk," Shiba said, "is indeed qualified to be Master of Mount Ta Wei."

But Kakushuza was greatly dissatisfied with Shiba's decision. He protested, saying that the true realm of satori could not be verified through that test.

Master Hyakujo said, "All right, then, I will give the test myself." He tested Kakushuza first, pointing at the pitcher by his side and asking, "What do you call this without calling it a pitcher?"

Kakushuza answered, "By no means can it be called a piece of wood."

"Reiyu! How about you?"

Without saying a word, Reiyu immediately kicked over the pitcher with the tip of his toes. Master Hyakujo broke into a smile.

"Kakushuza, you have been outdone by this cook monk."

So saying, Master Hyakujo appointed Reiyu to be founder of the monastery on the great mountain called Ta Wei.

There once was a warrior who visited the residence of Tanabe Hachiemon Nagatsune, the man who taught the art of spear-fighting to Tokugawa Yoshinao in Nagoya. The warrior was over six feet tall, his face looked demonic, his long unbound hair fell down his back, and he wore a lined white silk kimono and a red sleeveless jacket. In answer to the warrior's call, Nagatsune, the master of the residence, showed himself. The instant they met, their eyes flashed at each other as sharply as lightning.

"Well, well. How wonderful to meet you," Nagatsune, the host, greeted his guest first. Then he continued, "Mr. Musashi, isn't it?"[31]

With one look Nagatsune knew intuitively that the guest was Musashi. If Musashi's visit to Nagoya was around the tenth year of Kan'ei (1633), he must have been around fifty. Tanabe Nagatsune was sixty-five or sixty-six. It is said that Nagatsune was as tall and strong as Musashi.

Musashi was invited into the guest room. These two men, the master of spear-fighting and the master of swordsmanship began talking to each other. According to the study carried out by the last Matsufuru Meizo, Nagatsune said,

> When I learned you had come to Nagoya, I thought of having a match with you, but now that we are sitting face to face, it seems futile to do so. Instead, would you like to play go[32] with my son? Meanwhile, I will prepare a meal of fish for you.

Then, instructing his son Tsuneyuki to have a game of go with Musashi, Nagatsune withdrew to the kitchen. His son Tsuneyuki was evidently a better player of go than Musashi, and sure enough, Musashi soon found himself driven to bay. Staring earnestly at the surface of the go board for a while, contemplating his opponent's move, Musashi suddenly slapped his go stone to the playing board.

"I won't let you do it!" exclaimed Musashi as if scolding his opponent. Tsuneyuki was taken aback by the unexpected sharpness of the sound of the go stone as well as the tone of Musashi's words. As he furtively looked up at Musashi's face, however, he found Musashi in his usual self-composure looking down at the go board as quietly as before. At that moment the laughing voice of Nagatsune reverberated from the adjoining room while the clanking of the training spear he had tossed down could be heard.

"Ha! Ha! Ha! You won't let me spear you, eh?" So saying, Nagatsune threw the sliding door open and revealed his tall figure, taking off the strap he used to tie his sleeves with. In the entrance of the house, when they met for the first time, they both knew at a glance that if either of them tried to kill the other, he would have to kill him thoroughly. However, Nagatsune wanted to make sure.

According to the volume titled *Shin-shin Gakudo* in Master Dogen's *Shobo-genzo*, it is written that there are two means of learning the Buddha Way—one is learning with the mind and the other is learning with the body. We temporarily regard the methods of learning the Way as two. However, they are ultimately one, for they equally emphasize the realization of the true human body.

Master Reiyu had definitely mastered the way of self-liberation from life and death; his spiritual training was manifested through his daily activities. Musashi, however, entered through learning the techniques of swordsmanship and learned the Way physically. His physical training was reflected in his spiritual life as well.

After all, both men underwent spiritual discipline in the Way with their whole mind and body as one. The Way of learning with the body corresponds to the experience of physical realization of the Way. The Way of learning with the mind also is included in the realm of physical realization and must be interrelated to the body and expressed through our physical activities. Otherwise, it cannot be regarded as the true Way of learning with the mind. In the final analysis, the correct posture of the body in formal Japanese style—with mind, breath, and body in oneness—comes from this "five-foot body" and "fifty-year life span." The true human body just as it is, is none other than the manifestation of Buddha.

Yamaoka Tesshu[33] was an accomplished master of Kendo and Zen of the early modern period. According to his biography, he poured his heart and soul into training himself in Kendo as well as Zen. It is said that whether he was at home or traveling, he always did zazen every night until about two o'clock. The way he did zazen was truly rigorous.

Tesshu was well-known for the poverty in which he lived during the prime of his life. His residence was totally dilapidated. There was only one tatami mat in the entire house and, on the spot he usually sat, there was a round hole where one could see the straw filling. Of course, rats ran about freely without regard to day or night. According to *Zensho-an Kiroku Bassui* (Excerpts from the Record of Zensho-an), "He left all the doors, walls, and ceilings torn just as they were." This give us a vivid picture of Tesshu in the days of his poverty.

Once Tesshu began zazen, however, all the rats which had been running about until that time would disappear without a trace. Tesshu's wife, who thought it was strange, asked him about it. He said with a laugh, "My Zen has value as a scarecrow for rats." I think that he must have sat with a vigorous spirit as if ready to meet a strong enemy with his sword. When he sat, he seemed so ferocious that no one could approach him. That awesome power of Tesshu must have made it unbearable for the rats to remain in Tesshu's house while he meditated.

It is also said, however, that in his later years, rats would play joyful-ly, running along his shoulders and arms as he copied Buddhist sutras. The dignified, spiritual power of Tesshu's sitting is what Master Suzuki Shosan calls Nio-Zen. We should emulate his example.

The bronze *umpan* hanging outside the kitchen, Daihonzan Chozen-ji, Honolulu. The umpan is a gong, one of the several instruments used throughout a Zen monastery to signal such events as the start of meditation or the gathering for a meal. The quality of sound is a clear reflection of the condition of the person striking the instrument.

Omori Sogen Rotaishi practicing the Hojo.

CHAPTER 4

Things to Pay Attention to during Meditation

ADVISABILITY OF PUTTING STRENGTH IN THE *HARA*

I think you generally understand what I have written about *how* to sit, but when you actually try to sit, many questions will arise. While it is impossible to anticipate and answer all the questions which may arise, I can take up two or three concrete examples of mistakes that often occur in the practice of zazen. I hope this will help beginners avoid unnecessary detours by informing them of possible errors in advance.

First, there is a tendency for people to think that "to sit" means "to put strength in the lower abdomen." Though they are mistaken, a considerable number of people think that unless they fill the lower abdomen with strength, it is impossible to sit in Zen meditation. They strain the lower abdomen to the limit thinking it is zazen. When I was young, some of my fellow Kendo students would wind rolls of white cotton cloth around their waists to make their lower abdomens bulge out and thus pretend they had a well-developed hara (the effect, however, reminded me more of large toads or malnourished children).

In the Jiki-shinkage-ryu (the Straight-Mind-Shadow school of swordsmanship) there is a basic set of movements called *Hojo* which is indeed the most magnificent I have ever known. It is accompanied by deep breathing marked by the sound "Ah" when inhaling and "Um" when exhaling. When we began training in Hojo we put great pressure on the lower abdomen and would hold our breath for a long time. Those who were weak often would faint due to cerebral anemia, but they fell happily, imagining that they were in samadhi. In those days, the older students encouraged the younger ones to breathe this way. I myself experienced this so-called samadhi several times and was elated by the praise of the older students. Fortunately, I was still so young and full of vitality that I suffered no permanent injury.

I shudder when I look back on it for it was really a dangerous thing to do. Some of my Zen friends put so much pressure on their lower abdomens that they created hernias and suffered for a long time. In view of these dangers, we have to be very careful about these problems.

On the other hand, Master Suzuki Shosan lamented that it would be useless to practice dead zazen—sitting absentmindedly. There are some people who have practiced zazen for a long time but who do not radiate a power that pervades their entire being. This will not do. In this sense, it is not a mistake to infuse the hara with energy, for it is an effective method for entering samadhi. However, it is harmful and ineffective to exert ourselves so much that we become dizzy. Then, what should we do? Essentially, we should let our spiritual strength instead of our physical strength fill our entire body, using the lower abdomen as the source.

In the Yagyu-ryu (a school of swordsmanship), there is a secret teaching called "*Seikosui*." Yagyu Toshinaga, a master of the Yagyu-ryu, taught that it was especially important to concentrate vital energy and power in the front of the body around the navel and at the back of the body in the koshi (pelvic) area when taking a stance. In other words, he means to fill the whole body with spiritual energy. In his *Nikon no Shimei*, Hida Haramitsu writes:

> The strength of the hara alone is insufficient; the strength of the koshi alone is not sufficient, either. We should balance the power of the hara and the koshi and maintain equilibrium of the seated body by bringing the center of the body's weight in line with the center of the triangular base of the seated body.[1]

I explained earlier that we should put strength in the area above the coccyx. This does not mean that we should strain ourselves and put excessive strength in the lower abdomen. It means we should expand the area ranging from the coccyx to the area right behind the naval in such a way as to push out the lower abdomen, while at the same time contracting the muscles of the anus.

When I observe beginning sitters, I notice that they usually put strength in the stomach area. This must be stopped. Physical strength varies from individual to individual, so we cannot say that everyone is alike and instruct them in the same way. It may be the least trouble to say as a general precaution that strength should be allowed to come to fullness naturally as one becomes proficient in sitting. We should sit so that our energy increases of itself and brims over instead of putting physical pressure on the lower abdomen by force. The question becomes, "What is the difference between spiritual power and physical power?" It is difficult to answer. All I can say is that if we practice zazen for a long time and become proficient at it, we will naturally come to know the difference.

Master Suzuki Shosan berated his pupils, saying:

> Beginners should by all means strive for Truth. You must not force yourself to train or do zazen too vigorously before you realize the Truth. If you forcefully let out energy and practice Zen in violent ways, you will become fatigued, lose your energy, and it will all be of no use.[2]

He stressed the use of the energy of Nio, but this does not mean you should put excessive strength in the abdomen. When standing correctly and holding his sword in a stern attitude, Shosan taught that this was the energized working of Zen concentration. This matter cannot be fully comprehended except by learning it through one's own experience.

In short, all this should emphasize the concentration of power in the whole body by simultaneously placing strength in the tanden and by infusing

These two statues represent the two Nio, or deities, that often guard the entrance to Japanese Buddhist temples. They embody the intense concentration emphasized by Suzuki Shosan. Notice that the Nio on the left is portrayed inhaling, making the sound "Ah," and the other is exhaling, making the sound "um." (Permanent collection, Daihonzan Chozen-ji)

the whole body with energy moving away from the tanden. Thus, by means of the equilibrium of the centrifugal and the centripetal force, the whole body is brought to a state of zero and spiritual power will pervade the whole body intensely.

On Munen Muso (No-thought and No-thinking)

What I want to discuss next is the preconception that one's spiritual condition during meditation is devoid of any thought and thinking. As in the case of the use of strength in the lower abdomen, there are large number of people—so-called believers—who misunderstand the concept of "no-thought and no-thinking" (Jpn. munen muso).

These people make the mistake of literally interpreting the term no-thought and no-thinking as meaning without thought and not thinking of anything. They lament that no matter how they try, they cannot get rid of their thoughts or the act of thinking. In such cases I say, "Drink some *sake* [rice wine] and go to sleep; I am sure you will be free from thought and thinking," or "Take some sleeping pills and sleep soundly."

Once the mind is unified and thinking subsides, it is natural that we should hear the sounds which would otherwise remain inaudible. Sarutobi Sasuke (a famous *ninja*), is said to have heard a needle fall over 350 yards away as distinctly as if it had fallen right near him. You may not be Sarutobi Sasuke but if you can hear such a remote sound, the term "immovable quietness" would apply to you.

There are various levels, shallow and deep, in samadhi or Zen concentration such as the condition of no-thought and the condition where all affective disturbances fall away. Even half-opened eyes can naturally see things as long as their functioning is sound. From the physiological standpoint, even during zazen it is inevitable that as long as we have ears, we will hear sounds which come in contact with our eardrums. I do not mean to encourage anybody to purposely see and hear things during meditation, but as long as the five sense organs are working properly, it is natural for us to see and hear things if we are not sleeping. In a sense it proves that we are alive.

As Zen Master Hakuin writes in his *Neboke no Mezamashi*,[3] "Even if you become selfless, do not be a fool. Selflessness is not something external to you. Quit your selfish, one-sided thinking and uphold the principles of nature." This means that we should stop our selfish one-sided thinking, including the petty schemes and delusions which we ourselves create. Master

Bankei[4] writes about something similar in his *Bucchi Kozai Zenji Hogo*. A certain man asked Bankei, "Is it because my daily self-discipline is inadequate that I get easily scared at the sounds of things such as thunder? What measures should I take so that I do not get frightened by anything?"

In answer to this Bankei said, "When you get frightened, just be as you are. If you take precautions, you'll be dualistic." This is interesting. As long as our nerves are sound, we inevitably show a physiological reaction to any sound that suddenly reverberates around us. The problem is whether or not the noise will cause what Hans Selye calls stress diseases.

In *Neboke no Mezamashi*, Hakuin continues his verse, "Learning means to learn the origins of joy, anger, sorrow, and pleasure and to learn who uses the eyes, ears, nose, tongue, and body and moves the hands and feet." As he expresses in verse, it is not necessarily bad to let emotions such as joy, anger, pity, and pleasure arise. The point is that we should laugh when we are supposed to laugh and cry when we are supposed to cry in accord with the principle of moderation so that we may express ourselves with propriety. It is needless for us to be unduly afraid and to escape from the seven emotions. When we are faced with arousal of the seven emotions, we should trace it to its source, inquiring, "What is this?" This itself is Zen training, which is not to be idly set aside by the false adherence to "no-thought and no-thinking."

As for the images and sounds which arise during meditation, they are all right if they do not give rise to dualistic thought and if they do not cause thoughts to follow. An ancient saying goes, "The succession of dualistically conceived thoughts is called a disease of the mind." Master Bankei likewise says in *Gojimon Sho*,[5] "If you happen to get angry in spite of yourself, and thoughts of stinginess and greed arise in your mind, leave them as they are. Do not pile them up and let them grow, do not attach yourself to them, and they will have to disappear."

Master Bankei also taught, "It is better not to divide one mind into two." His words are indeed to the point. What is wrong is to retain thoughts and let them grow, to become attached to various thoughts one after another. For example, if we sit in meditation and hear the whistle of a train in the distance, we should let the sound of the whistle go through our ears as it naturally does. In actuality, we tend to let the whistle remind us of the train trips we made long ago and then recall the various experiences we had on those trips. Thus, various thoughts and ideas are aroused one after another beyond control, like horses running about wildly or monkeys jumping from branch to branch endlessly. It is this way of becoming attached to thoughts which is wrong.

However, even such a great priest as Master Hakuin could not help recalling such occurrences as the loan of some black beans to the elderly lady next door three years before. Indeed, as long as we have minds, we cannot help thinking of various things one after another. It is not right, however, to let one thought follow another endlessly and permit ourselves to develop those thoughts. What is worse still is to be annoyed by them and to pay attention to them. As soon as random thoughts arise we should say, "There they are again." In short, the best thing to do is, "not to meddle with delusive imaginings." It is said in Priest Honen's[6] verse:

> Ignoring disturbing thoughts and letting them arise
> If they happen to arise,
> I concentrate on invoking Amida Buddha.[7]

The best and most effective way to be free from disturbing thought and thinking is to be concentrated on our own business without being distracted by other matters. It is good to face our own problems with the courage of a warrior ready to jump alone into the middle of a great army of one million soldiers. He could encourage himself, "If disturbing thoughts and fantasies want to arise, I will let them arise. I am as free as ever to count my breaths and concentrate on my koan." The quiet state of "no-thought and no-thinking," like a punctured rubber ball, is not taken seriously in correctly transmitted zazen.

There is an expression, "the matter of eggs," which appears in the traditional book used in the Jiki-shinkage-ryu. This seems to mean that we should keep practicing our arts diligently like the chicken in the egg that imperceptibly grows day by day. I would like to interpret the above phrase in terms of the following passage from the Enanji,[8] ". . . as well integrated as an egg which contains an embryo even in its indivisible oneness."

I told my teacher Yamada Ittokusai about the following interpretation of the "egg" and he approved. Having no eyes or nose, the egg is in the indivisible state of oneness, but it contains one instantaneous opportunity for the potential chick to jump out of the cracked egg-shell crying, "Cock-a-doodle-do." Thus, the egg is invested with a priori vitality.

When one holds one's sword face to face with one's opponent, there is no separation between the two. The undivided indivisible state of integration is maintained with the Self as the one and only general striding over Heaven and Earth. However, at the same time, a living opportunity waits for one to act spontaneously at any moment in response to the slightest change in the surroundings. Sitter and surrounding must be like this. We should take care not to become like the stone images of Jizo abandoned to the loneliness and emptiness of mountains.

As I have already written, Priest Hakuin is said to have remarked, "If you indeed practice such rotten zazen, gambling is more effective for concentration and raising your energy level." According to the *The Analects of Confucius*, "Those who indulge in food all day long without disciplining their minds are hopeless. Isn't there something called gambling? They would be better off gambling than living like that." I wonder if Priest Hakuin did not take the essence of Confucius' saying and make it his own. No doubt the ancient sage and the Zen priest who came later shared the same principle.

Master Daie Soku (Ta-hui Tsung-kao)[9] wrote in one of his letters to Chosha Jogen (Chang-she Chuang-yuan),

> They sit in meditation in the Ghosts' Cave at the foot of the Black Mountain idly without preaching and without saying anything. Drawing their eyebrows together and closing their eyes, they say they are in the state of absolute samadhi and in the state of their fathers and mothers not yet born. Further, calling this state silence filled with eternal light, they identify their meditation with Zen.

In this way Master Daie denounced pupils of unorthodox Zen who were entrapped in sterile, empty opinions and in the state of "no-thought and no-thinking." He saw them as deprived of their freedom and alertness.

According to the *Keitoku Dento-roku*, a monk named Shisei (Chih-ch'eng) had at first been trained by Shinshu (Shen-hsiu) before he became a disciple of Master Eno (Hui-neng), the Sixth Patriarch. When Shisei came to Eno, the Master asked how Master Shinshu had taught him, Shisei answered honestly, "He taught me to calm the mind and contemplate. He made me sit in silence for a long time without letting me lie down." Hearing this, Master Eno scolded Shisei, "To calm the mind and contemplate is a Zen disease and not Zen. To what avail is it in principle to sit for a long time and suffer physical pain?"

The lay Zen Master Kawajiri Hogin also warns against this empty type of sitting:

> To begin with, most people who practice zazen consciously try to make themselves empty. This is a grave mistake because you have thoughts about becoming empty, and it is futile to sit however

long you may try to do so. For instance, suppose there is a bowl
of rice. However long you may stare at it wishing it to become
empty, the rice will never disappear. And the more you think of
some clever way to make it disappear, the harder will it become
for you to do so. While you keep on staring at it anticipating its
disappearance with increasing impatience, evening will come. On
the contrary, however, if you eat the rice right away according to
the Dharma instead of wondering whether you should get rid of it
or not, it will disapear as quickly as you wish. The same is true of
zazen. As long as you are conscious of your wish to be empty, you
will never succeed in becoming empty.[10]

The above is indeed true. Instead of thinking passively of ridding ourselves of our thoughts and thinking, as we read in Roankyo we should arouse
our spirit of the immovable Nio and Fudo who make the devils surrender, and
then liberate ourselves from afflictions of doubt by entertaining the mind of Nio.

Hogin continues, "As for the ordinary man of little capacity, he tries to
empty himself and see his own empty self. He is intent on staring at himself
only." Hogin further writes that by doing so "such a man practices zazen in the
wrong way." Here lies the mistake of the believers of "no-thought and no-
thinking." These people forget that the true meaning of the phrase comes alive
when they become one with susoku and koan. We should remember that by
being well integrated with any matter or thing, we will naturally come to be
liberated from our attachment to them. Being liberated from our attachment to
any matter or thing does not mean escaping from it. Far from it, in the true
sense of the word, "no-thought and no-thinking" means flowing steadily and
endlessly in the pure experience of the oneness of self and other. We must take
every care to be aware of this true sense of "no-thought and no-thinking."

Further, I consider the following words of Master Takeda Mokurai[11]
from Zen no Katsatsu to be quite significant:

They say that if you practice Zen, you will be calm. Some misunderstand these words because they are attached to the literal sense
of the word "calm." They think they will be completely unaffected even when struck by a thunderbolt. But this is not true. The
subtle meaning of Zen lies in spontaneous response. If thunder
peals, we peal, too; if an earthquake comes to shake us, we ourselves shake with it. It is childish to say that those who practice
Zen will never care nor fuss about anything.

The Direction of Zazen

In the preceding chapters I have referred to *Zazen no Shokei* written by the lay Zen Master Kawajiri Hogin. I would further like to introduce here one of the chapters from the same book. In the chapter, *"Zazen no Hoko"* ("the Direction of Zazen"), the writer reminds the student of the correct objectives of zazen. If we are correctly oriented in the right direction, there will be no problem. But, if we are misdirected and move diagonally, we will continue to proceed diagonally and not in a straight line. Therefore, it is not an exaggeration to say that though we meant to go to Tokyo, we might possibly arrive in Echigo instead.[12]

As I have already discussed in the preceding section, by trying to become "no-thought and no-thinking," we create the idea of "no-thought and no-thinking." This is one example of the wrong direction of zazen. Another example is found in those of us who fail to be completely selfless in zazen (when we are supposed to be aware of our selflessness). The longer we sit and the deeper we enter into samadhi, the more unmanageable our self-centered opinions will become. In this sense, the direction of zazen is a very important matter.

Kawajiri Hogin classifies those who sit for wrong reasons as:

1) those who sit in order to tranquilize their minds;
2) those who sit to be empty in their minds;
3) those who solve koan as if they were guessing games;
4) those who start sitting, motivated by their wish for escape
     from this disturbing world.

Some of these types of people are no longer found around us, for the world has changed since Hogin's book was written. Nonetheless, these classifications may still serve as a good reference. When all of the wrong directions are forgotten, the right and true direction will be revealed. This is indeed exactly so.

Regarding those who sit in order to tranquilize their minds, Hogin writes, "It is not a bad thing to quiet one's mind, for even in Confucianism there is such a term as 'ching-tso' meaning tranquil sitting. The Confucians sit in order to calm their minds." Today, very few people in general study Confucianism. Those who teach Chinese Classics at various schools may be the only ones who study Confucianism.

In my opinion, there no longer exists any such thing as Confucianism. That is to say, there seem to be very few people, if any, who sit in tranquil meditation in order to study Confucianism. I mean that those who are inclined to tranquil meditation are apt to think that they have sat long enough as soon as disturbing thoughts within them subside during meditation. But thinking that they have sat long enough in itself is dualistic. As long as they are captured by such a thought, they cannot be liberated from dualism however long they may wait. These people may be compared to debtors who are annoyed by their debt-collectors every day except in the evening. Although they are free from the debt-collectors in the evening, they will be disturbed by them again on the following day as long as they are indebted to them.

These days, we are apt to become irritated and restless spiritually because we are living in a complex and busy world. Moreover, as is clear in Hans Selye's stress theory, we often find ourselves over-sensitive, both in mind and body, to the stimuli of our social environments. Therefore, we are apt to become neurotic.

According to Takeuchi Daishin, we become susceptible to diseases when the acidity of our blood rises above normal. He contends that the three causes for acidosis are spirit, food, and environment and refers to this phenomenon as "three causes with one result." "Spirit" includes feeling, including will, emotion, and temperament. These three fundamental conditions of health must always function properly to keep our blood consistently alkaline. We must adjust our living so as to allow the function of these fundamental conditions to normalize our blood.

While Zen can be practiced as a means of maintaining health, it is necessary for us to know that the maintenance of health alone is not the final destination of Zen. We do not have to severely criticize those who get off the train halfway on their trip in order to appreciate the beautiful scenery before arriving at their destination. Nor should we force passengers to continue their trips while they do not have enough money (perseverance) to pay for their extra tickets. But as we have not yet arrived at our final destination, we cannot remain where we are to live in freedom and contentment for the rest of our lives. We must always bear in mind that our old unpaid debts will return to haunt us.

Next, we have to discuss those people who try to become empty. This problem of emptiness naturally comes up when we feel uneasy about human existence as such and search for its origin. Even today it is theoretically studied as nothingness or non-existence, but I think average practitioners of Zen turn to it as "no-thought and no-thinking." I have already mentioned their mutual analogies and differences, so I do not think it necessary to write about them any further here. Kawajiri Hogin writes,

> They take trouble to create something called "emptiness" which they regard as separate from their own being. They aspire to this idea of emptiness, and in addition, they try to be empty of mental activity again and again. Thus, their deluded knowledge will keep on increasing so much that it will impede their becoming empty even if they wait for one hundred years. Even if they succeed in becoming empty in this way, it will be to no avail. It is mistaken to believe that to become empty is satori. If to become empty meant satori (enlightenment), human beings would be enlightened every time they wake up in the morning because they become empty every night during their sleep.[13]

This remark is indeed to the point.

Now, I am going to write about those who practice zazen mistaking it for a means of contemplation and as a means of only finding the answers to a koan.[14] Kawajiri Hogin criticizes them, writing, "These people outwardly appear to sit in zazen, but actually they are confused in mind, being over-filled with wild imaginations. This kind of zazen is called the zazen practiced daily just to kill time." They are exactly like some of the people who are absorbed in solving quizzes in weekly magazines. The publication *Koan Kaito Shu*[15] (The Collection of Answers to Koan) has recently become controversial in one part of the Zen world. Thinking that a koan is something to be thought about and solved objectively is out of keeping with Zen teachings.

I always try to make clear to my disciples that one should become one with a koan; it is not to be solved intellectually. As a result, none of my disciples misunderstand the function of koan training.

If we were to briefly explain what a koan is, I would say it means *kofu no antoku* ("public decree"). "Kofu" is what is presently called a government office. Therefore, "kofu no antoku" means an official document or decree authorized by the government. Consequently, koan pertains to incidents or cases in which Buddhist patriarchs attained enlightenment. As Chuho Myohon (Chung-feng Ming-pan)[16] makes clear, "'*Ko*' of koan means that the footprints of all the ancient sages are one. '*An*' of koan means official documents about principles of the sages." Koan is thus to be interpreted as principles that people should depend on.

A koan is not at all the product of the personal assumptions or opinions of anyone. Whereas we now have a known set of koan, originally there was no such thing as a koan in Zen. In the early days, each Zen monk who was suffering from some unavoidable problem which urgently needed solution had his Master present him with some ways of solving them. In later years, Zen masters and their disciples followed examples set by their predecessors who had succeeded in solving their problems. These problems later helped Zen monks to solve similar problems and they came to be called koan.

Therefore, the classification of koan is not simple. It is said that there are as many as one thousand seven hundred koan. They are classified according to the specific styles of the different schools in which they have been employed. In our School of Tekisui, koan problems are generally classified into *hosshin* (The body of Dharma), *kikan* (dynamism), *gonsen* (verbal expression), *nanto* (difficulty in passing through), *kojo* (stage of refinement), and *matsugo no rokan* (the final gate).

It is now clear that koan are not to be solved intellectually like quizzes or mathematical problems. As already mentioned, we should solve them through kufu, trying to become one with them. For instance, Master Daie (Tahui) says this about kufu:

> In training ourselves to solve koan, we should neither make guesses or comments nor try to understand them. It is unnecessary to know the meanings of the words or justify our attitudes toward the koan presented to us. On the contrary, we should neither be empty and tranquil nor expect to be enlightened. It is still worse to be absent-minded. Whether we walk, dwell, sit, or lie down, we should always be one with the koan and try to keep in touch with them all the time.[17]

In the *Mumonkan*, Master Mumon Ekai (Wu-men Hui-k'ai) states,

> Arouse your entire body with its three hundred and sixty bones and joints and its eighty-four thousand pores of the skin. Summon up a spirit of great doubt and concentrate on this word "mu." In order to do so, hold to the problem from morning to night without letting it go even for one second, and become one with the word "mu" (void) with all your strength.

I am not going to discuss the koan problems which fall under the categories of gonsen, nanto, and kojo here. Those which fall under the category of hosshin are the first ones presented by masters to beginning Zen students. They are generally solved through kufu in the above-mentioned way. The word kufu means, as I have already explained, being without any *suki* (opening or flaw in terms of swordsmanship) or *yudan* (carelessness) and to become the thing itself.

As for the koan of mu originally presented by Joshu, we should apply ourselves to it with all our strength at every drawing of our breath until we no longer know whether mu is us or we are mu. In this way, we will individually enter into the state of oneness. We should never treat the koan of mu as the object of our thought.

If the trainee is ignorant of this meaning of koan and misunderstands the method of kufu, his teacher or instructor is to blame, and not the trainee. At the same time, we should not discuss whether koan is good or not, or whether it is necessary or not, until after we are through with the whole course of koan. If we superficially insist on the uselessness of koan without being thoroughly integrated with the koan mu, we would be called frivolous.

It is said, "The same water becomes milk if taken by the cow or poison if taken by the snake." Koan as such are not subject to praise or to blame. We should note that koan consist of the blood and tears shed by the ancients. Whether they become milk or poison depends on those who resort to them for guidance. Zazen is far from being a means of solving koan as if they were quizzes or games.

Last of all, I will write about those who sit in zazen because of their wish for escape from the turmoil and troubles of this world. Though these people seem to have existed in the Meiji and Taisho eras (1868–1926), we seldom meet these people any longer. I think that as the world becomes increasingly complicated and noisy, some people give in to despair and become nihilistic. Kierkegaard indicated that some become aware of the truth of being out of their despair with themselves. However, contemporary nihilists are different; many of them seem to be lazy in their attitudes. They are inclined to escape from the troubles of this world, but they do not seem to be willing to sit in zazen.

Kawajiri Hogin notes that Buddhism is not asceticism. On the contrary, the ascetic mind grows out of one's attachment to the body and, like all attachments, this is rejected by Buddhists. Therefore, even if you escape from the world to live in the mountain forests all alone, you will never succeed in entering into the essence of zazen for you are disturbed by your own attachment.

According to Kawajiri Hogin, if all of the above-mentioned mistakes are removed, you will find yourself oriented in the true direction of zazen. Zazen should never become a means of making yourself feel good nor should it be a tranquilizer to settle excitement and wild thoughts. What is of primary importance is what the ancients called "no gaining and no merit." Indeed, zazen consists in awakening us to our own essence so as to secure and express our true selves in our everyday conduct.

If being awakened to the true self is called satori (enlightenment) or kensho (seeing our true self), to reveal it after enlightenment in all of our daily conduct may seem a natural result of our strenuous efforts. But, even if we are aware of the essence of our being, we will not immediately succeed in reflecting it in everything we do in our daily lives. An ancient saying goes, "Mistaken theories can be as easily smashed as crushing stones, but mistaken feelings cannot be renounced so easily, for they are like the filaments that continue to connect a lotus root which has been broken apart." In other words, mistakes in our opinions can be removed fairly simply if we come to know our original being; it will be comparatively easy for us to make a change in our way of thinking. However, mistakes in our feelings or the habits of our emotions cannot be removed just as the filament of a lotus root unfolds itself endlessly whenever we break it crosswise.

As noted in the *Ten Oxherding Pictures*,[18] sighting the ox may not be very difficult, but catching and herding of the ox can take ten to twenty long years. During this time, it is necessary for us to mature steadily, continue to make many laborious efforts, and endure severe discipline. In the course of time, we will be able to be masters wherever we may be. If we succeed in becoming masters wherever we are, we will be free anywhere and everywhere. Everything then will become the concrete embodiment of truth wherever we may stand.

For instance, some of us are proudly aware of our own power of Zen concentration when we quietly count the frequency of our breathing, or when we become one with koan. However, if our power of Zen concentration is disrupted when we stop meditation and continue with the activities of our everyday life, we are apt to be confused and dismayed. Perhaps everyone has experienced this.

If we become the guests (at the mercy of circumstances around us) wherever we may go, and if we find everything untrue wherever we may stand, we are headed in the opposite direction from Zen. The true direction of Zen, then, must be found when we are fully aware of our True Selves, when we are the masters wherever we go, and when we are free wherever we are.

How Long Should We Sit?

I have so far written a great deal about zazen. Since this book is meant to be a guide book for beginners in zazen, I will continue to write in detail all that comes to my mind even if it seems to be trivial. Generally speaking, I think we can sit in meditation by ourselves at home if we try to do exactly as I have written so far. Yet, I am going to write further about some concrete matters concerning zazen.

The second chapter in Master Harada Sogaku's *Sanzen no Hiketsu* mentions that direct knowledge of the practice of zazen corresponds to those topics I have already covered. Indirect knowledge, however, consists of several more topics. For instance, the way to sit and face the wall, the place to do zazen, things to do before and after meals, and so on are discussed fully and in great detail by Master Sogaku. Some of them seem to be common sense and known to everyone, but many of them require our attention.

Concerning the length of time for sitting, those of us who are used to zazen are free to sit as long as we like. However, the duration of zazen is an important consideration for beginners. Master Harada Sogaku writes, "For beginners it is adequate to sit for about thirty minutes at a time."

When I was a beginner, I used to sit until one incense stick about eight inches long burned—that is, for approximately forty-five minutes. When I was twenty-two or twenty-three years old, I started studying calligraphy with the calligrapher Yokoyama Setsudo. Before we started practicing calligraphy, he used to make us sit in meditation for a much longer time, until three incense sticks burned one after another. To us it seemed too long to endure.

I used to sleep until the first stick burned out so the first stick did not matter to me at all. The most effective part of meditation was while the first half of the second incense stick was burning. When our teacher lit the third incense-stick, I could not help resenting him. Until the third stick burned out, all I did was look at the lighted tip of the third incense stick impatiently for I felt pain in my knees and I was tired of sitting. It was far from being the true way of sitting. I wonder if beginners will not have the same experience though they may want to sit for a long time.

Zazen is not test of endurance so it is meaningless to sit without concentrating and unifying mind and body. Psychologists say that a man's mental activity goes up and down at a regular interval of one hour or so. Therefore, thirty or forty minutes, corresponding to the length of time it takes one incense stick to burn, is an adequate time for beginners to sit. There is a saying, "If we sit one minute, we will be Buddhas for one minute." Even five or ten minutes will be sufficient if we sit seriously with all our energy. It is not how long we sit that matters but how we sit that is important.

At Tenryu-ji, the temple where I trained in Zen, a priest named Gasan often told a story when he served as *jikijitsu* during sesshin and other similar occasions. This kind of story-telling is referred to as *kokuho* (announcement) but it is meant to serve as intense encouragement to the monks in training. The story goes like this:

Once there lived an elderly lady who was wholeheartedly devoted to *nembutsu* (the invocation of Amida Buddha's name). She would recite "*Namu-Amidabutsu*" from morning to night whether she was seated or standing. She never neglected to visit the temple and never missed any sermon. Out of respect for her virtue, everyone called her "Nembutsu Grandmother."

When she died, however, contrary to everyone's expectations she was dragged to the Black Gate of Hell. Weeping, she begged Enma, the Judge of Hell, "When I was living, I never neglected to recite the Buddha's name, and so I was called 'Nembutsu Grandmother.' Since I have come with a cartful of nembutsu tablets, please let me go to Paradise."

Enma told the devils of Hell to check the nembutsu tablets which the woman had brought with her. The devils checked them one by one, but they found them to be empty nembutsu such as "Ah, my grandchild is pissing, Namu-Amidabutsu. Oh, the fire is burning, Namu-Amidabutsu. Oh, it's dangerous, Namu-Amidabutsu. It's hot, it's hot, Namu-Amidabutsu," and so on. The copious nembutsu tablets which she brought with her in the cart all turned out to be empty and she was on the point of being sent to Hell. Just then, a banging sound was heard at the bottom of the cart. Curiously, the devils took it out. It seemed to be a nembutsu with something in it so they closely examined it through a magnifying glass. To their great surprise, they found that it was a nembutsu recited by the woman when she was still a young girl.

One summer day, when she was young, she was walking across the wide field on her way to the temple as usual. Suddenly, the sky was filled with dark clouds, and a great evening storm came. Lightning crossed the sky in rapid succession and thunder pealed menacingly. She was afraid of thunder, and she could not stand it. So she cried out, "*Nammai-da, Nammai-da*," with all her heart and with all her might as she hurried along. Suddenly, with a deafening sound, a thunderbolt struck the ground right in front of her. "Namu-Amidabutsu!" she cried desperately at the top of her voice. Then she lost consciousness.

The last nembutsu was the only real nembutsu that she ever uttered. The rest of her nembutsu were all empty. But, thanks to this one real nembutsu, Enma permitted the elderly lady to go to Paradise.

During my early Zen training, our jikijitsu would both scold and encourage us, "How is your zazen? You look miserable, sitting like kneaded cow-dung. As long as you sit like that, you will never be able to pass even the first barrier to enlightenment. Imitate 'Nembutsu Grandmother' and practice saying, 'Mu,' with your hara [lower abdomen] filled with energy!" Such violent words of denunciation and encouragement would rain down on us.

This story of the elderly lady devoted to nembutsu was told to us many times. And I find in her nembutsu a very interesting analogy to zazen. Like empty nembutsu, empty zazen will be of no use no matter how long, how often, or for how many days we may sit during sesshin. It is far better to sit earnestly even for five minutes.

In order to measure time, an incense stick is better than a watch or a clock. A long stick of incense lasts for forty or forty-five minutes and a short one for twenty minutes. If we want to sit for fifteen minutes, we should adjust the length of an incense stick properly in advance so that it will last for fifteen minutes. If we have plenty of time and want to sit longer, we should divide our time, for if we sit alone for a long time, we are apt to get tired. Those of us who are used to zazen may sit for one or two hours at a stretch, but it is better for beginners to limit the duration of sitting to forty minutes at a time and to do *kinhin* (Zen meditation in walking) at various intervals.

Kinhin means walking in the Zen hall after sitting in Zen meditation for some time. We walk meditatively with our hands held against our chests. The closed right hand held lightly against the chest is covered with the left hand, and both of the arms are held up horizontally. In the Soto sect, they walk very slowly half a step at a time. In our Rinzai sect, however, we walk briskly enough to feel the wind hitting our ears. We sometimes even run hurriedly outside the monastery.

At the signal for kinhin, we quickly stand up, lock our hands over our chest, turn to the left, and start walking immediately. On one hand, kinhin is a kind of exercise to ease our fatigue after sitting, and on the other, it is training to bring about the oneness of movement and calmness. When we generally sit on the cushions in tranquility, we grapple with susoku or koan so that we may enter koan samadhi. We are apt to instantaneously come out of samadhi as soon as we are on our feet for a few moments. This is because we are lacking in the full power of Zen concentration.

By getting to our feet and walking in kinhin while we are one with susoku or koan, we discipline ourselves to realize the oneness of tranquility and movement so that we may not be controlled and upset by our environment in our everyday life. If we understand this well, will not take kinhin lightly.

Now, is it enough to sit once a day for the duration of one incense stick to burn out? I do not think that people really cannot find time to sit because of work pressure. Anyone can sit for thirty minutes or one hour before going to bed if only they are willing to do so. If possible, we should sit as often as we can every day. In case it is impossible for us to sit many times a day, we must find ways to sit in the intervals of our work or while riding buses and trains on our way to and from work in addition to sitting once a day before going to bed.

Tokugawa Ieyasu[19] is also said to have performed his religious training every night though, in his case, it was discipline in the chanting and writing of the Buddha's name instead of zazen. The National Museum in Tokyo has preserved one example of the nembutsu calligraphy that he carefully wrote every night. Perhaps because the books I had read in my boyhood used Ieyasu's nickname, "Old Man Badger," I did not like him. But ever since I saw the calligraphy in which he repeatedly and respectfully wrote the name of the Buddha every night, I have come to sincerely respect him.

The sheet of paper on which he wrote the name of the Buddha repeatedly is the size of a sheet of Mino paper.[20] The characters for "Namu-Amidabutsu" almost fully cover the page. The brushstrokes are beautiful, the the ink penetrates the paper, and from beginning to end there is no trace of loss of concentration. Indeed, he displayed increasing virtuosity toward the end. Such work can never be done except by one of great character.

One night Ieyasu went to bed neglecting his daily task of copying the name of the Buddha, but somehow or other he found himself ill at ease. So, he got up and started copying the characters as usual. Just then the blade of a sword was thrust upwards from under the bed on which he had been lying. He escaped his enemy's attack by chance because he was engaged in *nembutsu-gyo* instead of laying asleep in his bed.

Apart from nembutsu, we can cure our fatigue by sitting truly well in meditation, even if we shorten the time of our sleep. This has been proved by many who have experienced zazen. Ten minutes of zazen before reading and the momentary immersion in samadhi before work—how well they help us enjoy our work and reading, and to what a great extent they enhance our efficiency!

I am going to write next about sesshin, although it is up to you whether you will attend it or not. It is advisable to take part in one week's sesshin in a Zen dojo at least once or twice a year. In order to do so, you are usually advised to save enough time and money. As I have written before, the accumulated effect of zazen will be great, even if the duration of each sitting is short if you sit every day. Still greater will the effect of zazen become if you keep on sitting for one week, forgetting your work and worldly matters. If you succeed in sitting through sesshin even once, you will want to sit more often and longer still.

CONTINUE TRAINING LONG AND STEADILY

I do not know whether or not the term "mosquito pupils" is still used today. From the Taisho Era to the beginning of the Showa Era,[21] when I was doing severe training, Kendo and Judo[22] teachers often used the term "mosquito pupils." I do not know the exact meaning of the term, but it seems to mean those people who practice their arts only during the season when mosquitoes are plentiful.

When I was a boy, a friend of mine invited me to attend the midsummer course of Judo at a certain *dojo*[23] in town. There were a great number of pupils attending and it was successful. One day a visitor to the dojo complimented the master of the dojo by saying, "You have a great number of pupils, don't you?" The master of the dojo said in reply, "Well, all of them are mosquito pupils."

Passing by the dojo as we strolled in the town, we would hear the thudding sounds of the throwing and falling Judo pupils or the cracking sounds of the bamboo swords striking one another. Looking into the dojo through the open windows, we felt like joining them. But as we entered the dojo without any real wish to learn Judo or Kendo, we tended to disappear from the dojo together with the mosquitoes as the autumn wind began to blow.

When it grew warm again the next year, we were again tempted to join them by their vigorous shouts which flowed out of the open windows of the dojo and returned to resume our lessons giving the excuse that we had been ill to explain our long absence. In short, the term "mosquito pupils" means weak-willed and indolent pupils who attended or left the dojo as the mosquitoes did.

Master Harada Sogaku writes, "If the kettle is put over the fire and then taken off the fire, heated and cooled alternately, the water in it will never come to boil. Those who resemble such a kettle are called kettle-minded pupils."[24] Looking back over my past, I confess that I was one of those kettle-minded pupils. The term "mosquito pupils" used in connection with Kendo and Judo may correspond to the term "kettle minds" used in connection with Zen.

In our Zen Association, the number of advanced disciples remains constant, but the number of new disciples varies though they are neither mosquitoes nor kettles. Of course, we cannot force them to keep boiling. The problem may be the method of teaching which is incapable of bringing anyone from 80 degrees to 150 degrees in a moment. But those pupils who quit and resume their discipline alternately without being able to endure discipline continually must reflect on themselves. I remember that my former teacher Seisetsu Roshi once said, "Anyway, you have to do it sooner or later. If so, you should do it with all your might while you are still young and vigorous enough to twist and break the wisteria vines with your bare hands."

Zazen is called the Gate to Comfort. But it takes a considerable length of time to be able to sit in comfort and say, "Indeed, this is the Gate to Comfort." Being sleepy and suffering from stiff shoulders and painful legs, we find zazen strenuous at first and far from being comfortable.

When people read articles about the popularity of Zen outside of Japan, they feel like sitting for a while. If they hear that Zen is good for neuroses, they start sitting at once. However, when they start sitting, they find it hard to concentrate, and then they begin to feel pain in their legs. Thereupon, they stop sitting. After ten days or so they are reminded of sitting again and resume their practice of meditation. If we repeat all this as if taking a kettle on and off the stove, the water in the kettle will never come to boil. Therefore, it is necessary for us to be patient and continue to sit for a certain period of time even if we have to suffer in doing so.

Unless we are well equipped with three important things—great faith, great doubt, and great will—we will never attain Great Dharma. If we have great faith, we will be able to make steadfast efforts to fulfill our wish to attain Great Dharma at any cost. But, as I have said before, it is impossible to expect the average person to have great faith. At first great faith, great doubt, and great will may be beyond our reach. So, faith, doubt, and will are enough for beginners. If we are ever so eager as to start sitting in Zen meditation, we are strongly advised to have the will to sit every day for at least one or two years and continue to practice Zen without fail.

It is generally said that it takes ten years to master one art. Therefore, it is necessary to be trained continually for a considerable number of years in order to master any skill, however trivial it may seem. Furthermore, zazen cannot be mastered even by intelligent people in one or two hours or two months of sitting, for in zazen we are to attain our true selves and to be well aware of the nobility of human beings.

In order to continue to practice sitting for a considerably long period of time, besides having great faith and will, it is necessary to have a love for zazen. There is a time-honored saying, "Because we like something, we become good at it." If we reluctantly discipline ourselves in Zen without liking it, we will not be good at it nor continue it. However, there is another saying, "Though we are not good at something, we like it."

The word "like" has many nuances. Even if we do not yet have great faith, we should at least have love for sitting in order to continue zazen. In training sessions during World War II in Japan, even those who did not like zazen were forced to sit. But today we no longer force anybody to sit against their will. Here I am addressing only those of us who like zazen to varying degrees. In order to continue to practice zazen, we must develop a love for the Way. In addition, it is very important to continue to try to deepen our love for zazen. However, though we may love zazen very much, we must remember that we must endure a certain amount of pain.

In view of my own experiences, the will of human beings appears to be strong, but it is surprisingly weak in the face of physical suffering. Even when we attend sesshin with the intent to fulfill its requirements at any cost, we may soon feel inclined to be lazy, to avoid suffering, and to think of indulging ourselves as fatigue increases after two or three days. Sitting day and night during the *Rohatsu Sesshin*, the training that takes place from the first of December to the dawn of the eighth of December in commemoration of Shakyamuni's enlightenment, students often make excuses because of their laziness, saying, "It is worthless to sit so late at night if we then fall asleep tomorrow during meditation because of lack of sleep. Excuse me, please, for tonight." Even when they are disciplining themselves to renounce and kill their smaller selves, they become lazy and self-indulgent. This is very inconsistent, as is human nature itself.

About noon of the following day, they continue to sleep during their meditation, forgetting the excuse they had made the night before. During the sitting early in the morning of the last day of the sesshin, they nonchalantly say with regret, "We have failed again this time." Thus, unless we love zazen, we cannot continue to practice it. At the same time, we cannot continue to sit for a long time unless we remove the obstacles that could block our continued practice of zazen. It is necessary not to be tired, not to be relaxed, not to take a rest, and not to be lazy.

My teacher Bokuo Roshi, Abbot of Tenryu-ji at present, once said in reminiscence of his painful discipline in his bygone years, "The way to be liberated from suffering is to be quickly absorbed into it." Indeed, I think there are no better words than these.

Even during sesshin, when a number of people get together to encourage and compete with one another, it is hard to be free from suffering. Some of you may practice zazen all alone at home with this book of mine as a guide. If you do, you must be well prepared for suffering. If there is no suffering, your sitting will be futile and you will find it difficult to continue zazen. For this reason, I stress the importance of this point in particular.

SELECTING YOUR TEACHER

I would like you to note one important thing if you wish to be disciplined formally with a teacher in the near future—you should be careful in selecting your own teacher. Master Dogen, in his *Gakudo Yojinshu*, writes:

> The practice of Buddhism depends on whether your teacher is right or wrong. The potentiality of the pupil is like good material, and the teacher is like the master of art. Even if the material is good, good work will not be produced without a good artisan. On the other hand, even a crooked piece of wood will immediately reveal the skill of workmanship in the hands of a good worker. This will testify to the fact that true or false satori (enlightenment) depends on the adequacy of the teacher.[25]

As Master Dogen points out, it is reasonable to think that the success or failure of a Zen disciple depends on the qualities of the teacher. What sort of teacher should you select? First the right teachers who have inherited Dharma authentically transmitted from their masters should be considered. Master Torei insists on the importance of transmission in the chapter titled "*Shijyo*" in his *Shumon Mujinto Ron*. In the very beginning of this chapter Master Torei writes:

> Ever since the degeneration of discipline for enlightenment, they do not pay any respect to the transmission of Dharma from their masters; they have dualistic opinions of their enlightenment and kensho (seeing one's own self-nature); they discuss the merits and demerits of each other and indulge in their own knowledge deviating from the Way of the ancients.[26]

Thus Master Torei mentions the importance of transmission and warns against the dualistic opinions and proofs of enlightenment outside the teachings transmitted by authentic teachers. He quotes from Master Gensaku (Hsuan-ts'e)[27] of Tung-yang, who said to Master Yoka Genkaku (Yung-chia

Hsuan-chueh),[28] "It does not matter what happened before the King of the Great Sound, but after the King of the Great Sound, those who have no teacher and think themselves to be enlightened are all natural heretics."

According to Master Torei, Master Genkaku was taken to the Sixth Patriarch for his approval upon hearing the words of Master Gensaku. "The King of the Great Sound" means the first Buddha who appeared in the Past Existence, and the expression "before the King of the Great Sound" pertains to something like "before the separation of Heaven and Earth." The primitive age when Heaven and Earth were not yet separated and before any Buddha had come into existence does not matter. However, in later years, those who had not inherited Dharma directly transmitted through their authentic masters are deemed to be heretics. That is why the matter of transmission is so important.

Therefore, "those who have not yet inherited Dharma from their masters should look for great masters to whom Dharma has been transmitted from their masters and through their Buddhist ancestors." Such great masters generally mean those who have inherited Dharma through the masters of India, China, and Japan, namely, those whose enlightenments have been authorized by their enlightened predecessors.

We must choose masters who have transmitted the essence of Shakyamuni's authentic teachings through the generations of Buddhist teachers from India, China, and Japan in the same way as a bowl of water is poured intact into another bowl. Originality or "surpassing one's teacher in perception" means making an improvement after having mastered the essence of the teachings of one's teacher. It never means the arbitrary opinions of one's feigned enlightenment unauthorized by any teacher.

Seisetsu Roshi, who was formerly my teacher, first entered Tenryu-ji in the twenty-sixth year of Meiji (1893) at the age of seventeen. In the spring of the following year when he returned to his home at Tajima after one year's training in the monastery, the first thing he did was to visit his former teacher, Priest Hokuin, at Shobo-ji. He told his former teacher about many things that had happened since he last saw him. Priest Hokuin, who was listening to him with great satisfaction and interest suddenly asked him, "By the way, what is the name of your teacher in the monastery?"

"Well, he is called Priest Gasan."

"Oh, Gasan? It is an unfamiliar name. Anyway, he must be a young priest. Whose religious heir is he?"

"I am sorry I do not know."

The eighteen-year-old Seisetsu did not know anything about it, and so he honestly replied as he did. But Priest Hokuin looked sad and said, "What?

You don't even know the religious lineage of your teacher? Ah, what kind of religious discipline have you undergone? I have never felt so miserable." Saying this, he cried though he was a full-grown man.

Seisetsu, who came to be called Master Gao later, could not stand being there any longer. As soon as he returned to the temple where he trained as a monk, he learned the religious lineage of his teacher and then put on his straw sandals once again and hurried back to Kyoto. It was perhaps because of this incident that it became a rule at Tenryu-ji to chant the names of our Buddhist ancestors and hold a religious service for them the first thing each morning.

Teachers of old went to these extremes in revering the transmission of Dharma through the right masters. This means nothing other than valuing the Dharma more than anything else. In this sense, the question to be settled first of all for anyone is to select the right teacher who has clearly inherited Dharma through authentic masters.

However, this alone is not enough to make it possible for us to select the right teacher to train us all throughout our lives. Master and student must really match each other, their *kiai* (life force) being one as if they are in perfect agreement. However authentic the master may be, it will not be to the advantage of the student to remain with him for a long time if they are incompatible in personality and temperament like water and fire. It is, therefore, desirable for the student to love his master so much that he would dedicate his whole life to his teacher. Thus, it is important that the teacher and student be compatible and that the teacher be an authentic master who has received Dharma transmitted by genuine religious ancestors.

Once one decides to be a student, he should never change teachers until he has achieved an understanding and is on his way to maturity. But, as it is, even professional monks often wander from one monastery to another in search of their master. Many of them eloquently criticize this monastery and that teacher without ever achieving anything. There are many people who seldom reflect over how they pass off their own responsibilities to their teachers and monasteries. I must say that such people sorely lack the heart and mind to seek the Way.

From the start, we should not become a student of any master unless we sincerely come to believe in him. An ancient saying goes, "Spend three years without learning before you choose your teacher." We should select our teacher carefully enough before we become his disciple. Once we choose our teacher, we should follow him faithfully until we attain enlightenment. Instead of doing so, however, some of us irresponsibly choose our teacher, so that in two or three years we may have to leave him on the pretext of some fault or other on his part. That is like blaming others while we ourselves are to blame. And by so doing, we will inadvertently reveal our own faults eventually.

In the chapter titled "*Raihai Tokuzui*" in *Shobo-genzo* we find the following passage:

> Shakyamuni said, "If you meet your teacher preaching the highest Bodhi,[29] don't seek his identity, don't look at his face, don't blame him for his faults, and don't think of his conduct. Solely out of your esteem for *prajna*, let him have hundreds and thousands pieces of gold daily, hold a religious service presenting him with heavenly food, and hold a religious service showering heavenly flowers over him. Worship him three times a day, paying him great respect. And, further, don't let your delusions affect your mind."[30]

The above words of Shakyamuni mean that once we choose our teacher, it is not necessary to think about his identity, his features, or his conduct for we cherish prajna, the Buddha's wisdom and perception, which is the same as the authentically enlightened view of the truth of being transmitted by generations of Buddhist ancestors. According to Buddhist teachings, we should pay great respect to our enlightened teacher and refrain from troubling him. If we choose our own teacher, it is natural that we should hold him in such great esteem.

However, even if we clearly know as a matter of fact that our teacher has inherited the enlightened mind through generations of his enlightened predecessors, I am still doubtful of beginners who may not have an insight into the content of transmission of their teacher. That is to say, they cannot tell whether their teacher is eligible to preach the highest Bodhi or not.

I had the opportunity to be guided by Master Seisetsu of Tenryu-ji. One day, when I was so fatigued and tormented as to be on the point giving up my training altogether, the sight of my teacher worshipping the image of the Buddha filled me with courage. In his lectures, too, I felt a great deal of power emanating from his words. Thus, even beginners will experience this inspiration within themselves when they sincerely seek a true master.

I think that only a truly great person can inspire one in this way. If we can perceive such awe-inspiring power in our teacher, we will be able to follow him without fail like Shinran, who said, "Is nembutsu indeed the seed of our rebirth in Paradise? Or is nembutsu the karma that condemns us to Hell? Indeed, there is no knowing if nembutsu as a whole is good or bad." As for

Shinran, following his teacher's instruction, he chanted nembutsu in order to be saved. There was nothing else for him to do but to believe in his teacher. When we trust our teacher, the feeling of absolute obedience is born, which makes it possible for us to continue our religious discipline for a long period of time.

On Makyo (Disturbing Conditions)

As we get used to sitting and attain a certain degree of maturity, we first notice that our hands get numb, and next that our feet get numb. Thus, the barrier between us and our surroundings is gradually removed. A line in a song says, "*Daruma-san* has neither hands nor feet." When I was a beginner in zazen, the senior monk used to say that line referred to the physical condition of the sitter. The authenticity of his remark is questionable, but it is true that during zazen, beginning with the hands and feet, the whole body is lost and the distinction between sitter and surrounding is forgotten. When that happens we enjoy the realm of concentrated meditation and sometimes a kind of disease arises, which makes us become addicted to and intoxicated with that enjoyment.

As we become advanced in meditation, sometimes phenomena appear during our meditation. Some of them are favorable while others are not. As a whole, they have always been called makyo (disturbing conditions). For example, once when I was sitting in zazen with my eyes glued to the floor in front of me, the lines on the floor looked like the face of a man, varying in expression.

Kawajiri Hogin writes about makyo as ranging from wild imaginings and sleepiness to boredom that attack us during our meditation. Some disturbing makyo are evidently harmful to our progress in Zen discipline, but it is easy to think of some way or other to drive them away. Pleasant or enjoyable makyo on the other hand are harder to deal with. When students visit their master in his room to express their answers to the koan assigned to them, some of them often say in high spirits, "All the surroundings became purely white," or, "My body became empty, rose directly up to Heaven and spread all over Heaven," as if they had seen mu (nothingness). As for me, when I said similar things to my teacher in self-satisfaction, he teased me saying, "Perhaps you were asleep." Before we ourselves discover that this is makyo, we presumptuously think that our teacher is ignorant of this form of samadhi.

Kawajiri Hogin writes, "I hear the sound of the ash of the incense stick in front of my eyes. When it falls on metal, it sounds 'chari.' When it falls on wood, it sounds 'batari.' And when it falls on ash, it sounds 'pasari.'"[31] I think most people have heard the sounds made by the falling of the ash of the incense stick. It makes conspicuous sounds. If we can hear these sounds, as Kawajiri Hogin writes, it is partly because of the effect of our mature meditative power. Therefore, if we hear them, we should just let them be heard.

But many of us say, "Oh, I hear the sounds of the fallen ash. I have made great progress." Thus, we attach ourselves to the sounds when we should ignore them. Being delighted with our own merits is called makyo, too.

There is no such thing as makyo even in the good sense of the word if we enter deep samadhi. According to the record of Shakyamuni's Great Enlightenment, even Shakyamuni encountered various disturbances immediately before his enlightenment. This demonstrates that when our minds are not concentrated, makyo will not appear, but that when our power of concentration increases, various phenomena will arise to interfere with our enlightenment. When Shakyamuni overcame these disturbing phenomena and was unaffected by them, he was enlightened. Without a doubt, makyo is a proof of considerable maturity in Zen concentration.

In the chapter titled "Manifested Realms" in Shumon Mujinto Ron, Master Torei writes, "You students of the Way, if your power of concentration matures, your suffering will gradually subside, and pleasant phenomena will reveal themselves now and then. They are called good phenomena."[32] When our power of samadhi is increased, various thoughts and wild imaginings disappear, and admirable phenomena which we have never before experienced present themselves.

Master Torei says that the experiences such as "everything is empty," "the universe is one," "everything before our eyes is the world of satori," and so on, though varied in degree of our power of samadhi, belong to the domain of good phenomena. However, if one thinks that this is a good phenomenon and that is an admirable satori, they are immediately turned into makyo.

The Ryogon Kyo[33] states, "If you are not inclined to the idea of sacredness, you will find yourself in favorable surroundings. But, if you are affected by your idea of sacredness, you will be surrounded by various evils." This means that we come to have wrong opinions because the purification of our minds is not right. Thus, we are directed to the wrong road. An ancient saying goes, "If the Way is high, accordingly it has a great number of obstacles." Anyway, even good things seem to be without good effects. Conversely, if we become attached to good things, we make them bad. In order to avoid the ill affects of makyo, "it is right to wash our minds." It is well to wash away dirt from our minds so that no speck of dirt is left.

One of the things which is necessary for us to do is to actually detect makyo. If we are willing, we should be acquainted with the fifty kinds of makyo by referring to Volumes 9 and 10 of *Ryogon Kyo*. The excerpts from these chapters in translation are found in *Gakudo Jasei Meikan*,[34] which I recommend you read.

Master Torei lamented, "Students mistakenly affirm their present circumstance as if it was proof of their enlightenment. Because of this, the number of those who fall into the evil group of deluded people is not small." It was so in the days of Torei (18th century), and truer today, when there are a great number of people who mistakenly believe that they are enlightened because of makyo. It is a formidable problem.

Makyo is, in short, our attachment to favorable conditions that we ourselves approve of. It is possible to subdue them by ignoring them and eliminating them, as testified by the words of ancients.

Well, then, in what kinds of psychological states do makyo occur? We see, hear, and think of things from morning to night and think that this is the entirety of the actual life of human beings. But, as it is, this represents only half of it. According to the psychoanalytic theories of Freud and Jung, there is an unconscious life that is out of the reach of consciousness and that lies in the depth of the visible and tangible life of consciousness. It is there that all the records of life stemming from time immemorial are kept. This unconscious life is responsible for the formation of our personalities. For instance, if we compare the life of consciousness to the waves moving on the surface of water, the life of unconsciousness is comparable to the current below the surface.

Jung calls the central point of our consciousness the ego. But far below it there is the stratum called individual unconsciousness which is the element indispensable to the formation of our personalities. Even further below this stratum, there is the limitless and boundless stratum of unconsciousness called collective unconsciousness, in which the traces of the whole development of human beings, ranging from the very beginning of human life in general to the present circumstances, are registered.

Reading Jung, one is reminded of *Alaya-vijnana*, the eighth consciousness, discussed in the Buddhist treatise called *Vijnapti-matrata*.[35] According to this work, the first five kinds of consciousness pertain to the sense faculties of the five sense organs. The sixth consciousness is what we ordinarily call the consciousness which embraces and coordinates the first five kinds of consciousness. These six kinds of consciousnesses are ascribed to the superficial operations of the conscious mind.

The seventh consciousness is called *Mana-vijnana*. This is generally called unconsciousness and pertains to the unconsciousness of the smaller self, in which everything is perceived with the self as the center. It corresponds to what Jung calls "individual unconsciousness."

The eighth consciousness is called Alaya-vijnana, which is translated into Japanese as "*zo-shiki.*" It alludes to the storehouse of life, where all of our past experiences are imprinted and where the possible motivations of all of our conduct are also said to be stored. Thus, we may safely regard Alaya-vijnana as equivalent to what Jung calls "collective unconsciousness."

The original cause of all our actions is stored in the eighth consciousness which is called Alaya-vijnana, but the seed of that original cause is by nature neither good nor bad. It is indeed deemed to be the operation of the seventh consciousness called Mana-vijnana that tinges the originally pure Alaya-vijnana with evil by involving it in the life of egocentric desires and passions.

Now, when we go into samadhi through meditation, our thoughts become pacified. This means that the first five kinds of consciousnesses and the sixth consciousness have stopped their operations. When the operation of the conscious mind stops, that of the seventh consciousness called Mana-vijnana prevails to create makyo. Therefore, makyo may be regarded as something resulting from the power of concentration.

However, as we sit in meditation, to be authentically aware of our selflessness and realize our true selves at the same time we should not let ourselves be agitated by the operation of Mana-vijnana. Hence, it is said, "If you meet the Buddha, kill him; if you meet your ancestor, kill him." We must stir up our courage to be free from all the phenomena which arise to disturb our meditation. Makyo will then unconditionally surrender and perish and we will be admitted to the state of mind comparable to that layer of ice 25 million miles thick as described by Hakuin.

Though it may seem unnecessary to write any further on the same subject here, I am going to write a little more for it is the key to the distinction between right and wrong Zen. The state of tranquility and nothingness, which at first sight seems to be the right awareness of the selfless self, is nothing other than the depth of unconsciousness called Alaya-vijnana, which has come to prevail over Mana-vijnana. This is suggested by the following Zen verse composed by the famous Master Chosha Keijin (Ch'ang-sha Ching-ts'en):[36]

> Students of the Way do not comprehend the Truth
> Because they only recognize the existing Eighth Consciousness.
> Fools identify with the original man,
> The boundless origin of birth and death.

Collective unconsciousness corresponding to Alaya-vijnana is regarded as the "Eighth Consciousness" embracing all possibilities, and yet it is not proper to identify it with the true self. It is true of course that apart from the "Eighth Consciousness," which means the boundless origin of birth and death, and apart from Alaya-vijnana there is no original man. And yet, it is not right to say that they are exactly the same thing. They are one and yet they are different.

Master Hakuin taught, "Lower your sword right into the middle of the eighth consciousness field." By saying so, Master Hakuin must have meant that we should stop the operation of the eighth consciousness in order to realize its emptiness and selflessness.

Excuse my lengthy exposition, but in short what I mean to say is that we should regard everything that appears to us during our meditation as makyo. Even if Buddha appears, even if glorious light shines, even if the ash of the incense stick is heard as it falls six feet away, and even if the absolute nothingness reveals itself, they all belong to makyo regardless of whether they are good or bad, as long as they occur to us during our meditation. When we come face to face with makyo, we should brace up mind and body and become courageous so that we may smash them all into pieces paying no attention to them. We find the following passage in *Kaian Kokugo*,[37] "If you want to maintain your life, cut the thoughts of protecting your life. It is only when you cut everything that you will be secure for the first time."

How to Get to Your Feet after Sitting

When we sit for the duration of one incense stick, that is for thirty or forty minutes at a time, it is not necessary to pay any attention to the problem of getting to our feet after meditation. However, when we regard standing as a turning point from tranquility to movement, and from zazen to our daily activities, it is very important.

To begin with, I want to point out the following words from *Zazen-gi*, "If you want to get out of samadhi, move your body slowly, stand up calmly and not suddenly." These words mean that we should not stand up abruptly as if we suddenly remembered something important.

In Tendai's *Shoshikan*,[38] the way to get out of samadhi is discussed in detail. According to it, we must harmonize mind, breath and body in getting out of samadhi, just as we do in getting into it. When we start sitting, we should move the upper body back and forth and from side to side to balance it, and then put breath and mind in order. When we are going to get out of the state of samadhi, on the other hand, we should carefully relax the mind, and then exhale, and last of all move the body. Before we stand up after sitting for a certain duration of time, we should move the body in the above manner.

Contrary to what we do when we are going to enter into samadhi, we start moving the upper body from side to side a little at first and then gradually increase the degree of movement, which becomes larger and larger with the hips as the pivot. Next move the shoulders to ease stiffness, and then massage the face, the head, and the neck with both hands. Last of all, we should unlock the crossed legs to alleviate numbness and any other discomfort. When we sit alone, it is effective to do some exercises. What is important is to "stand up calmly." We should never stand up abruptly or move in a rough manner. If we carelessly stand up, we may sometimes feel dizzy and ill. For this reason, we are advised to be very careful when we get out of the state of samadhi.

Another more important reason why we must be careful is that if we stand up carelessly after sitting for a long time, our accumulated power of concentration may vanish all of a sudden, as in the saying, "A single moment may destroy what took a hundred days to accumulate." Thereby, in regards to the problem of how to get out of the state of samadhi, *Shoshikan* excludes discussion of frame of mind or breathing. That is to say, mind and respiration are always to be kept in good condition, regardless of whether we are in samadhi or not. It is especially desirable to let the concentrated state of mind, samadhi, operate in our everyday activities. Otherwise, the life of Zen Mind will be nullified as the mere product of delusive imagination.

Zazen-gi cautions us to come out of samadhi calmly and to move the body naturally. It further teaches us how to get to our feet with dignity and what to do after doing so. It writes, "Even after getting out of samadhi, you should always be on the alert to act responsively and protect your power of concentration as you protect a baby. Then, it will be easy for you to cultivate your power of concentration until it comes to maturity." The above passage means that even when we get to our feet after sitting in samadhi, we should be like the mother cherishing her baby tightly held in her arms as we continue to cultivate our minds or power of concentration which we nurtured during meditation.

Master Eno, the Sixth Patriarch, said, "Externally, detachment from form is called zen. Internally, concentration of mind is called *jyo*." It may be right to think that jyo means the unification of the mind. Concentration prevents the mind from being dispersed and brings it into a constant and unified state. That is why the power of concentration as such is not something visible to our eyes, but is the power with which we are naturally endowed and which reveals itself as we keep on practicing zazen for many years. In short, it is the power of samadhi.

Now, as for *hoben* (skillful means) and the preservation of the power of concentration, I am going to write about them later in the section, "Zazen without Sitting." Hoben does not exist anywhere except in integration with work. Each of us experiences it more or less in our everyday life. Therefore, I do not have to write any more about it now. What I want to note especially is our mental attitude toward transition from zazen to everyday activities after we get out of the state of samadhi.

When we ordinarily sit in zazen, our dispersed minds become resolutely unified, with the waves and winds in them calming down like the so-called "immovable water profoundly calm." However, as soon as the stick of incense burns out and we get to our feet again, delusive thoughts begin to reappear one after another just as before we started sitting. This is because we stand up abruptly and roughly. Therefore, we must be always on the alert to act carefully in order to preserve our power of samadhi even after we get out of it.

Usually we create some device to smoothly transfer from tranquility to movement, unifying them by means of kinhin (meditation in walking). When I practice meditation alone, I replace kinhin with one of the techniques used in iaido (swordsmanship). Each of us is free to use any means. The point is how to bring the power of samadhi, nurtured during meditation, into one with movement after meditation and how to preserve this power.

At first the power of concentration nurtured during sitting for thirty minutes may be lost in an instant as soon as we stop sitting. But later we will be able to retain it for five or ten minutes by means of hoben and kufu. After much strenuous effort in our training, we will come to retain this power for a longer time, say, one or two hours.

Master Choen (Ch'eng-yuan)[39] of Hsiang-lin passed away at the age of eighty. Immediately before his death, he is said to have remarked, "For the past forty years I have lived at one with everything." His words are indeed awe-inspiring. It is very important to discipline ourselves to become one with everything, even for a day.

However, the duration of the power of samadhi is not the same as the persistent preservation of one particular state of mind. Harada Sogaku writes in his *Sanzen no Hiketsu*,[40] "The cultivation of the power of concentration means to cultivate the power which makes us 'masters wherever we may be.'" We must not misinterpret these words. In the true sense of Master Sogaku's words, to become the master everywhere does not mean to make servants of others. If our right minds operate at any moment and in any place in such a way as to make us take the right attitude and act properly at any time without at all deviating from the Way, then we are said to be masters wherever we may be.

We become alienated from objects because we make too much of ourselves. If we negate ourselves and completely plunge into the objective world around us, all oppositions cease. The phrase goes, "The holy man has no self; and, therefore, everything becomes the holy man." By making ourselves empty and plunging deep into the surrounding world to be integrated with things, the surrounding world will in turn become ourselves. We and the world thus will be one, and we will be masters everywhere.

When we sit in meditation, our minds may be as clear as the polished mirrors on which form is reflected as it truly is. But as soon as we get to our feet after sitting and go to the middle of town, we will find ourselves in the world of dualities. Under the dominating influence of our surroundings, we find ourselves tossed about in the dualistic world of self and other, and in the five desires[41] and seven emotions.[42] Therefore, we cannot rightly judge nor properly deal with the things with which we are confronted. Some may say that this cannot be helped, but, unless we can transcend the dualities of this world, how can we explain the meaning of our sitting in meditation?

If we treat things as they should be without being upset by our surroundings and without letting our minds be dispersed by them under any circumstances, we may be called masters wherever we may be. This operating power of our minds is called *joriki*. It is, in short, the operation of no-self. Master Sogaku writes about it as follows, "The right mind operates at each time and in each place to make you take the right attitude and act properly without deviating from the Way."

Master Yamada Mumon,[43] in his lecture on *Zazen-gi*, explained the operation of the power of samadhi by telling the following anecdote about Master Toko Shin'etsu (Tung-kao Hsin-yueh),[44] who came to Japan from China in the Ming Dynasty. There was a Lord who learned Zen from Toko Shin'etsu. One New Year's Day, when the Master visited Lord Mitsukuni[45] to exchange New Year's greetings with him, Lord Mitsukuni said, "It is New Year's Day today. Please let me present you with a cup of sake (rice wine)." So saying, Lord Mitsukuni took out a large cup and had one of his servants fill it with sake to the brim. Just then, "Bang!" rang out from an adjoining room. A gun had been purposely loaded beforehand with a blank cartridge and then fired. The Zen Master, without showing the slightest dismay, drank up sake from the cup in calm silence. Lord Mitsukuni acted embarrassed and apologized, "It is customary to fire a gun in a warrior's house. Please excuse me." The Master returned the cup to Lord Mitsukuni in silent acknowledgment of his apology.

When the servant filled Lord Mitsukuni's cup with sake, the Zen Master suddenly gave one loud shout, "*Katz!*" Taken by surprise, Lord Mitsukuni spilled his sake in spite of himself. The Zen Master said in apparent seriousness, "It is customary for Zen men to give a single shout of 'Katz!' Please excuse me."

After relating the preceding anecdote, Master Mumon said, "The power of such a Zen master is called joriki." It was this power that Master Toko Shin'etsu displayed automatically and without any preparation beforehand. It was the same as the spontaneous action of his selfless self. In other words, it must have been the very power of the one who was the master of everything wherever he might be.

This joriki which anchors itself in samadhi and which thoroughly identifies itself with all matters of daily living, is, needless to say, a precious thing that comes from sitting hard in the midst of quiet. Once that state is achieved, it is protected like carrying a baby. One must not forget that its working is the result of hard training in everything one does. Therefore, the attitude that one takes when standing up after sitting meditation is very important—one must maintain the intensity of concentration that was achieved during meditation.

KUFU IN MOVEMENT—PRACTICAL TRAINING

Master Hakuin emphasizes kufu in movement or practical training in Zen. He says, "To practice Zen in movement is superior to doing so in the stillness of meditation." Master Ta-hui says, "You should always be one with everything instead of deviating, and must be awakened to your true self in your daily life while walking, standing, sitting, and lying down." He advises, "You should straightforwardly leap out of the duality of birth and death with one bound." The purpose of zazen is to realize this fact: "Sentient beings are all primarily Buddhas." After we find the essence of our being we must freely use it at any time and any place even in our everyday life full of troubles and inconsistencies. It is very natural to take kufu in movement seriously, for Zen must be activated in the very places or fields of everyday life. Or rather, we should say that our everyday life itself must be guided by Zen principles. If so, it is essential to strive for the workings of Zen Mind in our everyday activities.

I do not mean by what I have written above that practicing Zen in stillness is not important enough to deserve our attention. I simply mean to suggest how difficult it is to train ourselves in such a way as to be concentrated in mind while being active in this world.

It goes without saying that the authentic way of zazen involves kufu while in the stillness of meditation. We sit in tranquil concentration in a quiet place, counting the frequency of our respiration or contemplating the koan mu as we keep on saying to ourselves, "Mu, mu, . . ." The basic discipline in Zen lies in destroying again and again the oncoming delusions and worldly thoughts by making avail of koan and susoku as our sword, thus going into samadhi where Heaven and Earth are one and mind and body are dropped.

However, there are only twenty-four hours in a day. If we sit only for thirty or forty minutes a day, reciting, "Mu, mu, . . ." and are taken up by disturbing thoughts for the rest of the day which amounts to twenty-three hours, it will be difficult for us to advance toward the desired state of mind. Therefore, it is absolutely necessary for us to be always aware of our True Selves twenty-four hours a day, without deviation. "Always" means that we are constantly aware of mu. We cannot forget it even for a moment. The phrase "to be always aware" pertains to guiding someone so that he may hold to his True Self earnestly lest he should lose it.

As we will see when we actually sit, it is very difficult for us to concentrate on mu while we eat our meals, while we do our work, while we walk after sitting, and while we are on our way to and from the wash-room, even during the period of sesshin when all we are supposed to do is concentrate our minds. Some of us have our own professions, while others are employed by business companies. It will be next to impossible for us to remain in mu even for one second when we are not sitting in meditation.

In disciplining ourselves to practice Zen in movement, we never cease to become mu with all our might or count the frequency of our respiration at all times and in all places just as we do when we are in meditation. Therefore, it is our ideal to train ourselves to attain immovability in movement. As I have been saying, however, even professional Zen monks cannot always practice Zen in movement except those endowed with the greatest capacities. I know it is impolite to say this to the reader of a book titled *An Introduction to Zen Training*, but it will be impossible for the unexperienced person to practice Zen except when sitting in meditation.

Given that, what should we do?

First of all, we should find as much time as possible to sit in quiet places, wholly concentrating ourselves, in mind and body, on the contemplation of mu and on the counting of the frequency of our respiration. And even while we are engaged in the perpetually changing affairs and events of this world, we should devote ourselves entirely, in mind and body, to whatever work we are doing then. When we are in trains or buses, it is surprisingly effective for the development of our immovable power to practice contemplation or to count the frequency of our respiration, "One, two, . . ." in harmonious accord with the rattling sounds of our moving surroundings.

Kawajiri Hogin writes in his *Zazen no Shokei*, "When you are engaged in some work or other, you become one with it. In the intervals of your work, you immediately resume your contemplation on the koan. For instance, when you are smoking by the fireside or doing something like that, you are considered to be in the intervals of your work. At such a time you are absorbed in the contemplation on the koan free from dualistic thoughts and imaginations. This is one example of kufu in movement."

By emptying ourselves we become one with objects, deeply absorbed in our work. To be thus thoroughly one with everything with which we are confronted is the true essence of mu. It is the state of both physical and spiritual liberation, to which kufu in movement should point.

Master Iida Toin also writes,

> Make efforts for only sitting. "Only" alludes to the state of being devoid of anything in excess. When we are in zazen, all we have to do is sit. If we sit earnestly, free from any disturbing things and thoughts, we become one with zazen. There is no room left for anything to intrude between zazen and us. That is why they say, "If we search for our own self, we cannot find it."

> In the same way, if we are confronted with koan, we have to contemplate it in the same way. Such a time is not the time for zazen, but for koan only, and we have nothing to do with zazen as suggested by the saying that the virtuous woman does not serve two husbands, nor does the loyal retainer serve two lords. Thus, when we are supposed to act, all we have to do is to act. We have to act for all our lives. When our whole bodies act, there is no dualistic self in us. When there is no self, there is nothing which is in opposition to us. I do not doubt that the universe is one with the whole active self.[46]

To apply this principle to reading and other activities, we can say that when we read, we only read; when we write, we only write; when we walk, we only walk; and when we sleep, we only sleep. Whatever we may do, we do it only. When we walk, a clear wind arises in our wake at each step of our feet. Whenever we raise our hands or throw out our feet, we do so in strict conformity to the Way. Such a refreshing state of mind and body must be in perfect keeping with the aim of kufu to practice Zen in movement.

When we are absorbed in the work we love, we forget the passage of time. In the same way, there is no idea of time in the world of "only." The state of "only" transcends time. Under such circumstances we are perhaps unconscious of our whereabouts. That is to say, we transcend space as well as time. Therefore, if we are concentrated on our work only by way of kufu to practice Zen in movement, our work will be accomplished more admirably. Moreover, as we never work reluctantly, we can work more efficiently with the result of much less fatigue on our part. So, if we get used to kufu to practice Zen in movement, we may go so far as to catch two birds with one stone.

A Zen friend of mine who used to work for a telephone company once told me about the way he worked. It was more than thirty years ago, and so the circumstances have been changed since then, but the principle at work should remain the same. This friend of mine belonged to the division which was responsible for the maintenance of the telephone connection equipment. It was his duty to check the machines in his charge every day. He worked in such a way as to be one with the machines. He was in the state of no-mind in samadhi, as he made a round of visits to his machines. His hands would unintentionally touch certain machines, and, sure enough, on close examination, he found many of them either out of order or on the point of being out of order. Therefore, he made more strenuous efforts to practice Zen while working in such a way as to be one with his machines in his charge. This story well illustrates the term "only work."

By the way, there is the problem which has always been considered as one of the three essential conditions of Zen, that is, "to raise a great feeling of doubt." For instance, in the famous book titled *Kana Hogo*,[47] Master Bassui writes,

> It cannot be helped that your thoughts arise and perish. Doubt your own mind thoroughly in accord with your thought. It is in order to be aware of the truth of being that you doubt profoundly. When you try to know what is unknown, your wandering mind will lose its way, and you will be at a loss. It is then that you are said to be in zazen. They say that to doubt in this way is kufu. In kufu you are to doubt thoroughly, whether you are on your feet or not, and whether you are asleep or awake, for you are well aware of your own unenlightenment.

Judging from the above words, we cannot make our own kufu unless we "doubt ourselves thoroughly," or unless we come to doubt ourselves to a great extent. Then, what do the above-mentioned kufu in movement and Master Toin's "only action" mean in connection with this great doubt? To doubt mu thoroughly is after all to tackle mu itself with all our minds and all our might. Therefore, as a natural consequence of our great doubt we will necessarily become only mu. We cannot help becoming mu itself by doubting it to the point of interpenetration with it. What Master Bassui means by telling us to doubt, whether we are sitting or standing, being asleep or awake, is not to question suspiciously, "What is this?" It is not to think of anything as if we were trying to solve a quiz either. The word "doubt" may be interpreted as "becoming the object of doubt itself." When we have to doubt our own being, we should doubt it thoroughly, becoming one with mu. What we should avoid above all is the ambiguous attitude halfway between negation and affirmation.

It is in this way that the power of concentration, nurtured in the samadhi of "Mu" is applied to our activities in the movement of our everyday life, and the power of integration, cultivated in the practical affairs of our everyday life, is transferred to meditation in stillness. This way of bringing movement and stillness into one is called "the twofold discipline in tranquility and movement." Such discipline is like a pair of wheels of a carriage, neither one can be neglected. For instance, we get up in the morning, wash our faces, eat our meals, manipulate our abacuses, and do bookkeeping. Such everyday activities serve to prompt our complete integration with our work. We see and hear things by becoming one with them, and the working of the self of no-self occurs in activity without activity. Kufu in movement or Zen in movement is no different from such activity.

At times Master Hakuin repeatedly refers to the practice of Zen in movement, as testified by his own words quoted in the early part of this chapter and by his almost fiery words found in many parts of his works. I am going to quote below some passages from his *Oniazami*.[48]

There are certain schools of inauthentic Zen students here and there in recent years . . . But they are not enlightened, and they think they are justified to remain undisciplined as they naturally are. They say, "To what avail is it to study? Of what use is it to search for enlightenment? . . . If we remain as we naturally are, like the carved bowls made of unpainted wood taken from the mountains, we will not have to worry about the lacquer coatings pealing off."

So saying, they sit, with their eyes closed and with their heads bent low. And they sleep to their hearts' content every day in order to get rid of their wild thoughts. Why do they practice such quietistic and futile Zen just as you do? It is, after all, because they failed to meet any qualified teachers in the beginning and came to indulge themselves in the practice of various inauthentic kinds of Zen. They know nothing about kufu to achieve immovability in movement. They should indeed be called self-indulgent, unenlightened, stubborn, and dense stink bags and pseudo-Zen men.

Hakuin goes on,

. . . If trainees are immersed in the peacefulness of quiet places and are possessed with desire for favorable surroundings, they are attached to the Zen taste. And due to this attachment, their environments are turned into makyo filled with a great number of obstacles.

They are advised, therefore, to be free from such attachment by:

. . . working so hard as to sweat every day, for only by doing so will they find an effective remedy to their faults and enhance their power of concentration. This will make it possible for them to establish themselves in mind and body firmly and harmoniously. . . . Kufu to practice Zen in movement seems to be remarkably more difficult than kufu in the tranquility of meditation. But it will be helpful to us as long as we live, for if we know how to do kufu in movement, our inner power will be increased.

On the contrary, even if we are very successful in practicing Zen in stillness, our minds may be dispersed the moment they get in touch with the dust of this world of movement. Therefore, training to attain immovability in the stillness of meditation alone is not very effective. Those who are attached to the idea of the so-called "no-thought and no-thinking" in favor of quiet places for meditation should be regarded as "the trainees vainly trying to get rid of filthy dung accumulated for twenty years." The Third Patriarch said, "The lotus flower blooms in the flames of fire when Zen is practiced in the midst of desire," in evident appreciation of the immovability of the Absolute achieved through kufu in movement.

Daito Kokushi[49] writes in reference to kufu in movement as follows:

I watch horse races at Kamo.
How gallant the horses look
Coming and going
Just as in zazen!

Master Daito elsewhere denounces the passive type of meditation,

The stone Buddhas
Make me realize
How useless we would be
If attached to Buddhahood!

In the writings of Ikkyu[50] we find:

Don't pick up tea leaves, but practice zazen.
Don't read sutras, but practice zazen.
Don't clean the house, but practice zazen.
Don't ride on horseback, but practice zazen.
Don't make fermented beans, but practice zazen.
Don't sow tea seeds, but practice zazen.

These words do not mean that we should sit in meditation by renouncing all of our everyday activities. Talking, laughing, quarreling, and moving the limbs should all be integrated into the one and the same samadhi. If we can turn things upside down on the tops of rocks, we are superior. If we are turned upside down by things, we are inferior. This is what is meant by the above quotation.

Do not be submerged beneath the stagnant water even for a moment, trying to keep to the corrupt morals of these days.

The above words warn us against the danger of passively yielding to useless zazen, in favor of the true way of active zazen. In view of these words, our everyday life, filled with noise and lively activities of people, must be the most convenient dojo for kufu to practice Zen in movement. The tendency to avoid this Heaven-blessed place of discipline may be called defeatism which is hard to rectify.

Zazen Without Sitting

In Kendo there is a kind of disease called "*itsuku*" (to be attached). It means attachment to the specific postures of attacking and defending which prevent us from moving about spontaneously. In Zen, too, there is a disease called attachment to meditation. Another name of this disease is infatuation with Zen. When we are afflicted with this disease, we lose our vitality by sitting comfortably and half-unconsciously in meditation.

However, instead of discussing this disease now, I would like to recommend meditation, urging ourselves to sit more and more. One hour's meditation a day is evidently not long enough. Therefore, it is necessary to make adjustments to practice Zen even when we are not in meditation so that we may compensate for the inadequate time for meditation as mentioned above. In regard to this matter Master Shido Bunan[51] composed the following poem on the significance of Zazen.

> If we know how to practice Zazen without actually sitting,
> What obstacles should there be,
> Blocking the Way to Buddhahood?

I understand that "Zazen without Sitting" means Zen discipline performed in terms of our everyday activities.

A master of swordsmanship holding a bamboo sword in his hands, confronted by a powerful opponent, and a master of Tea Ceremony, preparing a cup of tea for his respectable guest, both are admirable in their unassailable condition. However, often to our disappointment, their attitudes change as soon as they get out of the dojo or the tea room. Likewise, some regularly sit in strict conformity to the specified posture for zazen for one hour a day but indulge in delusive thoughts and imaginations for the rest of the day, which amounts to twenty-three hours. Such people make little progress in their discipline. Like the kettle of water mentioned before, it will take them a long time to reach the boiling point. That is why zazen without sitting becomes absolutely necessary.

Teachers of old inquired into matters regarding the Self. In other words, they teach us that it is our urgent duty as human beings to be aware of our True Selves and that we must fulfill our duty as immediately as if "we were extinguishing fire that is burning our own hair." If our eyebrows or hair caught fire, none of us could afford to be relaxed and feel at ease, however carefree we might be. I am sure that we would drop everything in order to extinguish the fire first of all. Likewise, to know our True Self is the basis of our own being. If we realize this fact, we cannot afford to do anything before we solve this problem of knowing our True Selves. That being the case, we should naturally choose to contemplate mu from morning to night, forgetting everything.

However, in these harried times we cannot afford to do so without risking starvation and the tragic dispersion of our families. That is why we must make use of as much time as possible to practice Zen without sitting in meditation, in addition to sitting eagerly and regularly every morning and evening. As for zazen without sitting, then, we should choose our own fields most suited to us from out of our daily pursuits.

Let us now refer to *Roankyo* for a few examples for your instruction. *Roankyo* was written by Suzuki Shosan, a Zen Master whom I admire very much. He was born in the seventh year of Tensho (1579) at Asuke in Aichi Prefecture and ended his life of seventy-seven years in Edo in the first year of the Meireki era (1655). He served Tokugawa Hidetada[52] and was a warrior distinguished for his meritorious service in several battles. He became a Zen monk at the age of forty-two and was a very serious practitioner of Zen. Roankyo describes how he instructed his disciples. In the early part of this book he laments,

> In learning the Buddhist Law (Zen) in recent years, many people seem to have forgotten that Zen includes high spirits of bravery and great power. Therefore, those who learn the Buddhist Law become so tenderhearted, admirable-looking, desireless, and good-natured that they somehow tend to lose the will to react to any unfavorable stimulus as angrily as if saying, "Damn it!"

> One day, Master said to a certain man, "I am going to teach you how to make use of Zen spirit in your everyday life, though I do not mean to say that they are the rules and regulations of Zen training." Then, he further said, "When you think of doing anything at all, it is well to do it immediately without thinking if it is right or wrong to do so. It is not desirable to think of doing it later. The

same is true when you go out. If you happen to feel like going out, go out spontaneously as you wish. Don't change your mind, thinking of going out later. Even if it happens to start raining or snowing, just go out as you wish, thinking how pleasant it is to do so and remembering your childhood when you used to enjoy playing in the snow. If you get used to doing everything spontaneously without discrimination, you will be unexpectedly relieved of unnecessary worries."

It is without doubt that in the above words of Shosan there is an allusion to Nio's spirit of zazen applied to zazen without sitting. The term "without discrimination" in the above passage quoted from Shosan's book is identical with what Suzuki Daisetz[53] calls "discrimination of indiscrimination." It neither denies indiscrimination nor ignores our ability to discriminate. Far from it, it points to the realm of thorough discrimination. I dare say it means becoming one with discrimination. I think it is ranked with the fulfillment of Nio's spirit characterized by "great strength, religious devotion, and courage." It is the repleted state of mind related to dashing against the thing or event as such.

One day a Noh[54] teacher named Kanze asked Master Shosan how to be trained in Zen. Master asked the Noh teacher to sing a Noh song. The Noh teacher respectfully sang a song in strict conformity to the prescribed form of singing. Master Shosan, who had been seriously listening to him, said as he finished singing, "When you brace yourself up sternly, raise your voice out of your abdomen and sing, unnecessary thoughts and wild imaginings will not arise. Or, did they arise when you sang?"

"No, none of them arose at all."

"I see. Zazen is not any different from Noh singing. If you sit in meditation with the same kiai as you sang with right now, you will be fine. And as you come to maturity in your art, you will naturally be free from any thought and thinking. Then you will naturally become a master of Noh singing. You will thus master the Worldly Law and the Buddhist Law at the same time. Therefore, you should do zazen by practicing Noh singing."

In such a case as this, of course, the pupil is made to sit in meditation for a certain duration of time, burning incense sticks as part of the basic training in Zen; and the rest of the time is devoted to the professional training such as Noh singing. Even then, however, the pupil will be left to his own devices to sing as well as he can.

When the wife of a certain lord asked Master Shosan for his advice, he asked her first to sing for him. After she had finished singing, however, he scolded her, saying, "Don't try to make the tune sound beautiful by singing in such a plaintive voice. Sing firmly in such a way as to bring your voice out from your abdomen."

Shosan also instructed his disciples to cultivate the Zen power of concentration by way of reciting the *sutra*. Just as in the case of Noh singing, he encouraged his disciples, saying, "Straighten your bodies, concentrate your spiritual power on the area below the navel, and recite the sutra with your eyes fixed. Then your recitation of the sutra will be equated to Zen. However often you may recite the sutra, it will be to no avail unless you do so properly." Similar teachings of Shosan's are found in many parts of *Roankyo*. If we concentrate our whole spiritual power in this way and forget everything, thoroughly absorbed in singing or reciting the sutra with all our might, our power of concentration will naturally be nurtured, and our high spirits will be utilized even when we are not actually singing or reciting the sutra.

When Master Shosan visited Hosho-ji, a temple at Hatogaya in the Province of Musashi, he taught dozens of the local farmers in a similar fashion:

> Indeed, agriculture is a kind of Buddhist discipline. Therefore, you are daily undergoing the Buddhist discipline and do not need any other kind of discipline than agriculture. Your bodies as such are the bodies of Buddhas, and your minds as such are the minds of Buddhas. Work in itself is the Buddhist discipline as I said before. If you are not well oriented in mind, you will eventually fall into Hell even when you have the seeds of good things. Therefore, it is advisable for you to reorient your minds. In order to do so, you should first entertain a great wish to redeem your bad karma accumulated since before your birth, by means of agriculture. If you cry, "Namu-Amidabutsu," repeatedly at the top of your voice every time you plow the field with all your might, you will never fail to be enlightened admirably.[55]

If we entertain such a great wish not only in agriculture but also in all other fields of work and do our best wholeheartedly in the spirit of "only" and samadhi, we will be admirably enlightened and will come to enjoy the work of our choice without fail, beyond the duality of work and play as if we were playing while we are engaged in our work.

In a similar vein Shosan taught the warriors how to do zazen in the midst of their cries of victory. He said, "You can never be accomplished in any kind of art without exercising the power of Zen concentration. Especially in Kendo you cannot use your sword without your concentrated and unified minds." So saying, Master took up his sword and immediately took a position with the tip of his sword pointing to the eyes of his opponent, as he said,

> Look! This is the exercised power of Zen concentration. But a swordsman only exercises his power of concentration when he manipulates his sword. When he is without his sword, he loses his power of concentration. This is no good. On the contrary, the Zen man exercises his power of concentration all the time. That is why he is never defeated in doing anything.[56]

Again, he taught how to make use of this power of concentration in doing kitchen work, in eating, in talking, or in doing any other thing or work.

All of these teachings of Shosan can still be practiced today. If this method of teaching is considered to be what Master Bunan calls "zazen without sitting," namely, Zen practiced in any place other than on the cushions, there should indeed be "nothing blocking the Way of Buddhahood." All things, including man's natural disposition and industry, are considered to be Buddhist Laws. There is nothing in this whole world which is not Zen.

When a bank clerk counts the number of bills, when the office clerk keeps his books, when the pilot manipulates his control lever, and when the bus conductor clips the tickets, all they do will conform to Zen Mind if they work in the spirit of zazen without sitting. And thus the power of Zen concentration will be cultivated, promoted, and exercised in terms of practical work. Then human life will be exhilaratingly and fully permeated with Zen Mind. We always have to be alert enough to do everything in the spirit of zazen and with the concentration power of samadhi.

If we discipline ourselves continually in this way, there will be no reason why we should complain of being too busy to sit in quiet comfort. Moreover, the actual zazen practiced regularly for one hour or thirty minutes in the morning or in the evening in addition to zazen without sitting will help us make remarkable and rapid progress in cultivating the power of Zen concentration. This is absolutely true, for it means that one hour of zazen a day will be multiplied twenty-fourfold by practicing zazen without sitting.

Samadhi and Attachment

There is a question which must be taken into consideration now. That is, whether living unconsciously in "no-self" from morning to night is in accord with the principle of Zen or not.

If you look at a mother bringing up her child, you find that there is no "self" in her. The slightest fever of her sick child makes her sit up all night, nursing her child without feeling any fatigue or reluctance. She suffers only from the standpoint of her own child. The barrier between mother and child is completely removed, and she forgets all her agonies and sufferings in taking care of her child. Such a thing as this often happens in our everyday life. For instance, in the case of a fire, we become unconscious of ourselves and involuntarily give full play to our hidden power. Even apart from such emergencies, it often happens when we are so engrossed with our work that we forget the passage of time and are unaware of our hunger. We are then living unconsciously in no-self.

If this unconscious selflessness is authentic selflessness in the literal sense of the word, we may surely call it samadhi. Likewise, the mother absorbed in bringing up her child in selflessness and the ordinarily powerless man, involuntarily giving full play to his hidden power in case of an emergency, may be deemed to be in the same admirable condition as samadhi and zazen.

Some people who are engrossed in watching horse races and bicycle races also forget the passage of time and are not aware of their hunger due to their absorption. Can we say they are in samadhi, too? If interpreted in the wider sense, these terms might be included into the boundless scope of samadhi. However, even if it is possible to interpret them within the scope of samadhi, those who are merely engrossed in horse races and bicycle races can never be deemed to be in the state of authentic samadhi handed down to us by generations of Buddhist ancestors. Here lies the very important difference between the seemingly similar samadhi and attachment.

There is a very interesting dialogue between master and disciple illustrating this difference between samadhi and attachment in *Denshu Roku*[57] written by the Chinese Neo-Confucian philosopher, O Yomei (Wang Yangming). His disciple Riko-cho (Lu Ch'eng) once him about the meaning of the merit of primal oneness. In my opinion, this term generally alludes to samadhi. When Riko-cho asked his teacher, "If we become absorbed in reading books, and if we pour ourselves into entertaining guests, can that be called samadhi?" "No," answered O Yomei, "it cannot. If what you say were samadhi,

you would then have to unjustifiably admit that those who abandon themselves to a love affair or to making money are also in samadhi. To be wholly
given up to love affairs or money-making is 'chasing after things,' or attachment, which means having yourself pulled and spun about by something
external to you. This can never be called true samadhi. What may be called
samadhi must be invested with the Heavenly Principle as the master."

This teaching of O Yomei reminds me of "Kyosho Dofu (Ching-ch'ing
Tao-fu) and the voice of rain drops" as told in Article 46 of the *Hekigan Roku*
(Pi-yen Lu).[58] According to this story, Master Kyosho Dofu from the Province
of Che-chiang once asked one of his disciples, "What is that sound outside the
window?" His disciple straightforwardly answered, "The sound of raindrops."
Hearing this, the Master said, "People in general perceive things upside-down
and run after them without being one with them."

The expression "to run after things" means being at the mercy of
things. We are apt to fall into this state when the relationship of subject and
object is upset, when the former is caught by the latter and dragged around
by it. The meaning of the expression "with the Heavenly Principle as the
master" is just the opposite. It means that we should abandon our self-centered wills, be free from personal opinions, be absorbed both physically and
spiritually in whatever concerns us at the moment, and become completely
one with things.

Running after things is called attachment; following the Heavenly
Principle is samadhi. Not only in love affairs and financial matters but also in
all other cultural activities such as reading, we can be said to run after things
if we are read by the books and dragged around by them instead of reading
them. O Yomei said a similar thing elsewhere:

> In the way of learning we use the term "*chuan*," which means
> "concentrated" or "attentive." It is necessary to be concentrated
> on learning. But concentration is not enough. To be "*ching*,"
> meaning "to be proficient," is further required in learning.
> Moreover, to be "*cheng*," meaning "to be correct," is indispensable
> to learning.[59]

"Cheng" pertains to making our mind clean so that it becomes pure
and unconfused. Therefore, we can say that to be correct is ultimately the same
as samadhi which ultimately makes the Heavenly Principle its master.

Ordinarily, the Sanskrit term "samadhi" is translated into Japanese as
"*shoju*," which means "to receive correctly." If we encounter blue, we perceive

it as blue; if we encounter red, we perceive it as red. Thus "shoju" is the same as true perception of reality in terms of the oneness of subject and object. If so, when we hear a drizzling rain as the "sound of raindrops," is that correct perception? Is that samadhi? It certainly resembles samadhi, but it is subtly different from it.

Master Dogen remarks in the chapter titled "*Sho-ji*"("Life and Death") in his *Shobo-genzo*,

> If you renounce and forget mind and body, throwing them into the house of Buddha, Buddha will in turn come to your rescue. Follow him, and you will become a Buddha, liberated from the duality of life and death without making any effort both spiritually and physically.

The distinction between samadhi and attachment (following forms) depends on whether we are completely one with objects, liberated from mind and body, or whether we remain even slightly attached to the duality of subject and object.

One day, when Priest Ikkyu passed a shop of broiled eels with his disciples, he said in spite of himself, "Oh, what an appetizing flavor!" They walked on two or three blocks before one of his young disciples suddenly said to Master Ikkyu, "Excuse me, Sir, but you said in front of the eel shop, 'What an appetizing flavor!' Wouldn't it be below the dignity of such a great priest as you to say so?" So saying, he implicitly blamed Priest Ikkyu for his involuntary remark.

"Nonsense!" said Ikkyu, "Are you still walking with the pieces of broiled eels under your nose? I shook them off right in front of the eel shop."

The above story may not be a true story, for I read it in a certain book written for children. But it is interesting to think of it in connection with what I have been discussing so far. The viewpoint of Priest Ikkyu is exactly shoju or samadhi, whereas that of his disciple is attachment. The above anecdote well illustrates the distinction between samadhi and attachment. Thus samadhi and attachment, though hardly different externally, are nonetheless completely different like Heaven and Earth, or clouds and mud. That is why teachers such as O Yomei abhor attachment and strictly advise us to be free from it.

By the way, I would like to refer to a book written to encourage young Zen trainees.[60] It is a collection of the teachings of ancient Zen Masters and shows us how they endured and overcame many difficulties to become enlightened. Reading it, we often come across such expressions as "like a cat on the point of catching a rat," "it is necessary for you to discipline yourself perpetually

like a hen sitting on her eggs," and other similar expressions figuratively referring to the attitudes of Zen disciples toward their discipline. How should we
interpret these expressions?

Suzuki Shosan writes in his *Roankyo* the following passages, some of
which have been quoted before:

> In training in Zen in recent years many people seem to have for-
> gotten that Zen includes a great spirit of bravery and great
> strength. Therefore, those who train in Zen become tender-hearted,
> admirable-looking, desireless, and good-natured, but somehow
> they become divested of the will to respond to any unfavorable
> stimuli angrily enough to say, "Damn it!"

He continues,

> Unless great thoughts arise, various other thoughts will not sub-
> side. Contrary to the zazen practised by people in general who try
> not to let thoughts arise, my zazen is the thought-provoking
> zazen. Indeed, it is the zazen which provokes thoughts as great as
> Mt. Sumeru.

Are such intense terms as "Damn it!" and "thought-provoking" not
related to attachment? In my opinion, most moralists and men of religion traditionally try to guide their disciples to the highest spiritual realm from the very
beginning regardless of the varied degrees of their maturity. However, it seems to
me that the empty and tender content of such a teaching method unnecessarily
causes some disciples to be too gentle, virtuous, and good-natured, as pointed
out by Master Shosan.

They say that poison must be controlled by poison. For this reason,
beginners must be trained to penetrate their attachment thoroughly in order to
transcend it. They should not be afraid to pass gas out of their sheer wish to
be virtuous. They should be well aware of the fact that by thoroughly penetrating into themselves they will attain "no-self."

For instance, when we engaged in susoku (counting the frequency of
our respiration) or in kufu, practical training to be one with the koan of mu,
it is very difficult for us in the beginning to be one with it. We cannot help
chasing the frequency of our respiration or mu at first. We just keep on chasing mu in a thorough-going way instead of seeing into our true selves, namely nothingness itself. If we continue to pursue mu with all our strength, we will

eventually come to a complete standstill like a cat driving a rat into a tight corner. Eventually there will be a time when the pursuing self and the pursued mu are brought into oneness. It is then that mu becomes the self, and the self becomes mu. Both will then be smashed and transcended simultaneously. This experience may be called "becoming one."

Attachment, if pursued thoroughly enough, will be turned into samadhi. This means that the self will be sublimated into no-self (selfless self). Therefore, to pursue things of this world is not necessarily a bad thing. What is wrong is to pursue them half-way, with no definite will to do so thoroughly. Therefore, we should keep on pursuing anything until we become one with it. However, even in our own pursuits, we should be completely selfless, for otherwise, we may be endangered to fall prey to blind attachment. That is why O Yomei emphasizes the merit of primal oneness as the master. It means that we should act on the principle of no-self and no-self-nature.

The point is that whether we will come to pursue things in attachment to them or in non-attachment to them depends on whether our perspective is based on being or non-being. In the light of this basic principle, we should pursue things thoroughly without reserve and without deviating from the Way. If only we are well aware of this basic meaning of the truth of being in our pursuits, I am sure we will succeed in giving full play to our potentialities to a greater extent than when we are restricted to quietistic and fruitless meditation, just like the tart persimmons revealing their hidden taste of sweetness when they are dried.

SIT HARD AND SIT A GREAT DEAL

A certain man wrote that Zen does not count for much, that it means to free one's own mind from all attachments and keep it in a free state. But, he went on, because Zen priests in general make sitting their only aim, their minds become inert and distorted. Zen must therefore make a new start by returning to the original teachings of the Sixth Patriarch Eno (Hui-neng).

Indeed, I have no objection to these statements. What the writer says is certainly true. I quite agree with him except when he writes, "Zen priests make sitting their only aim." This is questionable. First of all, I really doubt whether Zen monks these days are that earnestly devoted to just sitting in meditation. In addition, if it is wrong to make "only sitting" one's objective, I think those in the Soto sect of Zen Buddhism who strive for sitting only for the sake of sitting in their discipline will take strong exception to that contention.

Besides that I must say something in my own defense for I have been encouraging beginning students to sit hard and sit a great deal. Contrary to what the above writer says, I have always insisted that it is because students of Zen do not sit enough that their minds have become so inert and distorted and they cannot reach the realm of freedom.

I quite agree with the above writer's contention that "we must make a new start by returning to the original teachings of the Sixth Patriarch." However, I wonder if the above writer does not denounce meditation for the sake of meditation on the basis of his arbitrary interpretation of the Sixth Patriarch's teaching that only seeing one's original self-nature is to be discussed, and not liberation by means of samadhi. Is it really true that the Sixth Patriarch did not sit in meditation? It is questionable that he did not meditate at all. It is nevertheless beyond our knowledge, for neither the above writer nor I have ever seen the Sixth Patriarch.

It is certain that the *Dan-gyo* (The Platform Sutra of the Sixth Patriarch), while encouraging many things, does not say to spare as much time as possible to sit in meditation. However, Ui Hakujyu, in his *Daini Zenshu Shi Kenkyu*[61] treats this problem in light of the older edition of the Platform Sutra excavated in Tun-huang along with other Tun-huang manuscripts. It is clear today that before Eno became a disciple of the Fifth Patriarch he must have been well cultivated in the way of harmonizing his mind. In short, the Sixth Patriarch contends that Zen aims at helping the individual see his original self-nature and know his true self. The individual should not become attached to zazen in form alone, but by no means does he propose to do away with zazen. It is inconceivable that there has ever been a Zen sect which taught not to do zazen or a Zen Master who prohibited it.

However, zazen must be freed from attachment to the external world and must be practiced with the spiritual discipline to develop both wisdom (Skt. prajna) and the power of concentration (Skt. samadhi; Jpn. jyo) within us. The Sixth Patriarch warns us not to practice quiet and sterile zazen, for some people erroneously take zazen for sitting quietly and blankly with their eyes closed. Of course, I also reject zazen as a means alone.

In the *Dan-gyo* we find the following passage:

Externally, when your mind is free from any thought of attachment to the dualities of all good and bad things, this state of mind is called *za* (sitting). Internally, when you are concentrated on seeing directly your own self-nature, you are said to have zen (Skt. dhyana).[62]

Bodhidharma said to the Second Patriarch, "Outwardly, the activities of all the senses are brought into repose, and inwardly, your mind is not agitated. Using your mind like a sheer wall, you should enter the Way." Further, it is said in Zazen-gi, "Throw away your various ties to the external world of dualities and pacify all things, then your mind and body will be one, and there will be no gap between movement and stillness." All these expressions point to the same thing. If we renounce our attachments to the external world of dualities, filled with all kinds of good and bad things, and if we are in a state of mind unassailable like a wall, we are said to be in "sitting." That is to say, even if we are stably seated like the wooden or bronze images of Buddha in form, we are not deemed to be in the true state of sitting if our minds are confused like the soldiers of the Heike Clan defeated at the battles of Yoshima and Dannoura.

What I have written above is substantiated by the following dialogue between Shakyamuni and Sariputra, the wisest of his disciples, as recorded in the chapter of "His Disciples" in *Vimalakirtinirdesha-sutra* (The Sutra of Vimalakirti).[63] Shakyamuni said, "Go and visit Vimalakirti to inquire about his health on my behalf."

By way of apology Sariputra replied, "I am not worthy to go." He explained, "I once sat in *enza* (serene repose) under a tree in the grove." This response attests to the fact that even Sariputra, the wisest disciple, sat in peaceful repose under a tree.[64]

Judging from this response, the sutra suggests that zazen is the source of Wisdom. This sense of zazen should not be overlooked. Wisdom does not come by chance without any cause. I think the fact that Wisdom originates in samadhi is what this sutra teaches us. Well, then, if we sat in silent meditation like trees or stone images of Buddha, would Wisdom really dawn on us? No, it would not.

This same Vimalakirti, a lay disciple of Shakyamuni, once said to Sariputra, "Beware of the fact that sitting in this way is not always called 'sitting in serene repose.' 'Serene repose' means sitting without revealing the dualities of body and will in the Threefold World." In other words, sitting in serene repose reveals various manners of dignity which do not stem from ignorance. Vimalakirti elsewhere preached that "enza" meant acting like ordinary men of the world without deviating from the Buddhist Way and Dharma. Thus, "enza" means living neither in mind nor outside it, mastering the thirty-seven teachings without being agitated by various opinions, and entering Nirvana[65] without getting rid of desires and agonies.

According to the dictionary, "en" of "enza" is defined "to be peaceful and to rest peacefully." Thus, "za" means "to rest in peace." Therefore, "enza" is "to sit peacefully." It is the same as samadhi.

As mentioned above, one time when Vimalakirti saw Sariputra sitting calmly in the grove, he reproached him, saying,

> Zen Meditation does not mean sitting in vain silence. True Zen Meditation consists in liberation from self-centered opinions stemming from our attachment to ego. You should not lose the frame of mind attained through sitting in tranquility and calmness, but true zazen is to be able to act freely in the movements and changes in this world.

In the above passage from *The Vimalakirti Sutra*, an important distinction between the authentic zazen and the fake zazen is pointed out. If my wording sounds too disturbing to your ears, I would instead say such quiet zazen devoid of movement as practiced by the Hinayana Buddhists. Sariputra, even at that time, still seemed to think of zazen as simply sitting quietly in the grove isolated from the noises of this world. Unlike Sariputra, Vimalakirti is known to have anticipated the dynamic standpoint of Patriarchal Zen, transcending the duality of movement and stillness while regarding sitting and standing as one. It goes without saying that the Zen practiced by the Sixth Patriarch is the same as that taught by Vimalakirti.

As long as we make the Truth and the Absolute our primary objects without transcending the duality of subject and object, we are not said to be in zazen, even if we formally sit in strict conformity to its requirements.

As the Sixth Patriarch teaches, "sitting" means to sit with our minds "externally . . . free from any thought of attachment to the dualities of all good and bad things." The true meaning of "sitting" then lies in the state of mind in which no thought of contradiction arises even when it comes into direct contact with all things. Conversely, it can be said that "sitting" is the training of the mind in terms of no-self or no-form in the true sense of the word. Further, to "see one's self-nature without being disturbed internally" is Zen. The Sixth Patriarch meant to say that Zen is seeing one's own self, realizing that one has originally no fixed form, clearly seeing no-self, and realizing its imperturbability. If we grasp this point firmly, whatever we do becomes zazen whether we are sitting or lying down.

Therefore, the teaching of the Sixth Patriarch has nothing to do with the prohibition and denunciation of zazen. What he meant is simply this: that one should not sit in the wrong way; that one should not be disturbed when one gets into contact with one's good and bad surroundings; and that one should not see one's self-nature as something round or triangular. Otherwise, even if one sits concentratedly and quietly like a great image or a bronze or stone statue of Buddha, one will not be regarded as sitting, nor will one have Zen. Far from discouraging us in zazen, the Sixth Patriarch would rather have encouraged us to sit more and more.

In Zen, liberation from all the dualities of this world is important. I am sure that, apart from this liberation, there is no Zen. Therefore, I quite agree with that certain man above who writes that Zen means liberation of our minds from attachment to all things. But, our minds are like bird-lime, ready to be attached to anything in our surroundings.

How then can we carry ourselves non-attached to all things in this world? Here, sitting in meditation comes to be regarded as absolutely necessary. Self-liberation is possible only when we perceive our own formless self-nature in tranquil meditation and discipline our formless selves in such a way that they will operate on all kinds of practical affairs of this world even while we are out of meditation. In view of this we cannot be said to sit too much even if we keep on sitting as if sitting were the sole purpose of Zen. We should sit hard and sit a great deal to such an extent that it may even be said that we are disciplining ourselves in sitting rather than in Zen.

THE RINZAI SECT AND THE SOTO SECT

A considerable number of people who wish to be trained in Zen under a Zen master wonder which sect they should choose, the Rinzai sect or the Soto sect of Zen Buddhism. It is necessary, therefore, for me to distinguish between them.

I am often asked why I chose the Rinzai sect. In fact, when asked in this way, I am at a loss to answer. It may sound strange to say so, but at the time when I first came to be trained in Zen, I was only concerned with Zen. I did not even know that there were the Soto and the Rinzai sects in Zen Buddhism. My first Zen teacher happened to belong to the Rinzai sect. Later, it so happened that I came to be trained by the teacher who was a descendant of the Inzan School of Rinzai Zen Buddhism. It was by good chance that I came to belong to my present sect and school, which I find suitable for my disposition. Therefore, I did not have to change my sect or school of Zen. That is why, when people ask me which sect they should choose, though I may sound very irresponsible, I have to say, "Choose whichever sect you like."

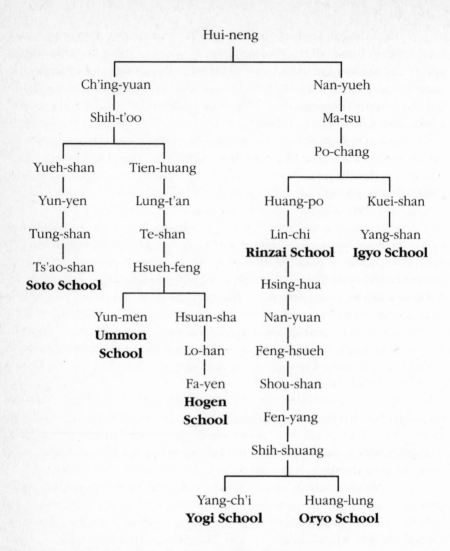

The Five Houses and Seven Schools of Zen Buddhism in China

There are twenty-four schools of Zen in Japan, all of which are alike in advocating Shakyamuni's Enlightened Mind—that is, the wondrous mind of Nirvana, the Eye and Treasury of the True Law. Their mutual differences are due to the teachers' differences in personality and educational backgrounds as well as in the method of teaching. Consequently, at present Zen Buddhism is divided into five houses, seven sects, and twenty-four schools but it is impossible to definitively distinguish between them.

Regarding the twenty-four schools of Japanese Zen, they were established in the course of one hundred and sixty years, starting from the second year of the Kenkyu Era of Emperor Gotoba (1191), when Zen Buddhism was introduced to Japan from China by Priest Eisai, to the sixth year of the Shohei Era of Emperor Gomurakami (1351), when Master Toryo (Tung-ling) immigrated from China. The classification of Japanese Zen Buddhism into so many schools is a very complicated matter, and it is of little meaning to the practitioners of Zen. Therefore, I will refrain from dealing with it. I will, instead, designate in a table the genealogical tree of the Five Houses and the Seven Schools of Zen Buddhism in China for your reference.

The Five Houses are the Rinzai (Lin-chi), Soto (Ts'ao-tung), Igyo (Kwei-yang), Ummon (Yun-men), and Hogen (Fa-yen) Houses. In addition to these, there are two sects stemming from Rinzai. These five houses and two schools later came to be called the Seven Schools of Zen Buddhism. Their characteristics and mutual similarities and differences are discussed in great detail in such works as Ninden Ganmoku (Jen-t'ien Yen-mu)[66] and Goke Sansho Yoro Mon.[67] I am not going to deal with them in detail here. However, because the differences between the Soto and the Rinzai sects seem to be due to differences between two major types of human beings, it will not be altogether in vain to look into their mutual similarities and differences instead of leaving you to your own devices to choose between them.

Prior to the division of Zen Buddhism into the Soto and Rinzai Sects, an encounter between Eno, who was later to become the Sixth Patriarch, and Jinshu (Shen-shiu)[68] took place, as is told in The Platform Sutra of the Sixth Patriarch. The differences in character between these two men presents a very interesting problem, even though its historical authenticity still remains debatable.

As we all probably know, the Fifth Patriarch Gunin (Hung-jen)[69] once said to his disciples, "If any one of you can compose a poem expressing your enlightened state of mind please bring it to me. I will give up my patriarchal robe to the one who succeeds in convincing me of his enlightenment, and I will nominate him as the Sixth Patriarch." Hearing these words of Gunin, the head monk Jinshu took the initiative to write a poem expressing his own enlightened view on a wall:

My body is a bodhi tree.
My mind is like a bright mirror.
Wipe it clean moment by moment
So no dust may collect on its surface.

The above poem means that our bodies are like the trees which will give birth to enlightenment, that our minds are as pure as mirrors, and that we must therefore always do our best to keep them clean by earnestly sitting in meditation. According to legend, a rice-pounder in the monastery named Eno composed his own poem in response, as much as to say what a stupid poem Jinshu had composed. Eno's poem read:

Bodhi is originally not a tree.
The bright mirror is not on the stand.
Originally there is nothing—
Where can dust collect?

What the above poem means is that satori does not come from the body. The mind is nothing like a mirror. Originally there exists no such things as body and mirror. Therefore, it is absolutely impossible to let dust collect on anything. It goes without saying that the difference between the above poems is due to the difference in view and degree of enlightenment between the two monks. Further, it is my opinion that there is the same dichotomy in the frames of mind of all human beings.

The above difference between Eno and Jinshu later came to cause the division of Zen Buddhism into two branches: the Southern School, derived from Hui-neng, and the Northern School, stemming from Shen-hsiu. The former advocated direct seeing into one's original Buddha nature—that is, sudden awakening to one's self-nature. The latter taught gradual awakening through perpetual endeavor to keep one's mind clean. The School of Eno later branched into the five schools as designated above, the Rinzai (Lin-chi) Sect, the Soto (Ts'ao-tung) Sect, the Igyo (Kwei-yung) Sect, the Ummon (Yun-men) Sect, and the Hogen (Fa-yen) Sect. In Japan, only the Rinzai and Soto Sects have survived today besides the Oryo (Huang-lung) Sect which was to develop later. The three great Zen Masters Daio, Daito, and Kanzan[70] are all found in the same line of the Japanese Rinzai Sect.

Now, as to the characteristics of the Rinzai sect, we read in *Ninden Ganmoku* as follows:

The great spirit of Zen, a fledgling almost falling out of its nest in its vigorous activities, dances about like a tiger, leaps like a dragon, flies like a star, roars like thunder, opens and closes the Gate of Heaven, turns the Earth on its axis, displays its high spirits to the extent of pushing up Heaven, and goes beyond the dualities of rolling and unfolding, catching and freeing, and killing and reviving in the exceptional way.

The above expressions are difficult to understand, but at any rate, these inspiring words seem to help me vividly imagine the activity of the spirit of Zen in all its inviolable freedom and vitality, almost to the extent of upsetting Heaven and Earth. Master Torei refers to this vitality in *Goke Sansho Yoro Mon* as follows: "The Rinzai sect lets its students vie with one another for vigor . . ."

According to Ko Ransei, a refugee from China who lives in Japan at present, the riot of Huang-ch'ao in 875 in the T'ang Dynasty of China devastated the greater part of over four hundred provinces. In those days the Chinese intelligentsia led a highly cultured life, indulging themselves in the play of ideas. Soldiers of Huang-ch'ao massacred as many as eight million of these intellectuals. In 845, about thirty years earlier, the incident called Hui-ch'ang Sha-t'ai had broken out, resulting in the destruction of Buddhist images by order of Emperor Wu-tsung. During this incident as many as two hundred thousand priests and monks were forced to return to secular life under great oppression.

The Rinzai sect of Zen Buddhism came to fruition during this extremely violent, war-ridden age, hence, its naturally sharp and vigorous spirit. Its special emphasis on independence from words came from its denial of the empty ideas and words cherished by the intelligentsia. And its insistence on thorough insight into one's original self-nature alludes to its protest against the intellectuals who spent their time repeating and criticizing second and third-hand theories without possessing any philosophy of their own formulation. At any rate, it may be safely said that the characteristic of the Rinzai Sect lies in its emphasis on the spontaneous operation of the spirit of Zen, arising from the standpoint of the awakened Self.

Regarding the Soto sect, it is stated in *Ninden Ganmoku*:

Its traditional manners and customs are minutely specified. And it aims at the alignment of word and conduct. It makes use of things in accord with circumstances. It comes in contact with other people in terms of their words and it judges their condition.

In *Goke Sansho Yoro Mon* we find the following passage regarding the Soto sect: "It aims at attaining the basis of the mind." Reading the above quotations, I feel I can well understand why the Rinzai and the Soto sects are referred to as the Rinzai General and the Soto Farmer respectively. The former is like the general on horseback who commands his army in all his magnificence and expresses the great spirit of Zen in its energetic operation as briskly as if holding up his unsheathed sword in high spirits, ready to strike his enemy right in the face. On the contrary, the latter reflects the careful and meticulous fashion in which farmers take the minutest care of their fields and make the best use of everything in response to the changing circumstances of every move of their hands and in every step of their feet.

When viewed in terms of its discipline, Rinzai Zen is distinguished from Soto Zen by its requirement of the realization of the True Self that transcends this five-foot body and fifty-year life span through integration with koan. For instance, there is the koan of mu which derives from Master Joshu's question about the Buddha nature of a dog. The contemplation on mu serves to help the student transcend the ego by thoroughly killing it as if with a sword. And when the Self is thus effectively killed, the experience of revival is realized (kensho).

In kensho, we see into our true selves and become awakened to our original self-nature. We need to be aware of our own viewpoints and see into our self-nature by being permeated with the poison of the koan to such an extent that we sweat and shed tears of blood. As Master Imakita Kosen[71] writes, "Imagine yourself as a go stone, shedding tears and blood." By starting with seeing our original self-nature through solving a series of koan, we should proceed to foster our discriminating wisdom.

Based on our living body, our True Self (our religious personality) will be established through the experience of seeing our original self-nature in enlightenment. Upon this realization of our True Self, we are supposed to return to secular life to enjoy freedom of choice on the basis of liberation from attachment to anything in this world. That means we are now living our full life in Zen fashion, "freely integrated with the old pine trees and serene clouds." Now, I may safely say that, viewed from the perspective of its discipline, the present Rinzai sect is characterized by its endeavor for the realization of the original self and also for the application of this realization to our everyday life.

In the Soto sect, however, the issue of kensho (seeing one's original self-nature) is seldom discussed for it is already evident in Shakyamuni's enlightenment attained under the bodhi tree. The content of his enlightenment later developed and was incorporated into Buddhist teachings. In view of this fact, everything should be correctly perceived in samadhi by all Buddhists.

Therefore, in the Soto sect, one is expected to sit in zazen, not out of necessity for seeing one's true self, but for the sake of discipline in enlightenment. All one is expected to do is to forget and abandon both mind and body, throw them into the house of Buddha and act as Buddha in every move of one's hands and in every step of one's feet. In this sense, one sits in meditation in such a way that by doing so one is regarded as a Buddha. It is for this reason that, in the Soto sect, neither koan nor kufu for the sake of enlightenment is required. Only in sitting with all one's might will Dharma be realized. Zazen anticipates nothing. The physical form of one in zazen in itself is the form of the enlightened Buddha. Very broadly speaking, the characteristics of Zen practiced in the Soto sect today seem to consist in what I have just briefly mentioned above.

In Master Shibayama Zenkei's *Rinzai Zen no Seikaku*,[72] the styles of the Soto sect and the Rinzai sect are respectively described as *honkaku* (original awakening) and *shikaku* (primal awakening). He writes, "It may be said that, as similar as they are, they are different. Rinzai Zen principally stresses discipline for enlightenment, whereas Soto Zen is principally concerned with discipline for descent from the height of enlightenment." Strictly speaking, then, it may be necessary to differentiate honkaku and shikaku by looking up these words in such books as *Daijo Kishin Ron* (Ta-ch'eng-ch'i-hsin-lun).[73] However, as this book you are reading is meant for the everyday reader, I am going to avoid their detailed differentiation in favor of their practical definitions.

Honkaku alludes to "the original existence of the equally and spiritually awakened bodies." In simpler words, it means that one's mind is originally endowed with an enlightened character. This character, however, remains concealed because of one's unenlightenment, that is, one's ignorance of the principle of things. Thus, one wanders aimlessly in the world of dualities. As for shikaku, it pertains to one who becomes awakened by some chance or other after having been in the state of unenlightenment. The reason why Soto Zen is characterized by honkaku (original awakening) is because it recognized zazen as the samadhi of various Buddhas in enlightenment, as mentioned above. If we carry this idea too far, however, we may risk overstressing our belief in our "natural enlightenment" at the cost of our need of discipline.

Moreover, "discipline for enlightenment" means strenuous endeavor for the attainment of enlightenment by denying and transcending this reality filled with agonies in which human beings are lost. "Discipline for descent" means the acceptance of this profane reality as the world of Buddhas under strict Buddhist discipline for reunion with this reality in enlightenment.

I hope that the general characteristics of the Soto and the Rinzai sects, briefly delineated above, are now clear. What we should discuss next is the problem of which sect we should choose.

If these two different sects vied with each other for superiority, nothing would be more deplorable. Each of these sects has its own merits as well as its own weak points, as we can plainly see. The Rinzai sect regards kensho (seeing one's original nature) as the indispensable condition in enlightenment. In the Soto sect, which emphasizes the body of the enlightened mind, the minutest care is taken to enhance the effects of discipline and to maintain Dharma for the creation and salvation of human beings. For this reason, it may fall into the danger of turning zazen into something inflexible, inert, weak, or even lifeless. The Rinzai sect, if excessively inclined to seeing one's original nature and action, may likewise fail to prevent zazen from becoming the mere means of attaining enlightenment. For the one who is truly awakened to the truth of being, discipline and proof of enlightenment, as well as body and action, are originally one.

Having read some of the merits and weak points of these sects, we should choose either one according to our own dispositions and preferences. Thereafter, there is no other way for us but to leave ourselves to the care of Heaven in our belief in causation. I would like to point out in conclusion that apart from the above-mentioned differences between the two major Zen sects, it is essential for us to choose our right teacher, that is, to choose the right Zen master as our teacher.

By the way, the Rinzai sect once prided itself on having as many as twenty-four schools, of which only one is surviving today in Japan. This school is in the line of Priest Hakuin. The greatest Zen master that lived in the past five hundred years, Master Hakuin led a simple and rustic life in the Shoin-ji Temple in Hara near Numazu. We are impressed with his unusual spiritual power which indeed overwhelmed the whole Zen world. Master Hakuin's religious heir was Master Gasan Jito (1727–1797), whose outstanding disciples Inzan Itan (1753–1816) and Takuju Kosen (1760–1833) originated the two major currents of Zen teachings, namely, the Inzan School and the Takuju School, respectively.

It is into these two schools that Hakuin's Zen is divided at present. The teaching of the Takuju School is characterized by the mysterious symbolism of words, whereas that of the Inzan School is reputed for the severity of its dynamic action. They say there used to be another school, that of Master Suio in the line of Master Hakuin, but it seems to have dwindled down to almost nothing today. Additional genealogical trees, similar to the foregoing one of the Five Houses and the Seven Schools of Zen Buddhism in China, have been placed in the Appendix.

DISCIPLINE AND PROOF

I have written above that it is quite all right for prospective students of Zen to be motivated at first by desires for good health, composure, iron nerves, and so on. In time they may possibly be inspired by chance to become aware of the primal significance of zazen, thus weakening their attachment to their purposes of less importance. And it is the responsibility of their Zen master to lead them in the right direction during their practice of zazen. Therefore, I have hitherto written in favor of these mistakenly motivated but potential students of zazen, for it is better to accept them than to reject them.

However, to tell the truth, it goes without saying that since time immemorial it has been forbidden to practice Zen as a means of accomplishing some purpose or other, for Zen should be without purposes and without acquisitions.

There is a famous story in the history of Zen Buddhism, recounting that Bodhidharma once said in reply to the Emperor Wu Ti of Liang that Zen is "without merits in spite of its strict requirement for endeavor on our part." Furthermore, it is not too much to say that the true spirit of Zen is expressed in the "incrimination of the robbed one rather than the robber himself." This comes from the parable about the man who was imprisoned on the accusation of being a fool just because he had reported to the police that he had been robbed of his purse. It is said that "satori is regarded as something to be one with." These words seem to have an allusion to enlightenment, or kensho, for the sake of some "proof" of enlightenment. Strictly speaking, however, even the "proof" of enlightenment should not be sought outside "discipline."

The Zen idioms, such as the "oneness of discipline and proof" and "true proof and wondrous discipline," directly express the above-mentioned point of Zen. The cause—namely discipline itself—contains the effect, the proof. And, in proof is found discipline. It is said that proof is not the destination to be reached by means of discipline. We are not permitted to seek anything external to discipline in sitting correctly. In our very moments of sitting in meditation, we are Buddhas. We are not to be proven enlightened for the first time as a result of many years of discipline in meditation. Master Dogen writes in "*Bendowa*" in his *Shobo-genzo*, "There is no limit to proof, as it is the proof of discipline. There is no beginning to discipline, as it is the discipline of proof."

What Master Dogen means is this: human beings are all originally Buddhas. Our discipline in itself, therefore, is an event that occurs in the midst of enlightenment. Therefore, there can be no demarcation between enlightenment and unenlightenment, and there is no knowing when discipline starts. Indeed discipline (in enlightenment) at each moment is proof (of enlightenment) at each moment. Discipline and proof are thus simultaneous, and purpose and means are one.

Shakyamuni, after long years of strenuous discipline, experienced his ultimate enlightenment at the sight of a bright star. He declared, "Look at this world of Dharma; I find everything in it has become a Buddha." Based on these words of his, Buddhist teachings were established. Therefore, it is no longer necessary for us to renew our wishes for salvation, resume our discipline, or reinvestigate the contents of Shakyamuni's enlightenment. All we should do is abandon our selfish attachment to the Self, and wholeheartedly accept and believe in the teachings of Shakyamuni through meditation in oneness with Dharma. It is here that we can realize that discipline and enlightenment are not two.

Zazen, in this sense, means becoming a Buddha under the Buddhist discipline, and it should be earnestly practiced in order to return thanks to Buddha continually. The Zen practiced in anticipation of enlightenment is undesirable. This theory of the Soto sect is indeed a logical, correct, and lofty one. As I have mentioned before, however, it may not necessarily escape the danger of becoming the peaceful and inert Zen marked by sheer insistence on equality at the cost of the realistic sense of cause and effect.

The mythological gods and goddesses of Japan from the very beginning lived in their heavenly abodes in Takamagahara.[74] When they became aware of their own missions, all they had to do was to descend directly into the society of wandering and lost people. In the case of Zarathustra, however, we should remember that he had to live a secluded life for ten years in a mountain cave, where he untiringly rejoiced in his own spirituality and solitude before he descended to the world of dust and smog upon experiencing self-awakening.

In this reality, filled with serious inconsistencies, complicated problems, and hardships, we are desperately confronted with our own limitations. In order to overcome our agonies and transcend our limitations, we just cannot descend unprepared into the world like the gods and goddesses of

Takamagahara. It is true and realistic for us to act like Zarathustra, who "lived a secluded life in the mountain cave for ten years," that is to say, we should necessarily be disciplined for enlightenment by abandoning ourselves to the Absolute in order to be one with it, and then find our own true selves in Buddhahood so that we may confirm our original true beings anew.

For instance, in the *Ten Oxherding Pictures*,[75] the first eight stages toward enlightenment, ranging from "Searching for the Ox" to "Both Man and Ox Completely Forgotten," may correspond to the above-mentioned Buddhist discipline in enlightenment. The ninth stage, representing his return to the original place, and the tenth stage, representing his entrance in to the world of dust, may refer to the divine descent of the mythological gods and goddesses from Takamagahara as well as the descent of Zarathustra. These last two scenes in the *Ten Oxherding Pictures* point to the essence of the true life of Zen so well expressed by such Zen idioms as "true proof and wondrous discipline" and "discipline in proof." The scene of turning one's back on enlightenment found in the *Ten Oxherding Pictures* pertains to our blindness to the world of enlightenment. We are now struggling in the muddy water of delusion in this reality, but we must once and for all return to our primal unity and directly regain our original selves at a leap or at a sideward leap in any case, before we become qualified to enter the world of dust with our helpful hands extended in abrupt awakening to our original selves.

If kensho means the rebirth of an ordinary man of the world in Buddhahood, awakening to our original selves may be mistaken for the discovery of something hitherto unknown to us as the object of our discovery, or the acquisition of something hitherto out of our reach. This is a great mistake. All of us are originally endowed with our own fertile Buddha natures, from which we are temporarily alienated in our unenlightenment. Kensho, therefore, means nothing other than the rediscovery of our temporarily concealed Buddha natures.

If the nature of kensho is such, discipline to enlightenment based on kensho should be differentiated from the undesirable Zen which aims at acquisition. The aim or purpose of Zen is not to be sought outside the self. If we aim at becoming one with our true inner selves, the proof of enlightenment will be naturally obtained only in the process of sitting in earnest meditation, for the purpose as such, which gradually reveals itself before our eyes, is the same as the means of attaining it.

Master Rinzai said, "While we are on our way, we are not away from home." In the above case, being on our way may be considered to be the means, and being not away from home to be the purpose. If so, being on our way is the same as being at home; the means in itself is thus the destination. It is in this sense that purpose and means are originally one. Discipline and proof are likewise originally inseparable, as Master Dogen said. This, however, does not mean that discipline and proof are completely one, for, if they are, their oneness is not the true oneness and will not deserve our serious attention.

In Rinzai Zen, satori is regarded as something to become one with. This does not necessarily allude to zazen as a mere means of pursuing the proof of enlightenment. But it means to completely penetrate our delusions and mistaken ideas of selfhood, transcend them, and attain enlightenment, the proof of the true self. The relationship of discipline and proof in the Rinzai sect, in short, is evident in their difference in direction. The upward-directed discipline to enlightenment reaches its height in proof (seeing one's original self-nature), whereupon the direction of discipline is to be turned back again to the actuality of this world.

I will illustrate this twofold direction of Zen discipline by referring to the following example, although it may not serve as a very appropriate example to us. For instance, when a man becomes ill, he enters a hospital for medical care and treatment. On recovery, he returns home from the hospital. The upward-directed discipline, on reaching the summit called proof, turns back to become one with the new downward-directed discipline. That is to say, the newborn world of enlightenment is different in dimension from the deserted world of unenlightenment in spite of their essential oneness.

Eno is noted in the *Dan-gyo* to have remarked, "I concentrate myself only on the problem of kensho, and not on that of self-liberation through Zen Meditation." In the face of these words, some people misunderstand. Some think that sitting in samadhi is not essential to Zen on the pretext that discipline in meditation is not necessary for the proof of enlightenment, whereas others contend that it is not necessary to get kensho in favor of discipline by means of sitting in samadhi. In my opinion both of the above-mentioned groups of people are one-sided and need to be corrected in their outlook on Zen. I think that the essential point of Zen lies in "proof," which is variously called "right awareness of no-self," "seeing one's original self-nature," and so on.

Zen Associations

In my opinion, a thorough reading of what I have so far written in this book is enough to help any lay student of Zen practice zazen by himself. In the case of those who are under special discipline in a traditional Zen dojo, there is no other way for them but to practice zazen in accordance with the specific rules and regulations of the dojo to which they individually belong. In this context I am going to write briefly for the laymen about the meetings of Zen Associations.

In any meeting of Zen Associations, the students sit along the two or four parallel walls of the Zen hall, face to face in the Rinzai Sect with their backs to the walls, and back to back in the Soto Sect with their faces to the walls.

The *jikijitsu*, the leader in charge of the meditation hall, takes a front seat with an incense stick in front of him to show the passing of time. The rest of the meditators take their proper seats with the senior students sitting closest to the jikijitsu and the more junior students sitting further away. When all are seated, the jikijitsu claps the *taku* (wooden clappers) once, followed by the four successive rings of the small metal bell called *inkin* at measured intervals. This is the sign of *shijo*, which means the beginning of samadhi or zazen. In the ensuing period of quietness, the slightest movement of our bodies, even coughing, is forbidden.

After the passage of a given length of time, the jikijitsu again rings his bell once and claps his clappers twice. Then comes a short break of about ten minutes. Sometimes during this break kinhin (meditative walking) takes place in the meditation hall. It helps us recover from our fatigue. (The way of walking in kinhin has been described before in this book.) During this short period of kinhin we are allowed to go out of the meditation hall temporarily, if we need to use the lavatories, for example. When we hear the crisp sound of the wooden clappers again, we should resume our meditation immediately.

Meditation is ordinarily followed by a lecture. This lecture is specifically called *teisho* in Zen terminology, for it consists of the Zen Master's commentary on some literary work of an old Zen Master, such as *Mumonkan* or *Hekigan-roku*. The term teisho means "to bring to show," and it is applied to the above kind of lecture which is very different from any other kind of religious or secular lecture. The word "teisho" is derived from the nature of such a lecture, in which the Zen Master tries to bring to light before his disciples' eyes the ultimate meaning of the Zen teachings.

The sutra such as *Hannya Shingyo* and *Zazen Wasan*[76] are recited by master and audience before the lecture. When a number of people recite a sutra in one accord, they are told to recite it with their ears. It is good to recite the sutra in such a way that the voices of those sitting next to us enter our ears, and, passing through them, come out of our mouths by becoming our own voices. After the lecture, the testimonial teaching of the past Zen Master related to the temple or the lecturer, or *Shiku Seigan Mon*[77] are recited by all present.

Sometimes *sanzen* takes place in the intervals between formal zazen. Sanzen is the personal interview of each pupil with his Master for the purpose of presenting him with his own account of his realization in terms of the koan already given him by the Master. This account must be based, not on his intellectual assumption or interpretation, but on his own personal experience of enlightenment through integration with the koan given him by his Master.

It seems to me that the formality of the pupil's interview with his Master varies with the style of each Master's teaching. In the Tekisui line which advocates the style of "only Buddha Imparting Buddha," teacher and pupil sit, looking intently into each other's eyes, as two Buddhas seated face to face, to fight a decisive battle. In sanzen, the pupil tries to give full play to his potential to satisfy his teacher with all his strength.

As for the manners and customs of sanzen, they are so flexible and variable that each pupil must be instructed individually in advance of his interview with his Master. In a Zen monastery where professional monks are trained, sanzen takes place twice a day, in the morning and in the evening. During the period of sesshin the disciples are allowed to participate in sanzen three or four times a day. Of course, in some dojo, they may be permitted to interview their Masters more often.

Each disciple is expected to devote himself wholeheartedly to his interview with his Master, be it morning or evening. During the period set aside for private interviews the Master rings his bell once as the signal "come" to the disciple who is ready to visit him. In answer to this ring, the disciple usually rings the larger bell twice, meaning "here I come." The Master then knows that a disciple is coming to see him.

Sanzen is classified into *sosan* (mandatory interviews for those with koan) and *dokusan* (individual interviews). For instance, at the beginning of sesshin all the participants are required to visit the Master's room almost by force to fulfill their duties of sosan. Dokusan is restricted to those who are self-confident and willing enough to interview their Master individually.

It goes without saying that sesshin is held for a certain period of time even by the Zen Associations organized by lay Zen disciples and students. On such occasions, all the activities are run according to the schedule prearranged by the leaders in charge of the Zen meditation hall. Therefore, it is advisable to be oriented in advance to the manners observed in the Zen meditation hall. In short, we are always required to act with our minds concentrated in samadhi on all occasions and in accordance with the striking of wooden clappers and the ringing of bells.

The December sesshin is held for the period of one week, from the first of the month to the dawn of the eighth of December, in honor of Shakyamuni's enlightenment. It is called Great Sesshin of *Rohatsu*. It has been traditionally observed with great respect and enthusiasm as the Great Fatal Sesshin. Since the time of Master Tekisui,[78] at Tenryu-ji the Rohatsu Sesshin has been purposely held so that it may end on the dawn of the winter solstice. This is because the winter solstice coincides with the extreme of *yin* (negative force of darkness). According to the *yin-yang* theory in the old Chinese system of divination, the operation of yin in Heaven and on Earth reaches its limit on this particular day. And it conveniently offers a chance to Zen students for Great Deaths. On crossing the threshold of the winter solstice, yin (darkness) turns into *yang* (light), symbolizing rebirth to one's original self-nature after one's experience of Great Death.

There is another such transition acknowledged in Zen monasteries—*konsho*. It is marked by the ringing of the large temple bell in the gathering darkness at dusk when we can no longer distinguish any lines on the palm of one's hand. Then comes *kaihan* when the wooden board hanging under the eaves of the meditation hall is struck repeatedly. The beats are divided into groups of seven, five, and three.

It is said that we can sit most effectively during the interval between konsho and kaihan or between the time when the sun begins to set and the time when its sight is completely lost, for this is the time when the daylight is imperceptibly merged into the darkness of the evening, saturating everything with tranquility. It is during this time of day that Zen disciples sit in meditation for all their lives and with all their might. If any one makes the slightest noise or movement, someone sitting next to him hits him with an abusive remark. I think it is a real problem for any lay disciple who is employed and is occupied by job-related activities to practice zazen calmly by himself at home in the evening, but still I would like to encourage you by all means to make an effort to sit with the setting sun.

Statue of Yakushi Nyorai (Skt. Bhaishajyaguru), the bodhisattva of healing, holding a medicine jar in his left hand. The healing abilities of Yakushi can be interpreted medically but they carry a deeper meaning as well. Yakushi's main role is to cure all people of ignorance, the most fundamental of all ills.

CHAPTER 5

Physiological Effects

The following passage is a famous one from the *Tao-te Ching*,

> In the pursuit of learning, one must daily expand one's sphere of
> activity, but in the pursuit of the Tao, one must daily reduce it;
> reduce it and reduce it again until one attains a state of "non-
> activity." One attains a state of "non-activity," and yet there is
> nothing which is not accomplished.

The same is true of the Way of Zen. In the world of intellectual learning, a day of learning brings a day's profit and gain. We thus increase our
knowledge. In Zen discipline, on the contrary, the more we are disciplined, the
less delusive will we be and our discriminating consciousness will decrease,
until even we ourselves become mu (emptiness). It is said that "myriads of
things come to illuminate the Self." It is natural that we should completely
become mu, ku (emptiness), and zero before we are confronted with myriads
of things coming to us.

An ancient sage said something truly insightful, "Last year's poverty—
no land, but a gimlet. This year's poverty—no land, no gimlet." He meant that
until very recently he had been immature as a man, retaining the stink of
enlightenment which was visible like a little hole made with the tip of a gimlet. But, now, being advanced in enlightenment, he was completely free from
anything external to his enlightened self, and he found himself in the realm of
what Lao Tzu called non-activity. Zen Master Joshu (Chao-chou)[1] likewise
said, "I entered the Buddhist life when I was a small boy. Now, I have already
grown too old and powerless to get down from my chair." He also said, "I used
to discipline myself in order to save people; however, believe it or not, I have
become a fool." It is indeed very childlike of Joshu to admit that he has become
so stupid that he cannot satisfactorily respond in spite of his strenuous efforts
in self-discipline for the salvation of others.

Zen pertains to the experience of emptiness and nothingness where
neither a gimlet nor land is to be found; and we attain Zen when we realize
that no one is in need of our salvation. Zen has no merit and no effect. Zen is
realizing that we already possessed that which we were so earnestly seeking
and realizing that all our training was needless.

It has been said since old times, "Zen gives me nothing, not even a
drop of water," or "Zen does not even offer me Dharma." The above remarks
are very convincing and demonstrate that Zen has no merit or effect. Being
meritless and effectless, how can Zen give any Dharma or offer any drops of
water to anyone?

Concerning the effects of Zen, the preceding words are enough to convince practitioners of zazen to seek nothing external to it. It is certainly correct to seek nothing except zazen. However, this will not satisfy anyone who wishes us to preach or write something about Zen. It is for this reason that I have to deviate from the Zen way, in compliance with the needs of others, to present some knowledge of the meritless merits and the effectless effects of Zen.

The other day, I listened to the lecture by a certain scholar of education. According to his theory, education shares a principle with hypnotism in that education addresses itself to the deep stratum of unconsciousness which underlies consciousness. In his opinion, the same is true of the repeated slogans of politicians when they campaign for election as well as the announcements made for TV advertisements.

Master Rinzai, the founder of our Rinzai Sect, severly disliked propaganda. He often bitterly denounced the advertisements of the marvelous properties of medicines, calling them the "medicine sickness of the establishment and propagandistic statements." However, conversely speaking, the mere sight of the leaflets advertising the favorable effects of a certain medicine either helps the sick feel better or worsens their illness. Therefore, I do not make light of advertisements that describe the effects of medicines. In the same way, merely reading about the effects of zazen may encourage some Zen students to foster their religious yearning, yet it still may not cure neurotic patients.

To begin with, let us refer to Master Hakuin's remarks on the effects of zazen. He praised zazen from various perspectives in many of his works such as *Chobokure* (Ballad of the Beggar Monk), *Obaba Kona-hiki Uta* (Song of the Old Woman Grinding), but his *Zazen Wasan* is the most accessible to us. In his poem he publicizes the tremendous effects of zazen as follows: "Those who even once, in all humility, listen to this Truth, praise it and faithfully follow it will be endowed with innumerable merits." Of all this infinite number of good fortunes, the greatest one is described as follows: "Your form of no-form, your going and returning, takes place nowhere but where you are. Your thought being the thought of no-thought, your singing and dancing is none other than the voice of Dharma."

Master Hakuin suggests that through zazen, anybody can begin to enjoy this life, liberated from attachment to this world of dualities. The mere recitation of these passages makes our minds and spirits joyful. In other words, "Nirvana presents itself before you; where you stand is the Land of Purity. Your person is the body of Buddha." This is the greatest of all the effects of zazen. If we read aloud these passages on the effects of zazen before and after sitting in meditation, what other effect should we need?

I have briefly mentioned before investigations of the brainwaves of Zen monks during their meditation that were carried out by Professor Hirai and Professor Kasamatsu of Tokyo University. According to the results of their investigations,

> The brain-waves (the activity of cerebral cells recorded by means of the variation of the electric voltage) gently undulate, and the frequency of respiration decreases during meditation. Strangely enough, however, the number of pulses increases. Even though tension is alleviated, the body remains in an alert condition to act readily at any time instead of being inert as it is in sleep . . . In the case of advanced monks, the shape of their brain waves quickly changed to an astonishing degree 50 seconds after the start of zazen. Even after the finish, the effect remained. This could not be seen at all when amateurs tried to imitate it.[2]

Thus, zazen has recently begun to be recognized as something contributing to the mental health of some patients suffering from neuroses.

It has long been said that breathing becomes well regulated, blood circulation becomes normalized, the abdomen becomes filled with energy in a way that creates self-composure, and insomnia can be cured as the result of zazen. The unprecedented research of Professor Kasamatsu has succeeded in demonstrating theses empirical effects scientifically.

Hasegawa Usaburo's Igaku Zen[3] has also been highly acclaimed of late. As is suggested by its subtitle: "Hara to Kenko no Genri" (the Principle of the Abdomen and Health), zazen is viewed as a "strenuous discipline for the maximum activation of the parasympathetic nervous system." Dr. Hasegawa further writes that the ultimate goal of zazen is the cultivation of the hara in the well-unified man with sound pneumogastric nerves, emphasizing the nature of medical Zen quite literally.

Dealing even further with the relationship of zazen and the pneumogastric nerves, Takeuchi Daishin published a book several years ago regarding the method of Tendai discipline as taught in his dojo.[4] If the discipline practiced in the Tendai Sect is regarded as equivalent to Zen, it can be usefully introduced to my readers here.

The basic question Dr. Takeuchi seeks to answer is, "When you fill your tanden with power and with attention, what physiologic effects can be found?" The first effect he discusses suggests that, when the tanden is filled with energy and pressure, blood previously stored in the liver and the spleen is pushed into the capillaries. The physiological effect is such that one could say that the tanden acts like a secondary heart. Fresh blood, rich in red blood cells, is sent up to the cerebral center through the cervical plexus. As a result, the respiratory center is influenced in such a way that respiration is tranquilized.

The second phenomena in this circulation is the neutralizing regulation of adrenaline by the cholinergic nerves of the parasympathetic nervous system when they are stimulated by pressure on the tanden. In short, a new world, completely different from the one in which the body used to breathe with chest and abdomen, comes into being through the pressure applied to the area in and around the tanden. It is indeed a "revolution of the living body."

I would also like to introduce Hirata Kurakichi's *Suwari no Kenkyu*[5] and Sato Tsuji's *Shintai Ron*,[6] both of which deal with the physiological effects of meditation in great detail. These men both practice meditation in the fashion of seiza (sitting formally on bent knees). Therefore, they may not be correctly called Zen men. However, I have been helped by their works which explain the posture of the seated body and its relationships to respiration and to the function of the internal organs.

Ueno Yoichi published the book titled *Za no Seiri Shinri teki Kenkyu* in 1938. Although it is a small book consisting of only seventy-six pages, it is very well written and to the point. Ueno writes,

> It is my opinion that the purpose of regulating the body, respiration, and mind through zazen is to prompt the action of the automatic nervous system through the maximum suspension of the conscious processes of mental activity which are controlled by the central nerves in the cerebrum and vertebra . . . In zazen, therefore, the conscious processes of cerebral activity are temporarily suspended, and the activity of autonomic nerves is enhanced. It is like switching off cerebral nerves and switching on autonomic nerves. As the center of autonomic nerves is in the abdomen, you become one with the universe by acting with your abdomen instead of with your brain.[7]

Thereupon, blood descends in the body to keep the head cool and to cure excitement. If you breathe with chest and abdomen, with your power concentrated on the tanden under the navel, the area near the solar plexus (the center of the autonomic nervous system) is properly stimulated to keep your feet warm. In this way, the three poisons—greed, anger, and folly—disappear. When autonomic nerves are fully active, the natural vitality of the human body operates to make us healthy and alert enough to attain enlightenment.

As I have little or no knowledge of medical science, I should refrain from presenting any further secondhand explanations here for fear that I may inadvertently impose my personal opinions and interpretations on you. They say, "True gentlemen do not stand beneath rock-strewn cliffs." So, here I will just let the above quotations suffice. However, in the following chapters, I will try to make amends for my insufficient explanation by introducing some of the effects of zazen traditionally pointed out by Zen masters of old.

IN SERENITY BEYOND LIFE AND DEATH

To begin with, let me introduce three men—Deishu, Kaishu, and Tesshu—who were called the Three Boats (*shu* means "boat" in Japanese) and who lived toward the end of the Tokugawa Shogunate.[8] All of them were masters of Zen and swordsmanship.

Deishu was a man of broad scale. He lived in obscurity, devoting himself to the Tokugawa Family. Although his name is familiar to us, his biography is hardly known. However, in a book recently written by Kobosawa Kan, Deishu is minutely described as a great man of accomplishment in the arts of spearfighting and calligraphy.[9] As for Kaishu, he writes about himself, strongly stressing the effects of Zen on him as follows:

> I, Katsu Kaishu, owe what I am today to my discipline in swordsmanship and Zen, the basis of my spirituality. The merit of my twofold discipline spontaneously revealed itself at the very time of the downfall of the Tokugawa Shogunate. It helped me remain well composed even in moments of my encounter with various enemies and rascals. It also made it possible for me to tide over the difficulties successfully during the Meiji Restoration when I was roaming between life and death.[10]

Tesshu likewise devoted himself to swordsmanship and Zen, practicing his swordsmanship in his dojo during the daytime and sitting in Zen meditation until around 2 a.m. Moreover, as I have written before, he sat in meditation in such an earnest way that even rats ran away from his house. In his youth, he would sleep sitting up through the whole night, with one of his shoulders supported by the upper end of his bamboo sword. According to his wife, she never saw him sleeping in his bed for a period of about ten years from the time of their wedding.

In his last years he trained in Zen under the guidance of Master Tekisui of Tenryu-ji Monastery. At the age of forty-five, he could see into the ultimate meaning of the following eulogy on *Goi-Kenchuto*:[11]

> When two sword points are crossed, there is no need to ward off. The master swordsman is like the lotus flower blooming in the flames of fire. Then, the energy of heaven-soaring spirits spontaneously comes out of your original nature.

At the same time, Tesshu reached the height of mastery in swordsmanship and he was able to act freely thereafter wherever he might be for he was one with everything. Ever since then, he called his school of swordsmanship Itto Shoden Muto Ryu.[12] The swordsmanship of Tesshu was so fierce as to be called "Devil's Sword." But he must have reached the stage of full maturity by the time he established his own Muto Ryu.

My own teacher of swordsmanship, Yamada Ittokusai,[13] once said to me, "Old Tesshu was sluggish in manipulating his sword," and I can well imagine him slowing down in his later years. But even then Tesshu had not yet reached the ultimate stage of swordsmanship, which is called *ainuke* (mutual passing) by Harigaya Sekiun.[14] I wonder if Tesshu could resist temptation to vie with his opponent for victory whenever he was confronted with him. This thought happened to occur to me as I remembered his remark that the slightest thought of habitual duality between man and woman still remained indelibly marked on his mind. I suppose, however, that when he reached the age of forty-nine or so, he was completely free from any dualistic thought, attaining the mastery of ainuke.

Judging from the above assumption, Tesshu's spirit of Zen seems to have reached its maturity during the period ranging from his forty-fifth to forty-ninth year. When most men reach their eighties or nineties, they are free from various desires both physically and psychologically. They are also free from concerns about fame as well as of life and death. It is indeed amazing how Tesshu could attain *his* full maturity at such an early age, while he was still in the prime of his manhood. At the age of forty-five or forty-six he could drink almost four gallons of sake at a time and he must have been still full of his sexual powers. In stature, he was a giant, over six feet tall and close to 250 pounds in weight.

A student of his, Chiba Ritsuzo, thinking he should be free from passions in order to concentrate on self-discipline, once unburdened his concerns to Tesshu. In response Tesshu said, "What a bright idea you've got! It is indeed passions that cause the duality of life and death. Unless you get rid of them you will never succeed in attaining enlightenment, however hard you may practice Zen. Well, then, how are you going to get rid of your passions?" Chiba replied, "I'm going to get rid of them by keeping women at a distance and trying to avoid contact with them." "That does not mean," said Tesshu, "getting rid of passions but repressing them; it is merely putting a cover over undesirable things." He continued, "If you really mean to get rid of your passions, take courage now. Go and jump into the rough waves of your passions and see through them." It so happened that Master Bokujyu of Daitoku-ji (temple) was in their company. When Tesshu asked the master, "Please tell him what to do," the master replied apologetically, "I'm sorry I'm quite in the dark about such a matter."

Years later, Tesshu recalled his own efforts, "I used to make such strenuous efforts for the solution of this problem. Ever since the time when I was about thirty, I have never been susceptible to female charms, but the awareness of the duality between man and woman haunted me until I became forty-five and finally succeeded in seeing through the ultimate meaning of the words: "When two sword points are crossed, there is no need to ward off . . ." It was then that I became one with all things in all places. Even then, however, there still remained in me a faint trace of the habitual thought of duality, which, I could at last discard at the age of forty-nine, at a chance sight of a flower blooming in my garden."

One spring, all of Tesshu's students held an informal dinner party in commemoration of the opening of the training in swordsmanship. One of the students went up to his teacher to have a talk with him. As soon as he put down his hands on the floor to bow, however, he vomited. The teacher stood up immediately, and pushing away the other students in his way, ate the vomit without leaving any bit of it. One of his students tried to prevent him from doing so, "What on earth are you doing, Sir?" The teacher answered very serenely, "Well, I have just undergone discipline for the integration of purity and impurity."

On another day, a man visited Tesshu and said, "I have come to ask for your instruction in Zen."

"For what purpose," asked the teacher, "do you intend to practice Zen?"

"I would like to attain the enlightened state of freedom and serenity, with non-attachment and adaptibility," he replied. Tesshu said, "My Zen becomes the Way of Warriors when practiced by warriors, and the Way of

Merchants when practiced by merchants. If you want such Zen as you have described, you might ask the professional clown Rohachi for instruction." The visitor was embarrassed and took his leave.[15]

I think there is a considerable number of people in this world who think of Zen in the same way as that visitor to Tesshu. It often happens that some people think it the purpose of Zen to be free and serene or to be natural and obedient. They often regard those who show such qualities in attitude as adept in Zen. This type of people are often found among old-fashioned lay Zen disciples. In my opinion, they are rather stereotyped and distasteful.

There is another story about Tesshu which I feel is characteristic of the man. A lay Zen disciple, who had long trained under Tesshu's guidance, once asked his teacher for his teisho (formal Zen lecture) on the *Rinzai Roku* (Lin-chi Lu.) Tesshu said in refusal, "You should ask Priest Kosen in Kamakura."

But the lay Zen student insisted, saying, "Well, I have already had the pleasure of listening to Master Kosen's lectures. Please let me listen to yours at any cost, for I hear you have been recently granted an approval of enlightenment by Master Tekisui." So saying, he persisted in making his request.

"All right, then, you shall have my teisho." Tesshu suddenly stood up and took his visitor to his dojo with him. After a match with their swords there, they returned to the room. The teacher asked his visitor, "How did you like my teisho on *Rinzai Roku*?" The visitor did not know what to say in his embarrassment.

The teacher raised his voice, "I have just given you a lecture on *Rinzai Roku* in Swordsmanship, as I am a man of the sword. The Way of swordsmanship is my own professional field. I am a warrior. That is why I don't follow the Way of priests. Imitation in any way is false, however good it may look. For instance, the games of *go* and *shogi*[16] are of no use unless they are internalized and put to practical use. The same may be true of Zen. Even Zen, if it is a dead Zen, is after all nothing but a useless object of pleasure. I hear you have been practicing Zen for years. I am sorry to learn that you take *Rinzai Roku* for the mere collection of words."

So saying, Tesshu laughed aloud. It is said that the visitor was much ashamed of himself and apologized.

In the summer of the twentieth year of Meiji (1887), when Tesshu was about fifty-two years old, he was suffering from a large tumor in the right side of his abdomen. The doctor diagnosed it as cancer. Around July of the following year, his illness suddenly turned for the worse. Tesshu summoned his disciples on the eighth of July in anticipation of his approaching death, and gave lessons in swordsmanship to all of them individually.

In the early evening of the seventeenth of July, he took a bath and asked his wife to bring him a white kimono to wear in preparation for his approaching death. She hesitated to obey him at first, but he insisted on wearing it. When she finally brought it to him, he put it on and returned to his room. After bowing toward the Imperial Palace, he lay down in his bed.

Around 1 a.m. the tumor in his stomach ruptured. It resulted in the perforation of his stomach, causing peritonitis and placing him in critical condition. On the morning of the following day, the eighteenth of July, more than two hundred people including his relatives and friends gathered around his death bed in quiet sorrow. All the sliding doors and partitions had been removed to make more space for the visitors. Just then, Katsu Kaishu arrived in a rush. At the sight of Tesshu surrounded by so many people in his death bed, Kaishu shouted in a loud voice, "You have been torturing Tesshu all his life. Are you going to torture him to death when he is suffering in such a critical condition?" Everybody withdrew into another room.

Kaishu then said to Tesshu, "Are you leaving me behind and going ahead without me?" Tesshu replied, "I am through with my work. Excuse me for taking my leave before you." When Kaishu asked him, "How about asking your favorite priest to come and talk with you?" Tesshu answered, "He is now far away on journey." Tesshu referred to Master Tekisui, who was then absent from his home temple to attend the religious service held at Unju-ji in Izumo.

Tesshu sent his children off to school at 8 a.m. as usual, and ordered his students to practice swordsmanship. He himself unsheathed his sword to practice a patterned fighting exercise called *Sho-goten* in the Itto Style of Swordsmanship. Then, at 1 p.m., he set about his work of copying a Buddhist sutra to fulfill his self-imposed daily task. His brow was wet with perspiration. When he at last finished half a page, his family doctor Chiba Ritsuzo said, "How about leaving off copying now? It does not matter if you finish half a page or a full page." "That's right. I agree with you." So saying, he immediately put down his brush on his desk.

Tesshu spent that night leaning against the quilts piled up behind him. On the morning of the nineteenth of July, he showed the following haiku poem to Dr. Chiba:

In my suffering
From my swollen stomach,
"Caw"—the crow at dawn.

"Well, this is about all I want to say," said Tesshu. At 9 a.m. he asked Dr. Chiba to leave his side. The doctor asked, "For what purpose?"

"Well," answered Tesshu, "I do not want to be disturbed when I take a nap."

When Tesshu was left alone, he slowly got out of his bed, and sat down on the floor with his face turned toward the Imperial Palace. Slowly, he held out his right hand. Sitting a short distance away and understanding the meaning of this gesture, Dr. Chiba handed him a flat fan. Tesshu closed his eyes meditatively, trying to write some letters on his left palm with the end of the fan, but he suddenly began to pant for breath. Dr. Chiba quickly offered medication to him, but in vain. There was no longer any strength left in Tesshu to take the medicine. Finally, at a quarter past nine, he died a Great Death while sitting in zazen. It was on the nineteenth of July in the twenty-first year of Meiji (1888). He was then at the age of fifty-three.

It goes without saying that what made it possible for Tesshu to die the so-called "Grand Death unsurpassed by anything in this age of religious degeneration" is nothing other than the operation of his invincible power so strenuously and so patiently nurtured in samadhi during the long years of his life.

DYING IN MEDITATION

In this section, I am going to introduce an article written by Nakano Shuntaro that appeared in the Buddhist periodical *Daihorin*.[17] In this article Master Seisetsu of Tenryu-ji presents his account of the life and death of his teacher, Takagi Ryoen.[18] Although he is counted among the most outstanding Japanese Zen Masters of recent years, Ryoen is not very well known to the general public.

According to Master Seisetsu, Priest Ryoen served as Archbishop of Tenryu-ji for twenty-one years (except for a two year period when the younger Priest Gasan held the position). Outshone by his teacher Tekisui in religious virtue,[19] and surpassed by his student Gasan in meritorious service, Priest Ryoen ended his life in obscurity. Nonetheless, he was a man of superior character as well as a scholar.

Priest Ryoen was born in the northern part of Kyoto Prefecture, Japan. At the age of seventeen, when he first left home on his religious journey, he made the vow "never to return home before distinguishing himself considerably." At Chion-ji, a temple in Kirido, he fasted for one week and then copied an excerpt from the *Suramgama-sutra*[20] in blood instead of in ink. After dedicating his copy to Bodhisattva Manjusri,[21] he made his start in religious training. Priest Gettan of Chion-ji later said of Ryoen:

> I struggled to be a mature Zen monk for a long time, but because
> I was not a man of merit I have lived in obscurity in the country
> all my life. Ryoen made an admirable start while he was still young
> because of his iron will. But, no matter how strong he may be, he
> will end up in obscurity in the country if he does not have merit
> as well.

Soon after, Priest Gettan began to make monthly pilgrimages for the sake of his student, traveling widely for three years.

Ryoen at first intended to be a disciple of Priest Imakita Kosen of Eiko-ji, a temple in Iwakuni, in order to be trained in Zen as well as in Buddhist scholarship. However, hearing from home that his first Buddhist teacher had been praying for him for three years, he was greatly touched. "What should learning mean to me?" So saying, he went to Bairin-ji in Kurume, where he stayed on until his teacher passed away.

He then went to train with Priest Gido at Tenryu-ji. Shortly after Ryoen's arrival at Tenryu-ji, however, Priest Gido passed away and responsibility for Ryoen's training was transferred to Priest Tekisui. It was Tekisui who later granted him approval of his enlightenment. Ryoen was appointed to priesthood in Jizai-in, a sub-temple of Tenryu-ji, at the age of twenty-nine.

At that time there was a retired priest named Shozan at Jizai-in who said to Ryoen, "You seem lacking in character. How about building a public bathhouse to please people so that you may increase in virtue?" Priest Ryoen thereupon built a bathhouse in a wide vacant lot near the Middle Gate of Tenryu-ji.

To get the water, he would row a boat to the cold artesian spring which came from Mt. Arashi. He would heat the mineral water from the spring in the bathtub and invite neighboring farmers and peasants to take a bath. He continued this act of charity for three years. In spite of his strenuous efforts, however, his meager virtue did not grow to attract public attention.

I said earlier that he served as Archbishop of Tenryu-ji for twenty-one years. During this period, however, he served in name only. The Bishop actually served as the manager of the temple. One accomplishment for Ryoen, however, was the founding of the temple called Tokko-in in Kobe, where he lived with his student Seisetsu.

It is customary in the Buddhist temple to heat the water in the bathtub with chopped wood as fuel. When the water was moderately heated,

Seisetsu would invite Priest Ryoen to the bathroom, calling to him, "Priest, the bath is ready." Every time Seisetsu offered to scrub Priest Ryoen's back, the latter would refuse and say, "No, thank you, never mind."

One day, Seisetsu entered the bathroom immediately after the priest went out of it but he found no trace of the priest having taken a bath there. He wondered why, but he did not pay much attention to it in the beginning, for he was still a young boy, busy with his work in the temple. But, as the same thing happened more than a few times, he became increasingly concerned with it. One day, he said to the priest, "It seems you are not taking your bath." The priest said in reply,

> I make it a rule not to get into the bathtub. All I need is two buckets of warm water. It is impossible here to draw water from a well. I have already tried to dig a well thirty-six times, but in vain. Not a drop of water can I get from the ground here. That is why we must take the trouble to obtain water from the waterfall. As we live in such a place as this without producing any water at all, we must make the best use of every drop of water. So, I am content with only two buckets of water and keep from dirtying the water in the bathtub.

The above words of his are awe-inspiring from the religious point of view, although people in general these days may laugh at him for saying such a thing.

Another noteworthy thing about Priest Ryoen is that he did not eat more than one bowl of rice at a time, though there are some who often crave more than two or three bowls of rice at a time. They would ask, "Do we have mixed rice today?" Priest Ryoen, on the contrary, used to say,

> No, one bowl of rice is enough for me, for I usually eat the same amount of rice. In fact, I could eat two more bowls of rice if I tried, but I would like to save as much rice as I can for posterity. A certain monk in the Soto Sect whose name I've forgotten weighs the quantity of rice every time he eats it. He thinks that it is not necessary for him to eat more than he needs in order to live, and he leaves the remainder of his rice to posterity. I do not take the trouble to weigh my portion of rice each time I eat it as he does, but I make it a rule to eat just one bowl of rice at a time. However much rice there may be, I will always leave extra rice for posterity.

Priest Ryoen thus neither took his bath in the bathtub nor ate enough rice to satisfy his hunger completely. He was also a priest of great patience. It was probably the fifth year of Taisho (1916) that he began to complain that something was wrong with his bowels, often soiling his loincloth because he was unable to control himself before he reached the lavatory.

A certain physician in Kobe named Matsushima examined him and said, "Please go to the University Hospital in Kyoto for an examination." When Priest Seisetsu accompanied Priest Ryoen to the hospital, the doctor said to him that a cancer had developed in Priest Ryoen's rectum. The doctor said to Priest Seisetsu,

> What an unconcerned air he has been assuming! He has only a couple of months to live. If ever he happens to live longer, he will hardly live for more than a year at most. The rest of his life span is limited to two or three months. It is too late now to operate on him. There is no effective medicine for him either. Therefore, let him live as he pleases.

When they returned home by car, the priest asked Seisetsu, "What did the doctor say to you?" Unable to tell the truth, Seisetsu answered, "The doctor did not say anything in particular. All you have to do now is to lie quietly in bed and continue to receive medical treatment. The doctor said there is no medicine for you."

"You are telling a lie. The doctor must have said that it is all over for me. Tell the truth!" Thereupon, Seisetsu could not help but tell him the truth. The priest then said, "That's exactly what I thought. As a doctor he can diagnose my sickness as cancer of the rectum. But, as far as my life span is concerned, it is beyond his knowledge. I won't die yet. Don't worry, please."

Thereafter, he quietly set off alone on a pilgrimage to the thirty-three sacred sites in the western part of Japan as well as to the other temples in Saitama Prefecture and in the eastern part of Japan to pay homage to one hundred images of Kannon (Bodhisattva Avalokitesvara).

Later, in August of 1918, just when Seisetsu returned home from a visit to China, he received a letter of invitation from Priest Ryoen. Seisetsu lost no time in returning to the Tokko-in in Kobe where he found Priest Ryoen ill in bed. Hearing Seisetsu's account of his visit to China, the priest said, "How interesting! Please tell me more about it tomorrow." To the great distress of Seisetsu, Ryoen seemed to be greatly weakened at that time so Seisetsu was obliged to stay in the temple for a week.

On the twenty-eighth of August he was invited again to visit him with Master Takagi Tagaku,[22] Archbishop of the Tenryu-ji in those days, and Yamazaki Ekishu. Priest Ryoen said to them, "I will probably die on the first of September. So, I must distribute my mementos before I die." He had a list of all his belongings, including his robes and his equipment, prepared in his notebook, together with the names of whom they were to be bequeathed. He then expressed his wishes for his cremation and other matters concerning his prospective funeral. He said, "The sutra should be chanted on a Sunday regardless of what day of the week I die. You need not spend too much time on it. That's all there is to take care of, so please withdraw now." The invited guests consulted with each other, and agreed to take their leave.

The next day, Priest Ryoen got up out of bed. He sat in Zen meditation on a folding straw mat slightly elevated above the ground. He said, "We are not expected to die in bed but in zazen." Finally he fell into a critical condition. His nurse and disciples suggested many ways to make him feel comfortable, but he would not hear of it. When morning came, he went up to the Main Hall to recite the sutra.

He crawled from his room to the Main Hall, a distance of about 25 yards. Frequently lying on the floor to take a rest, he finally reached the Main Hall, where he chanted the names of the ancestral Zen masters to whom we owe the transmission of the Illuminated Mind. Chanting each of their names, he bowed in reverent worship of each master. He took a rest after every three or four names. In this way, he repeated his chanting day after day, until the dawn of the eleventh of September when he simply could not go to the Main Hall. When he passed away later that day, however, he was found seated in zazen.

Every Day a Good Day

We frequently encounter the phrase, "Every day, a good day" written mainly on the hanging scrolls used in the tea rooms. Zen men also write this phrase frequently, but tea masters are especially fond of it. It literally means that every day is a good day as it is. It is certainly considered to be very appropriate as the content of the hanging scrolls used in the tea rooms. It is there that people enjoy themselves in tea ceremony apart from the world of dust, forgetting their troubles and suffering for a while.

Master Unmon Bunen (Yun-men Wen-yen)[23] once said to a gathering of his students, "I am not going to question you about the things which happened before the fifteenth, but bring me one appropriate phrase composed after the fifteenth." Things that happened before yesterday have already gone by, and no matter what one says about them now, nothing can be done to bring them back. It is no longer of any use to pass any remarks about them. Therefore, Unmon did not intend to question his disciples about them. Now, when he asked them to say something now and hereafter, though I do not know how many of his students were present, not one person could answer. Therefore, Unmon himself offered an answer to his own question: "Every day, a good day."

If this phrase had been superficially taken for "every day is a good day," at least one of Master Unmon's disciples might have been able to answer him directly, even if it was said that there was a scarcity of talent under him. But, as it was, none of them could answer him to his satisfaction. Why was it so?

Our lives do not consist of favorable days alone. We have rainy days and windy days as well. We are sometimes sad and other times glad. There are a greater number of disagreeable things than agreeable things in our societies. The news is filled with murders, corruption, and suicides as well as the agitation of school teachers waving red flags or fighting with policemen. That is why the late Zen Master Sugawara Jiho[24] from Kamakura said, "I would answer that each day is a bad day."

Did Master Unmon mean that we should consider anger to be our enemy, and reminisce about times we were happy when we are sad, making an effort to live each day as a good day? That could not be! It would be impossible for Master Unmon, distinguished as he was, to make such a petty attempt at moralization.

Well, then, what does Master Unmon's phrase really mean? In reference to this question, Master Setcho Juken (Hsueh-tou Ch'ung-hsien),[25] composed the following poem:

> Cutting One (The Absolute), grasping Seven (Relativity),
> Above and below, and in the four directions.
> Smoothly walking
> He treads on the sound
> Of flowing water;
> And discerns as he pleases
> The traces of flying birds . . .

The numbers "one" and "seven" are not important here. The first line of the poem should mean that the Absolute is negated and the Relative is affirmed. Truth remains constant. Even if you take something away it does not decrease and even if you add something to it does not increase. Truth fully reveals itself at any time and at every place. All events and all things are self-sufficient in themselves. A pan is always a pan and nothing else, at present as well as in the past. Paper is likewise paper in its exaltedness under heaven. Ink is ink, unique in its being in the whole world. There is nothing under Heaven which is not absolute in its existence.

This fact should throw some light on the hidden meaning of the phrase, "Every day, a good day." To describe it more beautifully, when we walk along the stream, we become one with it and flow with it; and when we look up at flying birds, we become birds and fly freely all across the far extending sky with them.

> We are white dew drops;
> If we lay ourselves just as we are
> On the maple leaves,
> We are red beads.

The above poem points to the hidden meaning of the phrase, "Every day, a good day."

Zarathustra, as described in Nietzsche's *Also Sprach Zarathustra*, left home and climbed into the mountains at the age of thirty. After he spent ten years there, alone with his spirituality and solitude, he said,

> Look! Now I am satisfied with my wisdom. I am, as it were, like a bee overloaded with the honey of its own gathering. All I need now is somebody who will extend his hands to me in need of it. I wish to give and share it with someone else. Oh, setting sun, like you must I also descend. Those who are waiting for me to join them call it "descent."[26]

Ten years previous to his descent, Zarathustra had carried the ashes of his own lifeless body up the mountain where he now found himself reborn. One morning he got up at a rose-streaked daybreak and talked with the sun. He filled his goblet to the brim with the fountain-water of his overflowing life. And, with this feeling, he descended the mountain for reunion with the world of human beings.

On his way back to the world, Zarathustra met an old sage in the woods and exchanged words with him. After parting from him, he resumed his journey back to the world, saying to himself, "Is it possible? That old sage, living in the woods, has never heard of it yet—that God is dead!"

What is important to note here is the word "descent." Takeyama Michio comments on this word "descent" as follows:

> (Descent) has a twofold meaning. It simultaneously suggests Zarathustra's descent to the reality of the human world from the world of ideas in the mountain, and his tragic self-destruction for the sake of self-development and self-transformation in the sense of coming back to life after death.

Speaking from the Zen point of view, Zarathustra descended to the human world again, with his mind and body brimming with boundless life and well-ripened wisdom, upon his rebirth after his Great Death. That is why he ran down the mountain in one breath, tearing himself away from the sage in spite of the sage's effort to detain him. The sage who lived in the woods between the heavenly world and the earthly world of human beings said, "It is God that I love," without knowing that God was already dead. Zarathustra ran down the mountain, laughing mockingly at the sage for his vain search for God—for that search was proof of his separation.

Many hardships as well as pleasures must have lain in ambush for Zarathustra on his way. It was like balancing himself along a rope tightly stretched between higher man and lower animal. But he would always appreciate his days just as they were with joys and sorrows, for his days in which skies were always blue were bright, good days.

The essence of the Zen teachings lies not only in upward progress toward God and Buddha, but also in downward descent to ordinary everyday life here and now. It is to be intuited through transcendental penetration into nothingness beyond the duality of upward and downward directions of Zen discipline. In that and that alone lies the natural beauty of the phrase "Every day, a good day."

Playing in Samadhi

It is a long time since the phrase "loss of humanity" first came into use. Among the books I valued in my early days, there was Tomonaga's masterpiece titled *Kinsei ni Okeru ware no Jikaku-Shi.*[27] In this volume, the author deals in the minutest detail with the process of our self-awareness, ranging from the

Renaissance discovery of the self to Hegel's idea of the Absolute Self. In this sense, Tomonaga's book may offer a valuable perspective on modern world history. It is not too much to say that modern world history has developed exactly along the lines of or on the basis of this theme of self-awareness.

As far as I remember, his book on self-awareness treats the dichotomy of Feuerback and the South-West German School of Philosophy as the splitting of the philosophy of the Absolute Self (which had reached its apex in Hegel) into the leftist and the rightist factions. In the late historical development of self-awareness, the Self has become lost among the machines which human knowledge has produced and we despair at our possible destruction at the hands of atomic power. Such curious phenomena are termed "loss of humanity."

It seems to me, however, that there are two different types of loss of humanity. The rightist type can be seen in a certain phase of the so-called American lifestyle. Those who become full of despair while chasing their insatiable desire for pleasure belong to this type. The nihilistic trend evident in the popularity of not only mahjong and pinball games but also in dances like "the monkey" and "go-go" dancing should be regarded as typical symptoms of this rightist type of loss of humanity.

The leftist type of loss of humanity is found in human beings who live mechanically like ants and bees, like men in Hell or in prison, just to perform their assigned tasks at the cost of their potential humanity, as in the cases of people in Communist China and the Soviet Union. At one time or another in Communist China, people in general were driven to extremes of fear and madness. They were forced to criticize themselves in their professional fields and were openly shamed in political classes and public debates. They were often berated by their wives and children when they returned home to rest. Is this not the way things are in the leftist type of loss of humanity?

Thus, in both the rightist and the leftist wings of societies today, human beings have lost the self and are suffering from loss of humanity in nihilism or despair. Modern world history began with the discovery of the Self and attained its summit in the eventual awareness of the Absolute Self. However, now that human beings in general have been so degraded in their self-deprivation, the pages of modern world history might well be closed.

According to scholars, history revolves on the axis of the question, "What is the nature of human beings?" It is certainly the right time now for the world to take a new turn. We can no longer cure the disease of our age by making a mere fuss about such problems as man-made satellites and the placing of the ultimate war weapons under international control. Our new epoch must dawn with the convincing answer to the question: "What are human beings?" The recovery of the loss of humanity should be the basis of (and fundamental to) our civilization yet to be reconstructed.

Among the contemporaries of Master Rinzai, founder of the Rinzai Sect of Zen Buddhism, there was an eccentric priest named Kingyu (Chin-niu).[28] Little is known about him today except that he was a disciple of Master Baso (Ma-tsu) and lived in Chen Chou. Every day, at lunch time, he would come dancing in front of the monks' training hall with a rice container under his arm, saying in a great laughing voice, "Well, well, please have lunch to your hearts' content!" He is said to have continued to serve lunch in this way for twenty years.

Years later, one of the monks asked Master Chokei Eryo (Ch'ang-ch'ing Hui-leng), "What did Priest Kingyu mean by doing such a thing?" Master Chokei answered nonchalantly, "He just meant to pay homage to meals!" This conduct of Priest Kingyu indeed strikes us as resembling that seen in dancing religions. It even appears mad to us.

When Zarathustra descended the mountain after drinking a toast to the rising sun, he met a sage in the woods on his way. At the sight of Zarathustra, the sage exclaimed, "He goes as if he were dancing, doesn't he?"

Also, our mythological gods and goddesses who appear in the *Kojiki*[29] performed sacred music and dances on all possible occasions, whether they were sad or glad. What is called *kagura*[30] must pertain to the ecstatic joy and pleasure expressed in the dynamic movement and vitality of life, as is well phrased in the following words: "Admirable! How clear! How interesting! How joyful!" In short, kagura corresponds to what we call "playing in samadhi" in Zen.

In my opinion, all matters in our life may be ascribed to the word "playing." Those who are healthy and animated with the lively movement of dynamic life, cannot help "going as if they were dancing." I think that a full life is revealed in every movement of our hands or every step of our feet like a healthy young boy involuntarily expressing his vitality in everything he does.

Just imagine the figure of Priest Kingyu as he danced about, carrying the rice container filled with steaming rice right from the cooking pot and saying, "Now, have some, please!" He was unaware of the lively movements of his dancing hands and feet. Far from showing a pale, serious face marked with lines between his eyebrows, and far from smiling the ambiguous smile which is neither a smile nor a sob, Priest Kingyu never showed any sign of melancholy or sadness. He laughed aloud and joyfully like the blue skies and the white sun. It is said in a poem that "loud and joyful laughter is found in the shadow of the white clouds." His laughter was so clear and thorough it seemed to move Heaven and Earth by its reverberation like the laughter of the gods and goddesses in Takemagahara. Likewise, if he had cried, he might have "withered all the green mountains with his tears" like the god Susano-no-mikoto.

This behavior of Priest Kingyu, if viewed from the special standpoint of Zen, contains the essential meaning of Zen. Nonetheless, it is pleasing all the same to take his behavior at its face value, as I do.

Priest Gensha Shibi (Hsuan-sha Shih-pei) said, "Many people have starved to death, with their heads stuck in rice containers, and many people have died of thirst, with their heads dipped in sea water." We should not ignore these penetrating words of Gensha, for is it not true that many people in this world today are on the verge of spiritual starvation in isolation from their True Selves, even while they have their heads stuck in the rice containers full of rice for life?

Dancing delightfully with a container filled with the rice of truth under his arm, Priest Kingyu laughed merrily from the bottom of his heart, quite unaware of his dancing hands and feet. I wonder if this very state of his mind and body would not offer a key to the solution for the problems of what true human beings should be and what the nature of true human life should be, at this radical turn of our world today.

SOLITARY SITTER: GREAT SUBLIME PEAK

Master Hyakujo Ekai (Pai-chang Huai-hai)[31] is said to have been the original "inventor" of the Zen dojo. His book of rules, Hyakujo Shingi (Pai-chang ch'ing-kuei), is still valid today; all the rules and regulations presently observed in Zen monasteries are in strict conformity with his work. Master Hyakujo is also famous as a great practitioner of Zen. Marx and Lenin said in an oppressive and exacting way that those who do not work should not eat. Priest Hyakujo, however, voluntarily led a self-regulated life more than one thousand years before them. He said, "If I do not work one day, I won't eat one day."

Hyakujo passed away at the advanced age of ninety-four, but until his last day he engaged himself in various kinds of work, ranging from sowing seeds to growing vegetables in the fields, together with the young monks of his monastery. His disciples, unable to bear the sight of their teacher working so hard at his age, entreated him to rest, but he would not listen to them. Therefore they agreed to hide his hoe and sickle one day in order to prevent him from working. Priest Hyakujo looked up and down for them, but in vain. So, he was obliged to retire to his room, where he remained sitting quietly all alone for a long time.

As he did not come to the dining hall for lunch as well as for supper, his disciples became worried and asked him why. Priest Hyakujo, thereupon, answered, "I am not a man of virtue. Therefore, how can I keep from working and eat the food produced and prepared by others?" It was on this occasion that the following famous words of his were uttered: "If I do not work one day, I will not eat one day." He spoke these words in self-admonition instead of insisting on his right to work as workers do today in the Marxist fashion. His disciples were so awe-stricken that they could not help but return his tools to him. Then, they asked him to continue to work in the fields with them as before.

One day a certain monk came and asked the same priest, "What is the most blessed thing in this world?" This monk may have expected such a matter-of-fact answer as God, Truth, or Morality. Contrary to his expectation, however, Hyakujo shouted in reply, "Solitary Sitter: Great Sublime Peak! I am now sitting here like this. How about it? Aren't you thankful? Well, then, worship me!" "Great Sublime Peak" is the name of the mountain where Hyakujo lived.

The monk made an overly polite bow to Hyakujo, as much as to say "Oh, how thankful I am to you!" However, Hyakujo lost no time in slapping the monk in the face in the fashion of "hitting immediately" as if he were scolding him for his attachment to his vain ideas.

At the beginning of the conclusion to Kant's *Critique of Practical Reason*, there is the following famous passage: "There are two things which fill my mind with ever-increasing and ever-regenerating feelings of admiration and veneration, the more often and the longer I think of them. They are the sky filled with twinkling stars overhead and the moral code within me." It goes without saying that what Kant called "moral code" alludes to nothing other than the operation of his own self as the free subject, in which he determined his own conduct with his own power. That is to say, Kant perceived something blessed in the starlit sky and in his autonomous self.

According to Kant, the autonomous and rational self which is the subject of the sacred moral laws because of its free independence is certainly a blessed thing to be cherished in this world. However, the "self" as meant by Hyakujo in saying, "Solitary Sitter: Great Sublime Peak," is quite different in meaning. It is the subject which is one with Absolute Nothingness and has cut duality of before and after while dropping all fetters from mind and body. The difference between Hyakujo and Kant lies in this point. Without detecting this difference it will be impossible to distinguish between the Eastern and the

Western modes of thought. Priest Myoe's words "as it is" suggest something akin to the selfless self represented by the words "Solitary Sitter: Great Sublime Peak."

Heaven is high and earth low. Willows are green and flowers red. It is foul weather on rainy days, and our elder brothers are older than we. All these are the tangible attributes of things as they are. And yet, Heaven in its highness is originally absolute beyond the duality of highness and lowness. Willows, beautiful as they are in their greenness, are independent and unique in their freedom from green and red. These facts point to the true state of things "as they should be," which is variously termed as "liberation from mind and body," or "mind and body in liberation."

Some people might say, on hearing the above words of mine, "That is why we say religion is opium." Others may even want to protest, saying, "What you want to say next is that capitalists are capitalists and workers are workers 'as they are.'" Well, I have trouble dealing with people who have dull heads.

In both America and the Soviet Union, the fact remains the same that capital and labor are both indispensable to the production of goods. When capitalists and workers who provide that productivity strive to give full play to their potential in their respective areas of specialization, they are said to be "as they should be." But, how can we ever deem them to be "as they should be" when capitalists and laborers in class opposition keep on accusing each other of exploitation or of undue demand for better treatment? The existing discrepancy between capitalists and workers may be regarded as a social phenomenon which is unavoidable in the course of the development of productive power. To say the least, however, neither capitalists nor workers are in the true state of being "as they should be." No religion would teach "it is the fate of workers to be exploited by capitalists and thus they should just endure it quietly."

Shakyamuni lived in the age when people in India were strictly divided into four castes. Nonetheless he asserted the fundamental truth of all living beings by saying, "Sentient beings are all essentially endowed with Buddha nature." His was a challenge to the discrimination of his time that artificially divided people into four castes. By no means was it an opiate for the sake of maintaining a caste society. All that he preached pertained to the equality of all human beings "as they should be." In Communist societies, however, "people work according to their capacities and receive their rewards according to their needs," and they are classified in distinction from one another, like tigers and wolves, under the powerful dictatorship of the single political party. Now, with regard to the phrase "as they should be," we must deliberately consider where its meaning can be more fully realized in the class-conscious Communist societies or in the free existence of individual human beings. In any case, nothing is more marvelous and gratifying for any of us than to be, as we naturally are, here and now.

A Clear Wind Arising in Every Step of Our Feet

Now, let me tell you about the early years of Priest Hyakujo. One day, Hyakujo was walking with his teacher Baso (Ma-tsu) as usual. Perhaps surprised at the sound of their approaching feet, a flock of wild geese fluttered away. It is the custom of Zen men to make use of anything at any time as material for training. Although Baso knew well that it was a flock of wild geese that attracted their attention, he asked his student casually, "What are they?"

Hyakujo, promising student though he was, at the time still did not have his satori eye and could not tell east from west. Thus, he announced, "They are wild geese."

"Where are they going?"

"Well, I wonder where! They have flown away in that direction."

No sooner had Hyakujo finished these words than Baso abruptly stretched out his long arm and pinched Hyakujo's nose. Hyakujo yelled, "Ouch!" in great distress.

"They haven't flown anywhere. They are right here."

These words of Baso are said to have immediately awakened Hyakujo to the truth of being.

Hyakujo, in reply to Baso's question, "Where are they going?" said, "They have flown away in that direction." These words of Hyakujo are criticized by Master Engo Kokugo (Huan-wu K'o-ch'in) as follows: "Hyakujo is being pulled and spun about in chasing after other things. What Engo Kokugon is pointing out is that Hyakujo was not aware of the ground he himself was treading on (the truth of being) because he was taken up by the geese and was being pulled and spun about all over the place by them. He could hardly be said to have been in the state of a clear mind arising in every step of his feet.

Most of us live our everyday lives more or less like Hyakujo before his enlightenment. In our pursuit of fame, rank, wealth, learning, knowledge, and so forth, which are like the geese which are flying away, before we know it our vital self has become a mere means to an end. Running after our goals endlessly, our own footing becomes less and less secure moment by moment. It was not until Hyakujo had his nose pinched by his teacher with the words,

"Don't look afar. The subject of your purpose is here," that he was abruptly awakened to the truth of his being for the first time. Master Engo Kokugon, in commenting on Hyakujo's pinched nose, said, "It is right here!" Our purposes do not exist ten miles away or eight years ahead. They are "right here" within us.

On the following day, Master Baso went up to his lecture seat to begin his talk on Buddhist Truth. Before he started Hyakujo suddenly rolled up the mat for worshipping and put it away as if the lecture had ended. Master Baso, Zen Master that he was, returned to his private room right away without delivering his lecture. Later, summoning Hyakujo, he asked, "Why did you put away the mat for worshipping as if the lecture was over when I had yet to speak a word?" Hyakujo was already not the Hyakujo of the day before. He answered with a straight face, "Yesterday, you pinched my nose and it really hurt."

"Where were you facing yesterday?"

"Well, my nose doesn't hurt a bit today." This answer must have highly pleased Baso. He praised Hyakujo, saying, "Now you understand. You know about today very well." He meant that Hyakujo truly realized the whereabouts of life.

If we come to know something like this, we will be able to stir a clear wind in every step of our feet whenever and wherever we may roam, for it is here and now that our destination lies.

In one of my books entitled *Ken to Zen*,[32] I write as follows:

Insofar as the Way of swordsmanship is a way of victory or defeat, it is characterized by the oppositions and dichotomies of self and opponent, winning and losing, victory and defeat, life and death, and so forth. This is the reason for the tension as well as the dead seriousness which arises from it. However, as long as we oppose and antagonize others, we will never succeed in finding peace and living peacefully, no matter how long we may live. We will have to live the rest of our lives in the state of insecurity and agitation. Swordsmen with kokoro (mind, heart, and spirit) from old have taken the greatest pains to transcend their dualistic discrimination and live in the security of absolute peace.

What I have written above is not limited to the Way of swordsmanship. It may well be said that the same is true of everything in our daily livelihoods in the human world which is based on the "will" to live.

Some people have said that Marx's dialectics is a process dialectics. Not only Marx's dialectics but also all things in reality, if viewed from a certain perspective, can be reduced to processes. In Kant's famous phrase, a human being is an end-purpose as such, and in his existence, should never be exploited as a means of attaining any end by any one else, even by God. In Marxism, on the contrary, human beings are exploited as a mere means of revolution. Be it education or morals, everything is supposed to serve as a means of attaining revolution.

I once heard of a certain Dutch gentleman who said that those who are not ideologically influenced by Communism in their twenties are fools and that those who are still wholly devoted to Communism in their forties are even greater fools. What he said is true. Those who are too insensitive to perceive the discrepancies of their societies and those who are lacking in the sense of justice to such an extent that they do not feel indignant at these inconsistencies in their youth are not a problem. However, when the twilight of life approaches and people are still unconscious of the futility of having had their never-to-be-relived lives vainly squandered as a mere instrument of process, something must indeed be wrong with them.

I should say that the phrase "a clear wind arising in every step of our feet" pertains to the revelation of the Absolute Self in each of one's affairs and conducts. In other words, it means that we are absolute even if we slip and that we are always at our destination even if we tumble down. It is here that the end and the means of attaining it are perfectly one. No matter which part of our whole life we dissect to examine there is not the slightest evidence of living as simply a means to an end or life as a mere process. Each step of our feet is absolute. Isn't our life truly rich and refreshing? The phrase "a clear wind arising in every step of our feet" indeed suggests each moment of the fully-lived life of the Zen man.

The will of human beings distinguishes between good and bad things as well as between self and other. In its discrimination of all things in this world, our will pursues the objects of its own choice endlessly. There is courage, but no leeway, in the human will. It inevitably points to futility, as is well suggested by Wakayama Bokusui[33] in the following poem of his:

> Crossing many mountains and rivers,
> Shall I some day reach the land
> Where there is no loneliness?
> I am still on my journey today.

The infinite pursuit of objects outside ourselves thus leads us to no end in our vain longing for joy and peace of mind.

STANDING UP IN RESPONSE

In a book written by Futabayama,[34] a retired sumo wrestler, there is a chapter titled "*Ukete Tatsu*" ("Standing up in Response"). This phrase "ukete tatsu" originally bore a double meaning. It literally means "to stand up in response" to the opponent's move to strike him down, which is possible only when there is a great difference in strength between the two wrestlers. As for me, it is impossible to stand up to defeat my opponent in this way for most opponents and I do not differ very much in strength. In my case, the same phrase should mean "to stand up in response to the opponent's cry of attacking" or "to stand up at the same time as the opponent." As soon as I stand up, however, I seize the opportunity, which is something called *gote no sen*. This means to encounter the opponent at the same time he stands up with a stance sufficient to meet his attack.

The phrase "ukete tatsu" describes a concept that deserves the attention of all great men of accomplishment. It has been especially studied with meticulous care in the various martial arts.

'It has always been a basic principle of religion to "stand up in response" to the surrounding world. However, if inadequately interpreted, the same phrase may mean a kind of defeatism called "the acceptance of environmental delusions" by Master Rinzai. This subtle shade of meaning is well conveyed by the following words attributed to Jesus in the Bible: " . . . When a person strikes you on the right cheek, turn and offer him the other. If anyone wants to go to law over your shirt, hand your coat as well. Should anyone press you into service for one mile, go with him two miles . . . ."

I do not know how Christians interpret these words of Jesus, but I think it would be interesting if these words are interpreted positively like Futabayama's "stand up in response" and therefore seize the opportunity. Otherwise, the same words are no more than the cry of a weakling.

If anyone strikes me on the right cheek, I am in the position of the object passively receiving the blow. However, if I turn the other cheek to him, saying, "Please strike me on this cheek, too," will I not become the subject by throwing him into the position of the object in turn and forestalling him by so doing?

Suppose we were employees and ordered by someone else to do a certain kind of work. It is like being "pressed into service for one mile," and we may find the work too exacting or too uninteresting to do. But, if we voluntarily do twice as much work as we are ordered to do, our work will then turn out to be our conduct stemming from our own free will instead of being the object of our reluctant undertaking, and we will no longer be in passive servitude, but in the standpoint of the active master of the work. It is my opinion that religious life pertains to such a positive state of being.

It was this living attitude of the subject that Master Rinzai referred to as the "master (subject) wherever he might be." I think that it is only when we are in such a state of mind that it could be possible for us to be "as if playing in a pleasure garden even when we are in Hell." If we were conscious of being in Hell, we should have to suffer immensely. But, if we could think of it as having come to Hell in order to inspect its facilities for the purpose of improving them, I am sure that, even in Hell, we should feel as if we were enjoying a stroll in the park.

In the T'ang Dynasty of China, there was a famous Zen man called National Zen Master Echu (Hui-chung),[35] teacher of the Emperor Su Tsung. One day the master called to his disciple Tangen Oshin (Tan-yuan Ying-chen) just as if he had thought of something for him to do, "Say, Oshin!"

"Yes, Sir."

But his master did not seem to be in need of his help. And yet, he again called, "Say, Oshin!"

"Yes, Sir." That was all Oshin could say in reply.

In this way master and disciple repeated calling and answering each other three times. Even today, the room occupied by the attendant of a Zen master in a Zen monastery is called *San-o-ryo* (The Hall of Three Answers). The Chinese characters for "Under the Three Answers" are often written side by side with the name of a Zen master in letters addressed to him. All these things have their origin in the above-told story of Master Echu and his disciple.

Here is another story to illustrate my point. Once upon a time there lived in the Province of Shinshu a man who was reputed to be the most pious and faithful to his parents in all of Japan. Another man, called the most pious and faithful to his parents in all of the province of Koshu once paid a visit to the pious man in Shinshu. It so happened that the latter was absent from home, but before long he came home from the mountain, carrying a big bundle of chopped wood on his back.

At this sight, his old mother ran up to him to relieve him of his burden. She untied the strings of his straw sandals and brought a pail of warm water to wash his feet in it. Meanwhile, he left everything to the care of his aged mother without doing anything himself. What was more surprising still was that, upon entering the sitting room, he casually lay down on the floor and let his old mother massage his hip. The man of filial piety from Koshu who had been watching him all that while, could no longer stand it. In great anger he exclaimed, "You fraud! You are not at all a man of filial piety, but a man of filial impiety, indeed!"

Thereupon, the son said, "To tell you the truth, I do not know exactly what filial piety means. So, I just behave as my mother wants me to in order to please her."

With these words the pious man from Koshu was sincerely impressed. He said to himself, "Indeed, he is right. What I thought to be filial piety before was only a matter of formality. I was, after all, imposing my selfish will on my parents."

"I used to think filial piety was difficult to practice. But now I see it means nothing but saying 'Yes, Yes!'" This ancient verse alludes to the truth that the way of filial piety is to be fulfilled of itself only when we are freed from our "will" in absolute obedience to our parents. It is interesting to compare the pious son's story with the way in which Oshin became the master by striding over Heaven and Earth while saying "yes" to his master without any self-consciousness.

In the Way of wrestling, in which victory and defeat are unavoidable, Futabayama "stood up in response to his rival," with a stance strong enough to forestall him with bare hands at the same time. As for Oshin and the pious son, although they share with Futabayama the same action of standing up in response to others, they are different from Futabayama in their manner of embracing others in absolute obedience to them.

There are those in this world who have superficially differentiated the Zen sect and the Shinshu sect of Buddhism as the Way of Self-Power and the Way of Other Power respectively. But even Zen Buddhism, which is known to advocate self-power for salvation is the same as the Shinshu sect (which preaches reliance on Amida Buddha's help for salvation) as far as "standing up in response" to others is concerned. Generally speaking, religion is regarded as passive. However, the word "passive" here is not negative and retiring in meaning. We must recognize that it is something positive coming from the standpoint of the Absolute Subject in alert response to others.

COMING WITHOUT ANY SOUND

There is the famous folk song called "A Drizzling Autumn Rain" that is sung in the district of Sendai. It goes as follows:

> Is it a drizzling autumn rain
> Or is the rain in the fields of Kayano
> Coming without any sound
> To soak us?

It seems to be sung at wedding parties or on similar occasions today. However, I hear that it was originally a war song, sung at the time of Lord Date Masamune's[36] departure for the battle front or his triumphant return to his castle. When I was young, my teacher used to tell us the secret of the art of swordsmanship in terms of this song. The point of this song lies in the last lines that read, "Coming without any sound to soak us."

In Chuyo (Chung Yung) it is written, "Things above Heaven are without voice and without smell."[37] Not only in the Way of swordsmanship but also in all other Ways of life, nothing is true unless it comes out of the voiceless and smell-less Absolute. Alienated from the Absolute, the swordsmanship of *Muso Ken* (No-thought Sword) will be degraded into *Moso Ken* (Delusive-thought Sword), and the Tea Ceremony of tranquility into that of greed. What spontaneously derives from the soundless and smell-less origin of life is the true Way.

There once was a battle fought between Uesugi Kenshin[38] and Takeda Shingen[39] at Kawanakajima. Kenshin challenged his opponent, Lord Shingen, to fight a decisive battle with him. He carried his famous sword, especially made for him by the swordsmith Nagamitsu in Bizen. Brandishing this sword overhead, Lord Kenshin raced all alone on horseback into the army of his opponent to attack his headquarters. It is said that he kept on shouting, "What is this, this thing above the sword?" as he slashed his enemies with his sword. It is open to debate whether this was a true story or not, for it was not put on record by anyone who witnessed him at that time. At any rate, this story has been handed down to us like this. The action of Kenshin is indeed impregnated with the same sentiment as the autumn rain, "coming without any sound to soak us."

Though taken by surprise by Kenshin's attack, Shingen was not dismayed at all. Seated in serene dignity, Shingen parried Kenshin's sword with a flick of his iron war-fan, replying, "A flake of snow fallen on the red-hot stove!"

Kenshin turned around on horseback in great majesty and then returned, brandishing his sword overhead as if trying to strike Shingen again. It is said that he then sheathed his sword, saying, "Melting and flowing into the murmuring water of the River Sai."

This story may sound too unrealistic to be true, even though it is about a battle fought long ago. And yet, there is no evidence to prove that these two generals did not say such irrelevant things during their fight. We cannot say definitely that nothing like this story happened between Kenshin and Shingen, for they were equally disciplined in Zen under the guidance of Master Soken[40] and the National Master Kaisen[41] respectively. It would be more interesting to believe the story, for heroes exist in another universe within this smaller universe and are truly at leisure beyond life and death, and beyond survival and extinction, even in their moments of danger.

The phrase "a flake of snow fallen on the red-hot stove" literally means a flake of snow disappearing completely as soon as it falls on a red-hot stove. That is, it pertains to nonexistence. There is neither enemy nor self, neither victory nor defeat. All are traceless like the evanescent flake of snow fallen on the stove. Myriads of varying and changing things deriving from nonexistence indeed must be ascribed to the very operation of "the one with a sword in hand." What is "coming without any sound to soak us" is none other than that.

Once upon a time there lived in China a man named Fuka (P'u-hua). He assisted in the maintenance of Rinzai's monastery. One day he was munching on an uncooked radish, leaves and all, as he basked in the sun in front of the Meditation Hall. Rinzai happened to pass by and said, "You are really like a horse." Fuka lost no time in neighing like a horse, "Hi-hi-hi-hin!" This shows how eccentric he must have been.

Fuka's death was indeed a very courageous one. One day he went into town, calling to the passersby, "Won't you make a robe for me, please?" People made robes for him, but none of them suited his fancy. Hearing of it, Rinzai had someone buy a coffin for Fuka. On his return, he gave it to him and said, "I have had a nice robe made for you." Fuka was very pleased to get the coffin. Carrying it on his shoulders, he went to the city to let everybody know what had happened. He said in a loud voice, "Rinzai has made a fine robe for me. It seems to fit me very well. I am going to die in it by the East Gate."

When a large crowd of people followed him to witness his death, Fuka went away with the words, "No, not today. Tomorrow I am going to die by the South Gate." He thus cheated the people three times, till at last nobody trusted him any longer. On the fourth day there was not even one person to follow him. Therefore, Fuka is said to have walked out of the city wall, and lying down in the coffin, he asked a passerby to nail the coffin for him so that he might die in it.

One day, Rinzai and some others were talking about Fuka's eccentricity by the fireside.

"Fuka goes to the city every day to enjoy himself. What on earth is he, a fool or a sage?"

As soon as these words were finished, Fuka appeared as casually as a wind. As the saying goes, if you talk about a person he will appear. At the sight of Fuka, Rinzai asked, "What on earth are you, a fool or a clever man?"

"What on earth am I, a fool or a clever man?" answered Fuka instantaneously. Rinzai then shouted, "Katz!" Thereupon Fuka began to criticize them mischievously, pointing at each one of them as he spoke. "Ho-yang is indeed a very timid fellow. He is like a newlywed wife, who is always too concerned with her mother-in-law's feelings to act freely. Mu-t'a is like a retired old lady who indulges her grandchildren. Rinzai is still an immature acolyte who wets his pants but he is, in fact, a very crafty fellow." Rinzai again shouted, "You thief!"

"You thief!" Repeating Rinzai's words calmly, Fuka went away as swiftly as a breath of wind.

Judging from the above-mentioned behavior of Fuka, he was indeed a man capable of "coming without any sound to soak us" like a drizzling autumn rain. He give us the impression that whatever he did came from and returned to nothingness in tranquility without making the slightest sound of the tree branches or of his own footfall. In this age of public relations when we are used to advertisements that show things as two times bigger than what they really are, the state of nothingness which eludes any attempt at propagation may not impress people in general. But, contrary to expectation, it may be effective to come without making any sound to shock them. To take one by surprise, therefore, may be counted among the effects of positive and active Zen.

BEING UNBORN

Lord Satake Yoshioki[42] once asked his retainers, "Tell me, is there is anything you want?" To his great surprise, a tea server expressed his ardent but futile wish, "I want to be born a great lord." At these words, the Lord lamented, "What an unbearable thing you want! I in turn want to be born a merchant."

According to the erudite Master Iida Toin, the Lord then composed a poem:

What heat of the day, even to me,
Venerated as a Lord though I am!

Those who are habitually dressed up and expected to live formally, in strict conformity to traditional manners and customs, in the innermost parts of their mansions where fresh breezes and sunlight seldom reach, must be very envious of the casual way the commoners live. In their poor and unlearned manners, many commoners are given to playing games of go and shogi on benches in the evening, cooling themselves off with nothing but their loin-cloths on. Even today, women are said to enjoy themselves best in the summertime, wearing their light clothes. The haiku poem which reads,

How fortunate it is to be a man,
Cooling off the heat of summer
In the evening!

is still a good description of a man's life in the summertime as long as he is within his home.

There once lived a *myokonin*[43] in Sanuki named Shomatsu. One hot summer day Shomatsu came home very fatigued, after weeding in his rice paddies all day. On his return home, he opened the doors of his small family shrine, took the statue of the Buddha out of it, and tied it to the tip of a long bamboo pole so as to hold it out into the fresh air, saying, "Amida Buddha, you must be comfortable now in the cool air." No doubt even the images of Buddhas enjoy cooling off when it is hot. Far from worshipping undependable wooden and metal Buddha images, as they do in popular pseudo-religions of recent years, Shomatsu stood on his thorough faith, finding the Absolute Vow to be reflected in his wooden Buddhist image. In its refreshing content, therefore, his faith has something in common with the Unborn Zen advocated by Master Bankei.

According to Master Bankei, our mind, as it naturally is, is the unborn and imperishable Buddha Mind. That mind can instantly recognize the difference between various phenomena and distinguish between the chirping of birds, the barking of dogs, the ringing of bells or the beating of drums as soon as it comes into contact with those sounds, without raising any thoughts about them. For instance, if anybody drives a gimlet into one's back when one least expects it and one feels pain, this may be considered to be the mind of nondiscriminating discrimination which Master Bankei calls the Unborn Buddha Mind. He writes, "To see and hear things without any preparation to see and hear them is called Unborn Mind."[44] In the world which operates through the Unborn Mind there is no duality between our minds and the minds of various Buddhas. Therefore, it is not necessary for us to take the trouble to undergo discipline for the purpose of realizing our own minds. On the contrary, "if you think only of seeking Buddha or attaining the Way you are simply turning your back on the Unborn and run counter to the nature you were born with."

> The Buddha Mind neither sees nor hears things with the intention of doing so, for it is reflected in the things which are visible and audible to us without any wish to see and hear them on our part. This very Buddha Mind is the Unborn Mind.

Thus, "the Unborn Mind does not distinguish between joy and anger, for it is no other thing than the marvelous Buddha Mind which illuminates myriads of things." Therefore, "to understand the principle truly and to be unattached to the myriad things is called the True Mind."

Shomatsu lived a refreshing life, walking, standing, sitting, and lying down in Buddha's infinite compassion, unconditionally embraced by Nyorai's great compassionate heart, whereas Master Bankei led a composed life completely abandoned to the care of destiny. He lived his everyday life with the Unborn Mind, and "let his thoughts arise and perish as they naturally do in his unattachment to them," after discarding all of his own schemes. What essential difference should there be between Shomatsu and Master Bankei? Though the former came from the Jodo Shinshu sect and the latter from the Zen sect, there is no difference between the two as far as the content of their beliefs are concerned. Truly, there is nothing strange to us in the true Dharma.

A man named Hachirobei once said to Master Bankei, "They say high-ranking priests of old performed many marvelous miracles. Do you know any secret way of performing miracles?" Bankei said in reply, "What do you mean by marvelous miracles?"

Hachirobei replied, "In the Province of Echigo, the founder of the Ikko sect of Buddhism had someone bring paper to the far side of the river while from his side of the river he wrote the six Chinese characters for *Namu Amida Butsu*. People in this world call it the Buddha's name written from across the river. It is still very popular today. This is one of the marvelous miracles."

At these words, the Zen Master is said to have laughed delightfully, saying, "As for such a matter, magicians do better than priests. But what has that got to do with the salvation of people? In the light of the authentic Dharma, isn't it like comparing dogs and cats with human beings?"

His words sound calm, but their meaning is very severe. It is embarassing that there still seem to be people in this world who cannot be satisfied with any religion unless it includes communication with the world of spirits, the oracles of gods and goddesses, and other marvelous miracles. Such necessary accessories add to our discomfort in the heat of summer. Anyway, human beings are at their best when they are naked, free from any external additions. I like human beings best when they remain as natural as they were at birth.

WAITING IN HELL

We are familiar with the name of Priest Joshu (Chao-chou) because of his koan about the Buddha-nature of the dog. Another time, a monk asked Joshu, "Will such a great enlightened man as you fall to Hell after you die?" Now, we do not think in Zen that the souls of the deceased wander between Paradise and Hell the way we take an elevator in the department store, neckties on the first floor and then having lunch in the dining hall on the seventh floor. In this chapter, however, I think it is best not to deal with this problem in detail.

To continue, when Joshu was asked by the monk about the possibility of his posthumous damnation, he answered seriously, "Yes, I will be the first to fall to Hell."

The monk who questioned him said in surprise, "How can it be that such a great priest as you should fall to Hell ahead of us all?"

"Who will save you when you fall to Hell unless I arrive there first and wait for you?"

I wish I could have seen the look on the monk's face when he heard this remark! Indeed, it is far from being a mere boast or arbitrary expression. It contains not only his full self-confidence and ambition but also the basic principle of Mahayana Zen Buddhism: "To save others first before saving ourselves." It is only here that the spirit of Mahayana Buddhism lies. Those people who are lacking in this feeling of compassion and love for others are no more than insignificant pupils of Hinayana Buddhism, however enlightened they are thought to be.

Once another monk said to Priest Joshu, "Shakyamuni must have been naturally free from all kinds of desires, as he was the Enlightened One and the greatest Ruler of the Threefold World."

"No, he is the one most attached to the greatest desire in this whole world," said Joshu, baffling our anticipation again. Viewed from a certain perspective, the above answer may strike some of us as a typical Zen expression of perversity. This, however, was not the case with Joshu, as is clear in the following dialogue with the astonished monk.

"Why do you say so?"

"Shakyamuni had a great desire for saving all human beings, didn't he?"

These words of Joshu are seemingly inconsistent with his words uttered elsewhere, "Alas! I have become a fool now!" But, in fact, these different expressions point to the same truth. The word "fool," in its true sense, has an allusion to the enlightened, for just like fools and blockheads, the enlightened make such futile efforts as trying to fill the old well with the snow carried on their backs, transcending the duality between their enlightened selves and others still wandering bewildered in their enlightenment.

Such a thing as the salvation of all human beings is a useless effort which resembles counting grains of sand on the beach. However, the exclusion of such unavailing efforts as piling up stones on the bank of the River Sai, and such foolish accumulation of karma (cause and effect) will prevent even universal scientific truth from illuminating the earth in its totality. What we need most in our world today is such compassion for others as felt by Priest Joshu, who insisted on voluntarily descending to Hell ahead of others in order to save them, as well as the Great Compassion as demonstrated by Shakyamuni.

Isn't it only upon the cultivation of such love and desire for universal salvation that all human beings will be equally able to share in the benefits of science and technology in the great, harmonious unity of this one world? I think that it is only in keeping with our need for universal love and salvation that Master Hakuin stressed, as he often did, the dignified manners of bodhisattva and our relationships to Buddhahood. He accordingly rejected the eulogy of Goi-Kenchuto as a distortion of Toku-un's (Te-yun's) original exposition of the Fifth Rank, writing instead,

> How many times has Toku-un, the idle old gimlet,
> Not come down from the Marvelous Peak!
> He hires foolish wise men to bring snow,
> And he and they together fill up the well.[45]

It is not too much to say that there is no Zen outside such a Great Vow and such Great Compassion for the world.

Hotei (Chn. Pu-tai) was originally an eccentric Chinese monk of the 10th century known for his compassion. Eventually he became revered as an incarnation of the future Buddha Miroku (Skt. Maitreya). The last of the Ten Oxherding Pictures (see Chapter 7) shows Hotei entering the marketplace, representing the goal of transcending life and death (dualism). Statue on the grounds of Daihonzan Chozen-ji.

Statue of Kannon (Skt. Avalokiteshvara) on the ground of Daihonzan Chozen-ji. Kannon, considered to be the embodiment of compassion, is one of the most important bodhisattvas of Mahayana Buddhism.

CHAPTER 6

Zazen Wasan
(A Song of Zazen)

Zazen Wasan was written by Master Hakuin Ekaku so that people in general may understand the essence of zazen. Therefore, it is clear and to the point. It is the quickest and simplest way to understand what zazen is. In addition, it is comparatively easy for us to understand its content, as it is presented to us in the form of verse so as to make it more convenient for us to recite it aloud daily. For these reasons, this verse has become well known to Zen students. It is common for them to recite it in unison before or after the meetings of Zen Associations and on other similar religious occasions.

I think it important to introduce some parts of the verse in order to make it easy for you to understand zazen. As a rule, I should say something about Master Hakuin's life at this point, but as he is so famous I will instead go directly into his verse below.

> All beings are primarily Buddhas,
> Like water and ice,
> There is no ice apart from water.
> There are no Buddhas apart from beings.

Shakyamuni sat under a bodhi tree, where, upon seeing a morning star at dawn, he was enlightened to the truth: "All beings are without exception endowed with Buddha-nature." To clarify the essence of this realization and to accommodate the vast variety of human beings, he left eighty-four thousand doctrines in over five thousand forty volumes of sutras. It is not too much to say that the statement of the opening line, "All beings are primarily Buddhas," can be called the primary statement of the essence of Buddhism.

According to scholars of religion, religion means the completion of the individual as the Whole. It makes it possible for each person to lead a human life as an individual who is also one with the Whole. Kato Genchi and other scholars like him contend that religion consists of two types: those religions which differentiate God from Man and those religions which equate God with Man. For instance, Christianity belongs to the first type where the distinction between God and Man pertains to the absolute distance between them. In Christianity the individual wishes to be saved by means of prayers which form the method of conforming with the Whole. Our Zen belongs to the second type of religion where equating Man with God pertains to the essential oneness of God and Man. In it the method of seeing into the oneness of the individual and the Whole is adopted, and by means of this method the distinction between the two is transcended.

The words "All beings are primarily Buddhas" mean nothing other than the fact that the individual is originally the Whole. What we should note here is the insertion of the word "primarily" between "all beings" and "Buddhas." This word corresponds to the strongly affirmative phrase "none other than" found in the last line of the verse reading, "This body is none other than a Buddha." Between the expressions "primarily" and "nothing other than," there is a subtle difference in meaning. This difference pertains to the distinction between those who are not yet aware of their original Buddha-natures and those who have been already fully awakened to their own Buddha-natures, even though human beings are all essentially equal in Buddha-nature and invested with absolute value as Buddhas. A good comparison is the difference between water and ice.

Water becomes ice if frozen; ice becomes water if melted. Between ice and water there should be no essential difference. However, externally speaking, water is flexible, flows freely, and becomes square or round in form according to the shape of its container, whereas ice is rigid and fixed in form. Water and ice are thus very different.

Ninomiya Sontoku[1] also writes in his work *Yawa*:

The Great Way is comparable to water. It enriches the world without being attached to any thing. But, if that valuable Great Way is written about and contained in a book, it ceases to enrich the world and becomes a useless thing to the world. It is as if water were turned into ice.

Well, the Buddhist scriptures have become something like ice. If you want them to be useful to the world you should melt their frozen pages with the warmth of your mind. Unless they are turned into water as they originally are, they will fail to enrich the world and will indeed remain useless.

We are primarily endowed with Buddha-nature, which is like the water that enriches the world. However, our Buddha-nature became frozen into rigid egos before we knew it. As long as we have egos we always find others in opposition to us. And thus we have come to live in perpetual conflict with them in clumsy and contradictory manners. "Buddha" (Hotoke) is said to mean "to come loose" (*hodokeru*). It is true that if the ego which is as hard as a piece of ice is melted, it will turn into Buddha, as free flowing as water.

Sontoku said that each attempt at commenting on the ice-like Buddhist scriptures meant adding another icicle to them. He told us that instead of doing such a useless thing we should turn our egos into water as they originally were by melting them with the warmth of our mind. It goes without saying that the method of melting the ice of our egos into water, as they originally are, lies in samadhi. We must prove ourselves to be Buddhas as we naturally are while immersed in samadhi.

Well, we are primarily Buddhas and are qualified to be the Absolute, which is nothing other than Buddha. The only reason why our virtues as Buddhas do not reveal themselves is because we have become frozen like ice. However, as there is no ice which is not water originally, there are no Buddhas outside ourselves, even though we have been turned into ice.

Master Yoka Genkaku (Yung-chia Hsuan-chueh) writes in his *Shodoka* (Cheng Tao Ko), "The real nature of unenlightenment (ice) is, namely, the Buddha Nature (water); the empty body of delusions (ice) is nothing other than Dharma (water)."[2] Master Genkaku is saying that there is no Buddha-nature outside our bodies given to desires and delusions. Indeed, there are no True Selves anywhere except in our empty bodies as such.

> Not knowing how close the truth is to them,
> Beings seek it afar. What a pity!
> It is like crying out for water,
> While in the midst of water.

There is the saying, "When I caught a thief, he turned out to be my son." When we are caught by the dualistic and delusive thoughts of God versus Man, we look up to God in Heaven far away from this world and long for Buddha existing beyond an innumerable number of lands. This is a great mistake. They say Buddha is "near." Indeed, Buddha exists right here as near as can be. "The ultimate meaning of truth is like our eyebrows. It is near, but we cannot ordinarily find it." It is just that we are not aware of how close it is. How silly it is to search for Buddha far away and outside ourselves! It is as if we were crying out for water because we are thirsty while we are immersed in swollen waters.

Confucius also says, "The Way is never separable from us. What is separable is not the Way." The Way does not lie in putting certain rigid moral teachings into practice in the same way as the train running mechanically on a prefixed railroad track. When the "selfless self" operates in no-mind (*mu-shin*) in every move of our hands and feet, the Way appears.

Master Dogen likewise writes in the section titled "*Genjo Koan*" in *Shobo-genzo* that there is no fish that examines water before swimming in it, and there is no bird that inspects the sky before flying across it; if "there were any such fish or bird, it would never find its way either in the water or across the sky." He continues to say, "This Way or this very place exists because it is neither large nor small, it is neither in the self nor in the other, and neither in the past nor in the present; it exists just as it is." He further writes, "If a bird departs from the sky, it will die in almost no time; if a fish leaves the water, it will die immediately."[3]

Thus, Master Dogen stresses the oneness of birds and sky, and fish and water. This is true of both human beings and the Way. Indeed, "What is separable is not the Way." I cannot help calling it foolish and vain to seek God and Buddha somewhere far way and apart from us and to regard the Way and Truth as something dual and opposite from us, as if "crying for water out of thirst while we are in the midst of it." As Buddhas and beings are like water and ice, all we have to do is to dissolve the hard lumps of ego into nothingness.

> It is like the rich man's son
> Who has lost his way among the poor.
> The reason why beings transmigrate through the six worlds
> Is because they are lost in the darkness of ignorance,
> Wandering from darkness to darkness,
> How can they ever be free from birth and death?

We are essentially the same as Buddhas. But when we reflect over our life in reality, we find many of us living from day to day in great difficulties and agony, far from being Buddhas. In the *Myoho Renge Kyo* (Saddharma-pundarika-sutra),[4] the unenlightened man is compared to the son of a rich man who lives among beggars without knowing their origin. The rich man here, of course, alludes to Buddha. All of us are the legitimate children of Buddha and naturally possess the right to inherit Buddha Mind. However, for various reasons at some point we become estranged from our parent, Buddha, and have only taken more and more wrong turns in our ignorance on the road of delusion. Therefore, our parent exhausts every means to search for us all over the world. His unceasing search for us corresponds to the so-called Amida Buddha's true wish for universal salvation cherished in the Shinshu sect of Buddhism.

The rich man finally discovers his own son among the crowd of beggars and takes him home. But his son finds it hard to trust his parent, meaning the unenlightened man cannot affirm his own identity with Buddha, or believe in the true Dharma. Therefore, the parent makes them begin with the menial work of servants, gradually promoting them to the positions of clerks, managers, and then heirs at long last, according to their progressive familiarity with the rich man's life. This parable illustrates the Buddha's (parent's) compassionate love for his children, which leads us step by step from the teachings of Hinayana Buddhism to those of Mahayana Buddhism, which culminate in our self-awareness as children of Buddha.

The *Myoho Renge Kyo* teaches that human beings are perpetually bound to the wheel of transmigration between birth and death in the six worlds of delusions (Hell, the world of hungry ghosts, the world of beasts, the world of strife, the world of human beings), because we are alienated from our original selves. This is due to our own lack of wisdom, or the concealment of wisdom due to our blind attachment to external things. Our transmigration between life and death is caused by our ignorance in which we are incapable of perceiving things as they truly are. Because of our ignorance and thirst for love we suffer from our bondage to the transmigratory rounds of birth and death, unable to escape from this world of darkness. Then, how can we escape this wheel of painful transmigration between birth and death or the alienation of the self from the realities of life? The method of escaping it is presented in the stanza quoted below from Hakuin's poem.

> As for zazen taught in the Mahayana,
> It exceeds all praise.
> The six *paramitas* beginning with giving,
> Observing the precepts,
> And other good deeds, variously enumerated as
> *Nembutsu*, repentance, and so on,
> Are all finally reducible to zazen.

Any religion, if it is to be called religion, has something corresponding to meditation or samadhi power. The rope-dancing feat in a circus can hardly be done except by one who is in samadhi. However, such samadhi belongs to the realm of Hinayana Buddhism. It is only the samadhi practiced in Mahayana Buddhism that is capable of awakening us to our temporarily concealed original Buddha-nature by liberating us from our bondage to the wheel of transmigration in the six worlds. The word "Mahayana" is called *Daijo* in Japanese. It can be thought of as a great vehicle referring to Dharma, which carries many people from this shore of delusion to the other shore of enlightenment.

The simple word "zen" varies immensely in meaning and dimension. It is possible that it consists of eighty-four thousand doctrines. What I call *zenjyo* (the power of concentration attained in samadhi) here is the largest in form, the richest in content, and the most excellent in quality. That is to say, it is the same as Mahayana Zen Buddhism, which is the largest, the most varied, and the most superb of all the Buddhist sects.

In regard to discipline in Mahayana Zen Buddhism, it is said that if we sit for one minute we are Buddhas for one minute, and that even in one minute of zazen the whole truth in its completeness is embraced. Indeed, it "exceeds all praise." Concretely speaking, the six ways of reaching the other shore of enlightenment from this shore of delusion are all contained in one duration of sitting. Such is the significance of zazen. Paramita means "reaching the other shore" or "salvation." It consists of charity, the observation of precepts, perseverance, diligence, concentration, and wisdom. The first two are mentioned by Hakuin in his poem.

"Charity" means sharing what we have with others in renunciation of our greed. It is commonly deemed to consist of giving the three things: possessions, Dharma, and freedom from fear. While charity is commonly interpreted to mean the giving of money and material things to those who are in need of them, in the true sense of the word, both the giving and the receiving must be equally in the same state of nothingness and non-attachment, free from their greed and ego. Sharing Dharma with others means to share our formless property such as reason and knowledge. Having freedom from fear in common with others alludes to leading others to the realm of no fear, as found in *Hannya Shin Gyo* (Prajnaparamitahridaya-sutra). This way of leading others to the realm of absolute security is the ultimate meaning of charity.

When a certain man asked Yamaoka Tesshu about the ultimate meaning of swordsmanship, Tesshu is said to have answered, "I have left it to the care of Kannon[5] in Asakusa." After searching all over for it, the man finally came upon a framed calligraphy of Tesshu's in which the characters for "Give Fearlessness" were written. The sight of this work, they say, spontaneously awakened him to the ultimate meaning of swordsmanship. Samadhi is the very realm of absolute selfless self, free from fear and insecurity. I may well say that the best and the only way to embody the feeling of fearlessness is to be in samadhi.

The precepts are the rules to be observed in the maintenance of correct living. Actually, they pertain to not blinding oneself further to one's original Buddha-nature and not lapsing into the duality between self and other. For instance, in Hinayana Buddhism, we are considered to be strictly observing the Buddhist precepts as long as we keep from stealing, even if we covet other people's property in our minds. But, in Mahayana Buddhism the mere thought of stealing in itself is deemed to be a breach of the precepts even if we do not actually steal.

However, in Bodhidharma's One Mind Precept, we are thought to be in perfect keeping with the precepts as long as we are free from the duality of stealing and not stealing, knowing well that self and other are one, and being compassionate for all others with which we are one. It is for this reason that in the samadhi practiced in Mahayana Buddhism, in which we do not distinguish between self and other wherever we may be, all the precepts are of themselves perfectly observed.

Moreover, there are no virtues that do not go with the samadhi of Mahayana Buddhism—perseverance in which anger is controlled in favor of modesty, diligence in which laziness is turned into wholehearted concentration on the thing of our concern, meditation in which our disturbed minds are unified and undisturbed under any condition, and wisdom in which we are able to see myriads of things as they truly are without yielding to folly and ignorance. All these virtues accompany the samadhi of Mahayana Buddhism.

Nembutsu is the invocation of Buddha's name. It is said, "When I invoke the name of Buddha, there is neither I nor Buddha." This is the true nembutsu. It pertains to the realm of oneness, rather than to that of dualism in which self and Buddha are deemed to be separate as subject and object of invocation respectively. Thus, it is not too much to say that the samadhi of Mahayana Zen Buddhism is the most supreme form of nembutsu.

In the next line of the poem, which pertains to repentance and discipline, discipline is regarded as the practice of the paramita. All of these good deeds go back to discipline and everything unites into one in samadhi. It is because samadhi as such is the way of realizing the Absolute, and it is the very origin of all things as one. Master Dogen emphasized this point by going so far as to write in the *Bendowa* volume of his *Shobo-genzo*, "Dharma, thus transmitted from person to person correctly and directly, is most supreme of all the supreme practices. Just sit and get liberated from mind and body without resorting to any such things as incense-burning, religious services, the invocation of the Buddha's name, repentance, and sutra-recitation, not to mention the acquisition of knowledge." It must be said that what "exceeds all praise" truly is "the samadhi of the Mahayana."

> The merit of even a single sitting in zazen
> Extinguishes the countless sins accumulated in the past.
> Where then are there evil paths to misguide us?
> The Pure Land cannot be far away.

Those who, even once, in all reverence,
Listen to this truth,
Praise it, and faithfully follow it,
Will be endowed with innumerable merits.

As the samadhi of Mahayana Buddhism is the way of realizing the Absolute and of fully appreciating the oneness of all Dharmas, it makes it possible for us to transcend the dualities of self and other as well as of good and evil in sitting for the duration of one incense-stick, however short it may be. It is fair to say that we will be freed from perpetual suffering from beginningless and endless sins we commit against one another in a single sitting of meditation. When our original selves—free from purity and impurity—are realized, the evil world of dualism cannot exist. That is why this very world, filled with hardships and sufferings, becomes the Pure Land of tranquility and light as it truly is, where there is no longer any evil to discard and any good to acquire.

The samadhi of Mahayana Buddhism is thus abundant with blessings. It is true that those who immediately believe and accept this essence of the Zen teaching with admiration and joy will be undoubtedly granted infinite bliss.

And yet, while it seems easy to praise the Teachings and faithfully follow them, it is actually very hard. In my book *Ken to Zen*, published some years ago, I refer to *Ken Dan* written by Lord Matsuura Seizan.[6] In this book the author discusses the truth of swordsmanship in terms of the following quotation: "If my father summons me, I just stand up with an immediate response, 'Yes!' instead of thinking of a reply." I also mention in the same book that Master Imakita Kosen likewise writes in the fourth chapter of *Zenkai Ichiran* that the consistent way of a superior man lies nowhere but in saying, "Yes!"[7] Master Takuan calls this mind that answers, "Yes!" Immovable Wisdom. I think that this spontaneous response to anything in the affirmative selflessly and with mu-shin (no mind) is "praising the practice of zazen and faithfully following it."

It is said that zazen does not mean the self sits in meditation, but that self has been made to sit by zazen. When doing zazen if you jump into the state of zazen and lose yourself in it as prescribed by the instructions, all at once you will experience Great Zen Samadhi. Master Dogen is said to have remarked in his return from China after finishing his training there, "I have gained a flexible mind." I think these words of his should be deeply appreciated. It can be said that only when our mind is free as water, liberated from our rigid ego, are we capable of "praising the practice of zazen and faithfully following it."

I have written before about the man of great filial piety in Koshu paying a visit to the man of great filial piety in Shinshu. This story should offer another example of the flexibility of the responsive mind.

> But if you turn your eyes within yourselves,
> And at once testify to the truth of Self-nature—
> The Self-nature that is no-nature,
> You will have gone beyond dualism.

After listening to the discussion on the benefits of zazen, we may have admiration and praise for it, but still more beneficial is the actual practice of zazen. In our search for things outside ourselves, our minds are turned toward the external world, but in zazen our minds take an inward turn of 180 degrees to "prove our original nature" by illuminating ourselves. Then our merit increases tremendously. Principles of things and the True Self are after all nothing but knowledge when we comprehend them intellectually, however well we may do so. Just like the ricecakes painted in a picture, intellectually conceived principles are not capable of satisfying our hunger. They are of no avail unless they are realized and substantiated in self-discipline on a personal basis.

We should note the words "at once" used by Master Hakuin in the stanza above on zazen. "At once" means "in this very place here and now." It suggests that the world of enlightenment exists nowhere but in our everyday life in which we are afflicted with many hardships and agonies as we keep on rolling and falling, and that this very reality under our feet is, as it really is, the dynamic field on which our own self-nature operates as when we are in samadhi.

Our self-nature realized in enlightenment is neither splendid nor blessed. It is no-nature. That is to say, it is empty. Ayusmat Nagarjuna[8] writes in his *Madhyamikasastra* to the effect that "things which come into being through the operation of Buddha Mind have no self-nature. Things without their own self-natures are empty. They are empty because of their no-self-nature."

I am sorry if I seem to be imposing my personal opinions on you, but that is not my intent. What on earth is self-nature then? Self-nature is said to be a perpetually constant and unique controller, which is expressed by the following Japanese phrase, "*joitsu shusai.*" "*Jo*" of "joitsu" means "eternal constancy;" "*itsu*" means "only one and not two;" "shusai" is "to control and decide." Thus, "joitsu shusai" should mean the "eternal, unchangeable, and unique ruler." What the term "no self-nature" suggests is that the true mind is free from any fixed idea of such an entity as self-nature. In other words, self-nature may not be found anywhere except in the perpetually changing and moving forms of things in which it is concretely embodied.

We are commonly apt to confine ourselves within the scope of our five-foot bodies and fifty-year life spans. But, in fact, our five-foot bodies and fifty-year life spans are supported by an innumerable number of lives. In a very commonsense way of speaking, my parents gave birth to me, and their parents in turn gave birth to them. If I trace back my life to its very origin in this way, I have two parents, four grandparents, eight great-grandparents, and so on. If we assume that one human generation lasts twenty-five years, I may be viewed as the one hundred and twenty-first generation springing from a man and woman of three thousand years ago. If the number of my ancestors included in 121 generations is calculated, it amounts to the tremendously large number of 26,549 followed by 32 zeros.

It would seem impossible, even for a computer, to compute the overwhelmingly great number of the ancestors of all the human beings in this world dating back to their very origin. Supported by so many lives of human beings of the past, for the first time I exist here and now in "my five-foot body and fifty-year life span." For this reason, I can safely say that the whole of the human race is embraced in this single life of me. What is true is that there is no "I" which is a purely independent ego that has a fixed self-nature. It is because of our attachment to our fixed self-recognition that "the other" antagonistically comes into being. And from our mutual opposition and antagonism stem various conflicts in the wretched life of ordinary men of the world.

However, if, in our quiet self-reflection, we turn our mind's eye from the external world to the internal life to realize our true self-nature we will clearly understand that the true nature of our Self, which we thought up until now had a fixed, real existence, is in fact no self-nature. Because we have no self-nature, there is neither self nor other. In the absence of self and other, there cannot be such passions as joy, anger, sorrow, and pleasure, all of which arise from the dualities of self and other. All things, just as they are in their very essence of no self-nature, function without any hindrance in freely flowing transformation.

This is the true condition of life and the reality beyond dualism. But dualism as such, even if it is originally the same as theorization, suggests nothing but the division of the whole. Therefore, it is natural that dualism is connected with analysis and abstraction that result in the death of living things. I think that what Master Hakuin means by his words "beyond dualism" is that it is not only we, who transcend such playful dualism, but also all other things in their own no self-nature that are in operation according to their selfless essence.

The gate of the oneness of cause and effect is opened.
The Way is straight,
Being neither two nor three.
In the form of no-form, we go and return
Nowhere but here.
In the thought of no-thought, we sing and dance
To the voice of Dharma.
The sky of boundless samadhi is vast!
The illuminating full moon of the Fourfold Wisdom will shine.
What then should we see?
Now that Nirvana is realized here and now,
This place is none other than the land of Lotus Flowers.
This body is none other than a Buddha.

In connection with discipline and proof of enlightenment, people in general believe mistakenly that discipline (cause) precedes enlightenment (effect). However, upon sincere contemplation we come to realize that the effect called enlightenment, even if it infinitely varies in degree, is inconceivable apart from the cause called discipline. I cannot help but say that the accumulation of causes as such is the effect. To speak more precisely, this is so because our very wish for spiritual discipline contains the essence of our original Buddhahood. Looking at it essentially, cause is none other than effect.

It must be in the samadhi of Mahayana Buddhism that the oneness of cause and effect, as well as the oneness of discipline and proof, is unmistakably realized. This is because when we are in samadhi, we transcend the distinction between the cause called discipline coming before in time and the effect called enlightenment coming after. Cause and effect are thus brought into one, as in the saying that if we sit for one moment we are Buddhas for one moment, and if we sit for one minute we are Buddhas for one minute.

Thus, the realization of our own true self-nature does not mean the acquisition of hitherto unknown knowledge of ourselves, but the renunciation of the hardened mass of delusion called our egos which we have borne so tenaciously up until now until we could hardly stand its weight. If satori is the experience we have the moment we renounce our egos and become one with the universe, that moment, needless to say, is when cause and effect are brought into one.

This state of being is termed the dropping of body and mind. As long as we are well integrated and liberated from body and mind in our everyday actions, each of our actions, however trivial it may be, will fully reveal the original nature of ourselves. "The clear wind arising in every step of our feet" directly alludes to the Absolute. Hence, it must be said that the Way is straight, being neither two nor three." Body and mind, liberated from tenacious delusions, still retains the same body limited to "five feet" in height. However, this body reveals the Buddha-nature, being the concrete embodiment of the Absolute. It has the form without form. In other words, it is "in the form of no-form." It is exactly what Master Dogen means by the following poem:

> The colors of the mountain,
> The echoes of the valleys,
> As naturally as all other things,
> All embody the voice and the form
> Of our Shakyamuni.

In enlightenment, every move of our hands and feet is the act of the Absolute. Even when we leap and jump, slip and fall, we always find ourselves in the middle of the Great Way, just as Master Hakuin says, "Your going and returning takes place nowhere but where you are. We go and return nowhere else but here." We are always sleeping or waking in the embrace of Buddha, whenever and wherever we may be.

When we are freed from our inflexible delusions, our True Selves are revealed in formless forms. Likewise, when we renounce all our delusions, our original true thoughts in turn begin to operate. Our true thoughts here mean no-thoughts. "Your thought being the thought of no-thought," when you act "your singing and dancing is none other than the voice of Dharma." Anything we do never fails to embody the truth in strict conformity to the ancient saying, "Whether we go to the left or to the right, we always return to our origin. Every clapping of our hands conforms to propriety." Hence, the following poem:

> Where did I sleep last night?
> Tonight it will be here.
> And in the rice fields tomorrow night,
> A pillow of grass.[9]

This absolute freedom of action in all places, like the passing clouds and the flowing stream, is referred to by Hakuin in the following line of his poem: "The sky of boundless samadhi is vast."

Samadhi, in short, pertains to complete integration with objects, for the subject and object will be no longer in opposition. Master Rinzai also deals with this problem in his famous Fourfold Perception of the Truth, which I would like to discuss some other time. Our perception of the truth of being varies with time and occasion. For instance, we take in all things subjectively with ourself as the subject at one time, and at another time we integrate ourselves into the objective view of reality. It is not uniform. Thus, we can enjoy our free and non-attached perception in any manner if only we are liberated from subject and object in opposition to each other. Just as airplanes fly freely across the spacious sky, we can act uninhibitedly, for "The sky of boundless samadhi is vast!" If we are in this state of absolute freedom, the illuminating full moon of the Fourfold Wisdom will shine clearly there.

The Fourfold Wisdom consists of the Wisdom of a Big Round Mirror, the Wisdom of Equality, the Wisdom of True Perceiving, and the Wisdom of True Working. These may be thought of as the four aspects of the workings of wisdom.

The first, Wisdom of a Big Round Mirror, pertains to the primal wisdom which is bright and clear all over like a big round mirror. It may be deemed as the essence of the mind, in which Heaven and Earth are one with us as in the phrase "the light of the great, round mirror brimming with black." It alludes to the oneness of myriads of things.

The second, Wisdom of Equality, is the wisdom in which it can be seen that all things in existence possess a nature that is equal. This kind of wisdom alludes to the mountains, rivers, grasses, trees, and all things as equally embodying the wisdom and virtues of *Tathagata*.

The third, Wisdom of True Perceiving, is said to be the wisdom which makes one observe the delicate operations of all beings by means of the analysis of their ways of existence, their structures, their forms, their actions, and so forth.

The fourth is the Wisdom of True Working. It is the wisdom capable of making our sense perception function properly, as in the case of the eyes seeing and the nose smelling. The operation of this kind of wisdom for universal salvation points to the integration of enlightenment and action, namely, the oneness of knowledge and conduct.

This Fourfold Wisdom corresponds to the eight consciousnesses with which we are originally one. The samadhi of Mahayana Buddhism is considered to be the only way of turning the eight consciousnesses into the Fourfold Wisdom and presenting it to us fully and clearly. The Fourfold Wisdom is not to be added to us from outside by the power nurtured in samadhi, but the power of samadhi itself is something to be cherished because it is capable of letting the Fourfold Wisdom operate fully and brightly like the full moon which shines clearly in the sky.

Well, having come to this pass, what else is there to seek? There should be nothing sought. The reason is that "nirvana is manifested" before one's eyes as the ultimate. Originally the term "nirvana" was used in the sense of blowing out or extinguishing fire, that is to say, blowing out the flames of our desire, agonies, and delusions to secure great peace. Nirvana is not pessimistic or negative like going to one's death the way most people think of it. Rather, it means gaining eternal life and entering the state of absolute security.

The attainment of this state of absolute security alludes to the land of Lotus Blossoms. The Land of Amitabha is called the Pure Land of Infinite Light, while the Pure Land of Shakyamuni is called the World of the Treasure House of Lotus Blossoms, or the Land of Lotus Blossoms. However, this Land of Lotus Blossoms does not exist outside us. It exists in the very place where each of us enters the state of absolute security by being awakened to our eternal life in nirvana, which is another name for samadhi. Therefore, there is no room for any doubt in our belief that this "very body is a Buddha," for we indeed live, breathing in the Land of Lotus Blossoms, which is said to exist right here under our very feet. Hence, "All beings are primarily Buddhas." Searching for Buddhas as they primarily are, we have at last come to realize that the original Buddha-nature is concretely embodied nowhere but in these very bodies of ours that live from day to day, waving our arms and walking with our feet.

The Ten Oxherding
Pictures

Zen Buddhism advocates an intuitive and direct seeing one's self-nature instead of the attainment of a certain degree of enlightenment after long and gradual discipline like climbing a ladder step by step. The essence of Zen lies in the realization of self and Buddha as one. That is to say, Zen, as a rule, teaches us to be aware of our original nature where we are standing right now and to uncover our True Selves right where we are. In this sense, there should be no difference in principle between Shakyamuni's enlightenment and our own enlightenment. It is not in keeping with the teachings of Zen Buddhism to require its students to go through hundreds of years and countless barrriers before attaining enlightenment like Shakyamuni and Bodhidharma.

However, if we closely examine the content of enlightenment or self-realization from another viewpoint, we cannot deny that there are various degrees in enlightenment because of the many kinds of people there are, as well as the innumerable levels and capacities they possess. Especially when it comes to circumstances, no matter how much we may insist that there are no degrees in Zen enlightenment, there are various degrees in it, and it would be a mistake to say that we are not mutually different in our enlightenment.

The *Ten Oxherding Pictures* is meant as a guide to students of Zen Buddhism. Here, the content of kensho is classified into ten stages which are illustrated by ten corresponding pictures of an oxherd who sets off to find his lost ox. He seeks it, finds it, catches it, and tames it so that it may not stray away from him again. We may be able to know the extent of our own enlightenment in comparison with these ten stages of Zen discipline. Since it gives us an idea of the extent of our own development, I am going to present to the reader a brief summary of the *Ten Oxherding Pictures* in this chapter.

In the original text of the *Ten Oxherding Pictures*, the introduction was written by Priest Jion (Tz'u-yuan).[1] He writes, "Principle produces discrimination and equality. Teaching generates abruptness and gradualness. It ranges from roughness to fineness, and reaches from shallowness to depth." He also writes in his note, "It is ranked as the discipline of the mind in terms of events." The above quotations from the introduction to the *Ten Oxherding Pictures* should make it clear to us for what purposes this volume was written.

There are several versions of the *Ten Oxherding Pictures*. In the Rinzai Sect, the *Ten Oxherding Pictures* drawn and commented on by Priest Kakuan Shien (K'uo-an Chih-yuan)[2] of Liang-shan are used for instruction.

Master Kakuan lived about eight hundred years ago. He was an honored priest of the Yogi School in the Rinzai sect. Kakuan was in the line of Master Yogi Hoe (Yang-chih Fang-hui) together with Master Hakuun Shutan

(Po-yun Shou-tuan), the Fifth Patriarch Hoen (Fa-yen), and his religious heir Master Daizui Gensei (Ta-sui Yuan-ching), whom Kakuan succeeded. According to the introduction, Master Seikyo (Ch'ing-chu) had already drawn the *Ten Oxherding Pictures* before Kakuan drew his own version consisting of the ten excellent pictures. Kakuan writes in regard to his pictures, "I express my inner self in following the good examples set by my predecessors." Here, let me leave references to the history about these pictures and get to the text itself.

1. SEARCHING FOR THE OX

> Searching for his ox in vain,
> The solitary oxherd
> Hears nothing but
> The empty voices of the cicadas.
> In the summer mountain
> Where the ox is out of sight,
> Only the cicadas are heard,
> Singing among the trees.

The ox has never been lost. What is the need to search for it? It is
only because the oxherd has turned his back on it that the ox has
become a stranger to him and eventually has lost itself in the dusty
regions far away from him. The home mountain has receded far-
ther in the distance. The oxherd finds himself confused by byways
and crossroads. The duality between gain and loss burns like fire.
Views of right and wrong arise like tips of spears in a battlefield.

The ox here evidently pertains to the true mind, which is variously
called the true nature, the original face, the true self. It is the search for this
mind which is to be discussed in this chapter titled "Searching for the Ox."

Shakyamuni is said to have renounced his secular life, over despair at
the four kinds of sufferings: living, old age, sickness, and death. It is commonly said that when a man comes face to face with suffering—the problems
of life and death, the consciousness of sin—and finds himself confronted with
the limitations of his mortal power, it is common for him to look to religion
for salvation from his sufferings. It seems to me that many people these days
are motivated to be religious by their suffering from living, namely, by the difficulty of life when faced by old age, sickness, and death.

It may be for this reason that the new religions which stress the immediate gratification of people's worldly desires are very popular. In addition,
with the progress of science, it is becoming more and more common for people to resort to medical science than to religion to take care of their suffering
from old age and diseases. Also, in regard to the problems of living, they may
seem more easily solved through social movements than through religion in
many cases.

For these reasons we often hear people say that there are no religious
leaders of great character these days. Indeed, I can find no words to defend
ourselves from such criticism. In old times, there were many great men of religion, such as Kukai[3] and Saicho.[4] In later years there was Abbot Tenkai.[5] In
addition to them, many patriarchs of Zen and other priests were engaged not
only in the spiritual salvation of people in general but also in practical work
including the curing of diseases, political counseling, the construction of high-
ways and bridges, and military counseling.

They had the most advanced and up-to-date knowledge and informa-
tion in the fields of astronomy, geography, and all other human affairs and
activities. Moreover, they had the authority and influence to direct others to
carry out these projects. Surprisingly enough, however, with the increasing
complexity of human societies and the remarkable development of science and

learning, specialization in professional fields came into being, till at last men of religion have become degraded into mere specialists to preside over religious services and funeral ceremonies.

Contrary to our expectation, the most far-reaching developments of science, such as the disclosure of the inner structure of an atomic nucleus, have made us realize that we are on the point of being ruined by the products of our own highly developed knowledge and technology. This is how the question "What is man?" has come to be asked anew. That is to say, it has become necessary for religion to illuminate the very basis of history and civilization. Gabriel Marcel writes in his *Human Beings: Their Self-Rebellion* as follows:

> Nietzsche once declared, "God is dead." Approximately seventy-five years later today, another declaration that "human beings are on the verge of ruin" is whispered in an agonizing way rather than in articulated words, as if it were echoing Nietzsche's declaration.

In my own opinion, it was only because "God is dead" that the egocentric modern civilization has come into being. Therefore, I think that unless another declaration, "Man is dead," is made in turn, no new civilization worthy of the name of the Age of Atomic Energy will be born. At any rate, the new problem about the existence of man has come up now owing to the fundamental insecurity of history or civilization rather than to the individually felt uncertainties and sufferings of people. We men of religion must provide a new perspective for a possible solution of this problem, and by so doing purge ourselves of the disgrace unduly cast on us as funeral specialists.

The "Searching for the Ox" pertains to the search of the lost human being, which forms the first step to be taken in Zen discipline.

In old times, men used to be regarded as the slaves of God. Deaths, births, and all other good and bad fortune in their lives were ascribed to the will of God. After the dawn of the Modern Age, however, men came to be awakened as free human beings, "never to be exploited by any other people, or even by God, as a mere means," so that they might "act in conformity to the principle of universally applicable legislation," as Kant writes. The tables have been turned, and in the reversed relationship between God and Man, subject and object, God has come to be deemed as dead, making way for the advent of the new age with man as its center.

This view of mankind, stemming from Kant, reached its apex in Hegel's Absolute Self (via Fichte[6] and Schelling[7]) and then branched into two groups. The rightist group led to Spann, and the leftist to Feuerbach. At present, both of these groups have been driven into blind alleys, or rather, to crossroads.

This search for Man has long been directed to something outside of ourselves instead of to the innermost depths of our minds. That is to say, our self-awareness in the Modern Ages has indeed been self-alienation, and not self-awareness in true knowledge of ourselves. We, in fact, have had our backs turned on true human beings. That accounts for our failure to find our original being in the smog and noise pollution at this turning point of the world.

How silly men have been, taking the ego for the true human being! We should retrace our steps toward our human home rather than find ourselves at the crossroads without knowing which road to take. But, even if we try to go on, there are so many roads that we do not know which leads home. If we try to turn back, we would find the sun almost set in the west, and it would be hard to find our way home. This is the present state of our being. Unable to think at all of what to do, we are at the mercy of our vain delusions that arise in rapid succession like so many bees flying madly out of disturbed beehives.

The "Searching for the Ox" forms the first stage of Zen discipline. It pertains to the question of what human beings are and what we are. We are awakened to these questions by various stimuli including our obedience and disobedience to our karma[8] relations. Beginning with these questions, we come to entertain the wish to solve them on the strength of various teachings and religious discipline. And yet, at this stage, we are still in search of our objects "outside of ourselves."

Even if we are in the Way of Zen, we have not yet gripped the essential point of Zen at this stage. And, even if we ever internalize our search, our searching self and the object sought are in dualistic opposition to each other. This is to no avail. It is a mistake. Nevertheless, it will not necessarily be futile for us to experience it, as it is a barrier which everyone should pass once and for all in his lifetime.

2. Seeing the Traces of the Ox

As the oxherd determinedly searches
Into the heart of the mountain.
He now delights in the sight,
Of the traces of his ox.
In search of his lost ox,
Thoroughly but doubtfully
Faint traces appear but
He knows not where they lead.

It is through the Buddhist sutras that we come to understand
the principle and through examining the Buddhist teachings
that we come to know its derivatives. By making it clearly
known that all vessels are of the same gold, we accord with
the myriads of things reflected them in ourselves. If we cannot
distinguish between what is genuine and what is not, then
our minds are too confused to distinguish between truth and

falsehood. We cannot yet enter the gate of enlightenment, and we must be compared to the oxherd who sees only the traces of the ox without finding it.

Most people are truly confident in their concept of existence that is limited to their "five-foot body and fifty-year life span." They regard all other people as separate from them, as "you," "he," and so on. However, more sensible people can easily understand that such a purely individualistic idea of the self, arbitrarily isolated from all its realistic relationships to other people and conditions, is nothing but a conceptualized and abstract existence which is as futile as a mirage.

For instance, our bodies cannot be conceived apart from our parents who gave birth to us as well as from our lateral relationships to the societies which supply us with food so that we may continue to live. Likewise, the consciousness of the "individual self" is not found in newborn babies. The operation of such a seemingly self-evident principle as "I think; therefore, I am," is formed in the course of our lifetime. That is to say, the operation of the principle of our thinking is inconceivable except in its relationship to our experiences accumulated after our births both in time and space. The consciousness of the individual, purely isolated from others, does not exist. It exists only in our thoughts.

Today, even elementary-school children know that everything is reducible to an atom, and they know about energy. Is it not commonly accepted, then, to think that all vessels, varied as they are, have the same metal in common?

Some people say that learning is not necessary in Zen discipline, but I think that Zen men are next to none in making use of words. Priest Hakuin said that if a mother's breasts were thin her baby would not grow healthy. Thus, he gained command of countless books written by men of learning in various fields, and he cherished them as his religious treasures.

By means of the sutras and the teachings of various masters, it will be easier to understand the principle of all things as one and all vessels having the same gold in common. At present, books on nuclear physics may be more convincing to many of us than my inadequate lectures on Zen when it comes to the principle that all vessels are one, being of the same gold. However, these scientific books will not be enough, for even the knowledge of the inner structure of an atomic nucleus leaves us ignorant of the root of life.

After all, our knowledge of the principle of all vessels as one, formed from the same gold, is no more than a piece of ricecake painted in a picture when it is acquired from books and lectures. Our intellectual knowledge of the origin of true life thus cannot satisfy our hunger. Therefore, the mere knowledge of the root of life does not mean "entering the gate to enlightenment." It is no more than "seeing only the traces" of the lost ox in our search for it. At the mere sight of its traces, we will not be able to tell whether the ox is white or black. Hence, "If we cannot tell between what is genuine and what is not, then our minds are too confused to distinguish between truth and falsehood."

This stage of "seeing the traces" of the lost ox pertains to the degree of self-awareness for those of us who have at last come so far as to find the right discipline after having tried to learn the Way through books and lectures and having asked our teachers for guidance. Now that we have at least found the traces of the ox, all we will have to do next is to interview our teachers and see through the koan given by them. It is all up to our efforts whether we will succeed or not. We just have to do our best to follow the traces with all our might, running forward at full speed.

At present many people are apt to be at a loss as to which religion and which discipline they should choose. It is an admirable thing to find the right direction to enlightenment, even if it is compared to the mere sight of the traces of the ox. There is no doubt that we will catch up with the ox sooner or later.

3. SEEING THE OX

> True Self, eternal and remote,
> Is seen embodied
> In the spring sunshine
> Permeating the tangle of green willow branches.
> Guided by the bellowing
> Of the untamed ox,
> The oxherd catches sight of it
> As he proceeds in search of it.

If he enters the Way by the sound he hears, he will see into the origin of things. His six perceptual faculties are in harmony and operate on his activities, revealing their individual characters, like salt contained in water and glue hidden in colors. If he raises his eyebrows by keeping his eyes wide open, he will become aware of the fact that all things are nothing other than himself.

The Modern Ages are said to be concentrated on Man, whereas the Middle Ages were centered on God. Modern history shows that human beings are treated first as individuals, and then as classes, and further as races. The confusion and pathos of the contemporary view of man, I think, lies in the fact that we human beings are seen to exist merely as individuals, as classes, or as races, with the exclusion of the others in opposition to us. If the essence of knowledge consists of judgment, and if judgment is thought to call for distinction, as in this modern civilization inclined to intellectualism, we are apt to recognize objects only by their mutual distinctions.

For instance, water is known as H_2O. It consists of the mixture of hydrogen and oxygen at the ratio of two to one. However, it is impossible for us to drink only the oxygen or the hydrogen part of water. They say that the bird named *hamsa-raja*[9] is capable of separating water from milk and drinking only the concentrated milk. We human beings, however, cannot perform such a feat.

The analysis of human beings in terms of individuals, classes, or races certainly serves to deepen our view of human beings. However, the one-sided emphasis on any particular one of the above groups with the exclusion of the others is undesirable. For instance, some define human beings as class-minded subjects, arbitrarily branding those who do not follow their unilateral view as lacking in social nature. There is no other way to reward such men of inflexible thought than by commanding them to drink the hydrogen component of water alone, if indeed they can.

The same is true of the absolute individualists, who one-sidedly define the concrete existence of human beings only from the individualistic viewpoint, as well as of the racists, who emphasize in abstraction the racial side of human beings. None of such phenomenological, abstract, and analytical views of human beings will succeed in guiding us to our origin.

At the dawn of the Modern Ages, people had become doubtful of the medieval mode of thought centered on God. They asked, "What is Man?" This question threw new light on the existence of the rational individual. And pivoting on it, the individualistic and liberalistic world-view centering on human beings came into being. However, those who had been socially mistreated by the capitalistic production system that had developed after the Industrial Revolution focused on classes of people. In post-World War I Germany and Italy, on the other hand, racism came into being in opposition to the class struggles which afflicted them. Today, the same question, "What is Man?" is asked anew in the face of the division of human beings into the three categories and their common affliction, namely, their self-centered view of human beings. Here, we must inquire into our "origin" and pursue it not only on an individual basis but also in terms of the foundation of civilization and history, transcending both the Medieval and Modern Ages.

Aside from our scholarly, logical, sociological, and historical pursuits, our retrospective pursuit of the deeply concealed "origin" of true life through samadhi has at last led us to the point of seeing something like it. This stage of self-awareness corresponds to the picture titled "Seeing the Ox."

It pertains to something selfless rather than egocentric, and to something like the integration of God and Man rather than self-glorification. It is the eternal "now," which is the origin of timeless time and from which history derives. And speaking specifically, it is "here" that the origin of our societies lies. Now, if we listen intently, we can hear the ox "mooing" at the top of its voice, can't we?

Ages ago, Kyosho (Ching-ch'ing), who was training under the guidance of Master Gensha (Hsuan-sha) in Fu Chou, could not understand this aspect of Zen. So, one day he asked his teacher, "From where should I enter Zen?" Master Gensha seemed to be listening for something without answering him. After a while he said, "Do you hear that sound of the mountain stream?" "Yes, I can, very well." "Well, then, how about entering Zen from there?" At these words, they say Kyosho was enlightened.

In the *Kongo Kyo* (Vajrachchedika-prajnaparamita-sutra) we read, "The sight of a form (color) illuminates our minds. Hearing a voice, we attain enlightenment."[10] We can perceive the form (color) of the all-embracing Buddha Mind (the ox) in a single flower, and we can hear, in the clear mountain river, the bellowing of the ox which finds its echoes in the whole universe. It is in such a way that we catch sight of the original "man," the fundamental "self."

Master Ikkyu said in verse, "In hearing the song of the silent bird in the dark night, I am fondly reminded of my father before his birth." Schelling also talks of "the dark night when all the cows and oxen turn black." Hearing the mooing voice of the ox of the mind in the dark of night means to "meet one's origin," that is, to get in contact with our origin. If we once meet our origin in this way, there is nothing under Heaven which is not our fundamental Self. Even in seemingly trivial phenomena, the basic principle is at work, as is well expressed by the phrase, "salt contained in water and glue hidden in colors."

Seeing the ox corresponds to kensho, or meeting this origin. However, at this stage, the depth of perception varies from person to person. Some only hear the remote bellowing of the ox, while some others catch sight of it vaguely in the mist or see its clear form in front of their eyes.

They say today that there is the method of rapid kensho, by which we may be awakened to our self-nature in four or five days. Still, in reality there are thickheaded people like me who take as many as eight or nine years just to get hold of the tip of the ox's tail. In the first stage, which deals with the oxherd in search of his lost ox, the oxherd becomes aware of the fact that unless he knows for sure "what he is," his whole life will be futile. Thus he sets off to seek his ox.

In the second stage regarding the traces of the ox, the oxherd succeeds in finding the traces of his ox and comes to know its direction. After following the ox at full speed through earnest zazen and religious discipline or through integration with his koan problems, he catches sight of the ox far away, as represented in this chapter titled "Seeing the Ox." But the ox is still out of his reach. If he is idle and absentminded, he will lose sight of it again. Therefore, he must raise his eyebrows with his eyes wide open in order to see into the "glue hidden in colors." It means that he must muster up his courage to do his best.

4. Catching the Ox

> If he tries to detain it,
> He does not feel good.
> That accounts for the truth
> Of their relationship.
> To what avail will it be
> To get hold of the raging ox?
> The harder he pulls the rein,
> The bolder the ox becomes.

Today for the first time the oxherd meets the ox which has been hidden for a long time in the wilderness. It is in such an inviting part of the wilderness that the oxherd finds it difficult to control it. It unceasingly eludes him, as it longs for sweet meadows. It still retains its stubborn mind and wild nature. If he wishes for pure harmony with it, he should not fail to whip it.

At this stage, the oxherd securely catches the ox by the nose. This alludes to his success in seeing his original self. Ordinarily, when a student passes the first barrier, the koan of mu, his kensho will be approved by his Zen master. He who receives the approval of kensho for the first time regards himself as enlightened. But real kensho must at least reach this stage of catching the ox, for seeing and catching the ox are as different as Heaven and Earth.

"If we contemplate one koan, our thoughts are extinguished and our wills become lost in vast emptiness and awe-inspiring nonexistence. It is as if we were on the edge of a very high cliff where there is nothing to support our feet or hands. When we are thus completely dead, we all at once become one with our koan, forgetting mind and body, with heart ablaze hot with agonies . . .," says Priest Hakuin. "We name this experience kensho and call it 'seeing one's self-nature.'"

The phrase, "become one with our koan, forgetting mind and body . . ." pertains to the Great Death, in which mind and body disappear in integration with our koan or susoku. Unless we experience this many times, we will not be considered to be at the stage of catching the ox, even after our kensho. It is far from easy to reach this stage of enlightenment.

A great number of books on Zen Buddhism have been published recently. Many of them are logically written with substantial proofs, and very little room is left for any unfavorable criticism and argument. However, it is very questionable that all of their authors have attained the stage of "catching the ox." I may well say that the discussion of Zen by anyone who has not yet caught his ox is off the point of Zen, however logical he may sound. What we should note here, however, is that to catch the ox is by no means the mere acquisition of the ox, as we have read so far in the preceding chapters, although the phrase may sound as if something hitherto nonexistent were gained anew.

This is clear in the following phrase from the first chapter concerning the search of the lost ox: "The ox has never been lost . . . it is only because the oxherd has turned his back on it. . . ." Even in our delusion, we are never separated from our True Selves which are compared to the ox.

Now the oxherd has at last rediscovered his True Self. But, as he has long neglected this ox of his mind, leaving it alone in the wilderness "with his back turned on it," it is still very wild in nature and seems to prefer the bushes of desires and delusions. It is inclined to run away to these seductive bushes. There is the saying, "Disturbing thoughts and opinions can be abruptly discarded like broken dippers; emotional delusions cannot be discarded except gradually like the filaments of the lotus root." As soon as we recognize our mistaken opinions, we can immediately get rid of them, but they say it is difficult to free ourselves from our deeply rooted prejudices and emotional habits. For instance, when we cut the lotus root crosswise, its filaments unfold themselves endlessly to our great annoyance. Therefore, emotional delusion must be removed gradually over a long period of time.

Likewise, it is not an easy task to orient the ox of our mind, our True Self, correctly as it originally is. It is said that the stubborn oxen corresponding to our inflexible minds and wild egocentric wills are very strong and we find it difficult to rein in their unruly and indecent natures. Unless we are always attentive and alert, after regaining our True Selves, we may be immediately thrown back into our previous state of unenlightenment in which we turned our backs on our True Selves.

Then what on earth should we do? Whip the ox if we wish for pure harmony with it. Pure harmony, I think, pertains to the delicate composure of the obedient and benign mind into which the unruly mind and the wild nature of the raging ox are to be turned after it is caught by the oxherd.

Master Shaku Soen says, "It cannot be possible except in the point by point by point succession of correct thoughts (Jpn. *sho-nen so-zoku*)." By these words Master Soen means, and I agree, that the experience of the complete integration of subject and object is realized by the subject throwing himself into the objective environment. It is the self-negation of the subject, which makes it possible for him to become one with the object. I think that "pure harmony" suggests such integration of the subject with the object as realized through his self-negation. In order to experience "pure harmony," self-discipline is necessary, so that we may be encouraged to be diligent and to be one with the objects in our everyday encounter with them. Integration, which means complete self-projection into objects, pertains at the same time to freedom from them.

In the picture illustrating this stage of catching the ox, the oxherd still holds the whipping rod in one hand and the rein in the other. The rein tightly stretched between the oxherd and his ox should suggest that they are still inclined to get away from each other. Therefore, at this stage, the oxherd has not yet succeeded in taming his ox even though he has gotten hold of it. This anticipates the possibility that he will have to strive for the proper operation of his original self on all affairs and matters in his everyday life. However, the oxherd has already passed the stage of catching sight of his ox. Therefore, even though the ox of his mind is apt to escape from him, tempted by the more seductive bushes, this can never suggest the possibility that he will abruptly fall to his former state of delusion and agitation. Rather, I can say that he is now in great self-confidence as far as his state of mind is concerned, and that he is now under discipline with various devices to secure the ox of his mind in great serenity even when exposed to the fiercest wind of this world.[11]

5. HERDING THE OX

>The wild ox, tamed
>After many days,
>Has become like the oxherd's shadow
>To his great delight.
>His long-sought ox is with him
>In the furrows of the fields.
>The longer he keeps it,
>The quieter it becomes.

The rise of the slightest thought is followed by further thoughts in an endless round. Through enlightenment all this turns into truth; through blindness it becomes an error. Delusion is not caused by the surroundings but stems from his own mind. He must tightly pull the rein tied to the nose of the ox so as to drive away any vacillating thoughts.

According to the *Ten Oxherding Pictures* by Master Shibayama Zenkei,[12] the fourth stage of catching the ox and the fifth stage of herding it reveal Kakuan's crude idea of the oxherd. Master Zenkei writes, "Originally this oxherd is not impure. He has just lost sight of his ox because he has turned his back on it. The ox in itself pertains to the Dharma essence, which is originally shared by all people, and which is above gain and loss, as well as purity and impurity. The ox means the truth which is compared to 'the dawn moon originally existing in the sky.'"

This is certainly an admirable remark of Master Zenkei and his point has long been unduly overlooked. I do not know any other person who has pointed it out so precisely as Master Zenkei. As he says, the ox, meaning the mind, is not something to be refined through "discipline" or to be secured physically by means of "herding." It is the realization or rediscovery of what has been so far concealed due to the blind ignorance of the oxherd. In this sense, fourth and fifth stages should be "interpreted freely and effectively in terms of the author's attempt to practice Zen in movement in order to bring action and knowledge into one." I quite agree with Master Zenkei in his contention that these chapters should never be deemed to suggest that enlightenment means the culmination of gradually undergone discipline. I take the same perspective as Master Zenkei in commenting on these stages of Zen discipline in this book.

For instance, if we truly understand the koan "Mu," we naturally come to realize the principle of all things as one. However, it is not always easy at first to apply this principle when we operate freely on all things and affairs in our everyday life of movement and change. Sometimes we are apt to lose hold of this power of operation. It is for this reason that we are taught to be disciplined for three years in the samadhi of the Precious Mirror, in which "all things illuminate one another," as well as in the samadhi in which discrimination and indiscrimination are integrated. The herding of the ox, for instance, means such discipline. Discipline in the samadhi of the Precious Mirror pertains to nothing other than discipline to practice Zen in movement in order to bring action and knowledge into one. This means that all things and ourselves are actually affirmed in our original oneness just like two mirrors confronted with each other. I think it important not to ignore this problem but to pay very minute attention to it.

Master Zenkei interprets the word "herding" as the throwing of oneself into one's circumstances and attaining no-self there. It is in this sense of oxherding that we discipline our selfless selves in all manners of transcending our attachment to things through becoming one with them, while we freely go in and out of the field of discrimination. Oxherding thus relates to the lasting discipline of a great master or one's discipline after enlightenment.

Reflecting over our everyday life, we notice that various thoughts keep on rising and ebbing in rapid succession without resting for even one moment. Master Gozu Hoyu (Niu-t'ou Fa-jung)[13] from Wen Chou in Yen-ling said, "The rising and ebbing of thoughts has no beginning nor end." Our imaginations and thoughts are stirred even in our sleep, causing us to dream.

However, our rising and perishing imaginations in themselves are neither bad nor good. What is wrong is only the succession of thoughts, one thought causing another. There is a poem reading, "The clouds of cherry blossoms! The sound of the temple bell! Is it from Ueno or Asakusa?" When we hear the pealing sound of the temple bell, we are inclined to wonder where it comes from, and whether it comes from the Asakusa Temple or from Kan'ei-ji, a temple at Ueno.

Such a series of thoughts aroused by the sound of the unidentified temple bell are followed by more thoughts in endless association with them, just like the horses of our wills and the monkeys of our minds. If left alone, these delusive thoughts will develop endlessly beyond our control. This is a very undesirable thing, for it will turn our minds into the nests of delusive thoughts. Master Gozu further said, "If another thought does not arise, the previous one perishes of itself." If we hear the sound of the temple bell, we should let it go and refrain from wondering if it comes from Ueno or Asakusa. If only such dualistic afterthoughts are kept from arising, one sound of the bell will send the preceding thought into nonexistence.

However, as it is said in the text, the "rise of the slightest thought is followed by further afterthoughts" ordinarily. And it is a very difficult task to prevent the afterthoughts from following the preceding ones. This series of thoughts may be due to the irresistible operation of the inborn human consciousness. The rising and falling of thoughts are, as it were, the proof of our being alive. Without them, we will be dead. Moreover, there is truth and there is delusion in these thoughts. The difference between good thoughts and bad thoughts solely depends on whether we are enlightened or not.

To quote again from Master Zenkei's words, I think that "throwing yourself into your surroundings" may be called "enlightenment." In movement, we are said to be enlightened if we are absorbed into the work calling for our immediate attention to the point of being one with it with no divided thought. In stillness, enlightenment means our being one with the frequency of respiration in counting it, as well as our oneness with the koan problems as such.

On the contrary, unenlightenment pertains to the dualistic states of self and work, of koan and self, and of all other things in mutual opposition and conflict. Lu Xin-wu[14] writes, "If we are one, we will see our self-nature. If we are two, we will generate passions." If we are one with all our surroundings, our originally pure, unified, and simple self-nature reveals itself. If we are subject to duality, the principle and its operation function separately, throwing us into the maze of delusions and passions.

What I have so far written must be enough to convince you that there is no clear demarcation in the objective world between truth and falsehood, or between enlightenment and unenlightenment. The fact that willows are green means neither enlightenment nor unenlightenment. The fact that flowers are red means neither truth nor falsehood. We live from morning to night, coming and going between hatred and love, and grudging and wanting. These, however, are never the intrinsic attributes of this objective world. It is just because we entertain such ideas in conflict with our objective world that we fail to turn ourselves into nothingness. Hence, the following words from the text: "Delusion is not caused by the environment but stems from our own minds."

The expression "the up-side-down dreams and thoughts" found in *Hannya Shin Gyo* also points to the same thing. Even though there is no duality between right and wrong, or good and bad, in this world, we are inclined to think as if there were such dualities, and we ascribe our subjective judgment of good and bad things to the objective world, unduly transferring our own responsibilities to others. It is no wonder we are called up-side-down.

It is said, "If we face Heaven and Earth in sorrow, all things in Heaven and Earth grieve. If we are in contact with mountains and rivers in joy, all the mountains and rivers rejoice with us." This makes it clear that it is not Heaven and Earth as such to grieve, nor mountains and rivers as such to rejoice. The poet Basho sings, "The full moon, I walk round the pond all night." He must have spent the entire autumn night, appreciating the full moon. The wife of a blind man must have sorrowfully appealed her husband's ill luck to the moon in singing, "The full moon . . . The night is for this blind-man's wife to grieve." The same full moon thus gives different impressions to the perceivers depending on their varying moods and situations. It is exactly in the same way that our enlightenment and unenlightenment have their common origin in our very minds, and nowhere else. This objective world is responsible for neither our enlightenment nor our unenlightenment.

"Because of enlightenment, Man becomes the Buddhas and the Patriarchs. Because of no enlightenment, Man continually is trapped by life and death (dualism)," said Master Soen. That is why it is so important to secure our standpoints without indulging in vain arguments. Now that we have finally rediscovered our lost ox at all cost, it is important for us to grip its muzzle firmly so that it may not stray away from us again. In other words, it is essential for us to be disciplined in samadhi with all our strength, tugging at the reins of our minds without diverting our attention, and being completely absorbed into the world of speech and silence, movement and stillness, and all other dualities.

6. Coming Home on the Ox's Back

Playing the flute to the sky
Of his clear, empty mind,
The oxherd turns his steps homeward,
The white clouds over the mountain tops.
Snow has melted on distant mountains.
Looking back over his shoulders,
The oxherd rides his ox,
On his way home.

The battle is already done. Gain and loss are also gone. The oxherd sings the song of the woodcutter. He plays the rustic tune of a nursery rhyme on his flute. Laying himself on the back of his ox, he looks up at Heaven. He will not turn back even at the call of others. He will not linger even if caught with a trap.

So far, the oxherd has undergone many difficulties, searching for his ox (his True Self), rediscovering it after looking up and down for it, and further, trying to discipline it. However, when he gets to know it, it turns out to be something like the head of a man. When we are confused we may think that we have lost our heads and search for them, whereas they have always been on our shoulders as they should be. In fact, we have never lost our head even for one moment.

The oxherd had likewise always turned his back on himself in search of his ox (his True Self). On coming back to himself, he realizes that he has been riding his ox all that while. Being one with his ox, he finds himself where he should originally be. That means he is back home now, where there is no longer anyone on the back of his ox nor any ox under his feet. Indeed, he is like the snail which is always at home wherever it may go. The oxherd finds any place to be his original home no matter where he may be. His home is at the same time the true world, the land of Buddha itself.

In Zen discipline, as well, we are not supposed to linger in the same world of dualities forever. We must at any cost experience our independent existence in Heaven and on Earth like the oxherd on his way home. In order to do so, we must first conquer the enemies in our mind as O Yomei (Wang Yang-ming) says. However, the termination of unenlightenment is not enough. If there is any trace of enlightenment left in us, we are not considered to be truly enlightened. Absolute peace must be realized after the end of the war between enlightenment and unenlightenment, and at the same time between gain and loss. Coming home on the back of the ox alludes to such a world of absolute peace, namely, the world of absolute security, as is well expressed by Master Rinzai, "Where I cease to long for the enlightened mind, there is security."

That is why Master Hakuin sings in his *Zazen Wasan*, "Your going-and-returning takes place nowhere but where you are. Your singing-and-dancing is none other than the voice of Dharma." Whatever we may do, be it the singing of folk songs, popular songs, or nursery rhymes, nothing is out of propriety as long as we are one with our hands and things around us. Moreover, like the oxherd who "looks up to Heaven," while "laying himself on the back of his ox," we exist in the very place to which we originally belong, even if we find ourselves in the midst of the ups and downs of this perpetually changing world. Therefore, our eyes are always turned upward to the remote world of the Absolute in aspiration to it. It is as though we were on the back of the ox.

Since we have come this far, we are no longer bound to the dualities of good and bad, enlightenment and unenlightenment, and so on. Even if Buddha called to us, we would not look back over our shoulders. Even if a demon wanted to detain us, we would not stay where we were. Indeed, we play in samadhi in all places. Such a world as this existing in Zen may seem remote to the average man of the world. Nevertheless, however, we should remember that Zen is the world for us to enter intuitively at one transcendental leap.

7. The Ox Forgotten: the Man Alone

How futile it is for him
To choose between good and bad
Without knowing that he is one of
The reeds washed by one rough wave!
There is a remote cave
At the end of the mountain road.
The longer the ox is herded there,
The quieter it becomes.

There are no two Dharma. The ox is temporarily portrayed here as a symbol of the principle. To differentiate the snare from the hare trapped with it or to distinguish between the fishtrap and the fish caught with it is like smelting gold from ore or seeing the moon come out of the clouds. A streak of cold light and a great sound existed even before the separation of Heaven and Earth.

Beginning with the stage of searching for the ox, Zen discipline has formally come to its climax in the preceding stage titled "Coming Home on the Ox's Back." On coming home on the ox's back, the oxherd finds himself reinstated in his original abode. This means that pursuing man and pursued True Self have become perfectly one. This is considered to be the climax of any religious teaching and discipline in respect to the unity of God and Man. However, the point of Zen lies beyond this experience.

Homecoming on the ox's back means the realization of the oneness of man and ox, human being and Buddha, and phenomenon and entity. Suppose this homecoming experience (self-realization) is directed toward the world of truth into which the ox, Buddha, and entities are embraced in their respective oneness with the oxherd, human beings, and phenomena. Then, the stage of "The Ox Forgotten: the Man Alone" goes a step beyond this homecoming

experience of the oxherd. At this very stage, the truth as such is comprehended from the standpoints of the affirmed man, human beings, and phenomena.

It is from such a standpoint that man observes the operation of the
Absolute on his own being in this reality, representing myriads of phenomena,
human beings, and the self in their oneness with their entities, Buddhas, and
the awakened self. In this case, the self no longer means the finite self existing
within the limits of "fifty years in time and five feet in space"; it is the larger
self occupying the whole space of the universe, as the host of Heaven and
Earth, and the unique and independent self in Heaven and on Earth. For this
reason, only the figure of the oxherd in all his solitude and self-sufficiency is
represented in this picture in which the figure of the ox is absent.

"There are no two Dharma." Searching subject and sought object cannot be two, for the Truth, as a rule, is one and absolute. However, the ox is here
regarded as the fundamental principle. It is expediently treated here as the
object of pursuit like a snare or a trap. A snare or a trap is a necessary tool
before a hare or a fish is caught. But, however good it may be, it is of no use
after the object has been trapped. Likewise, the ox, representing the mind, is
of no use, now that it is known on the strength of the sutras, Zen masters' dia-
logues with their disciples, and koan that the pursuing self is no other than the
pursued ox (the mind) itself.

Further, we can compare it to the smelting of gold from ore, or to the revelation of the full moon from masses of clouds. Once we get at it, we realize that it has never been lost all this while. The moon, like the truth, does not pertain to something which comes into being after the passing of clouds. But it has always been there beyond the clouds like the "dawn moon always there in the sky from the very beginning." Hence, "a streak of cold light and a great sound existed even before the separation of Heaven and Earth." A "streak of cold light" means the oneness of Buddha and Man. A "great sound " existing before the separation of Heaven and Earth means the eternal world before the separation of Heaven and Earth.

8. Both Man and Ox Completely Forgotten

> There are no clouds nor moon.
> The katsura and all other trees are withered.
> Everything is driven away
> From the empty sky.
> Originally, there is no duality
> Between Dharma and Mind.
> What should be meant
> By dreams and realities?

All worldly desires have been transcended and all holiness (enlightenment) has been negated. He will never linger in the place where there is a Buddha (enlightenment) and never fail to pass hurriedly by the place where there is no Buddha (enlightenment). Even one-thousand-eyed *Avalokitesvara* could not see through the one who is not attached to the dualities of these things and those things. The holy one to whom hundreds of birds dedicate flowers in reverence is, in fact, a man in great disgrace.

During the first four stages (Searching for the Ox, Seeing the Traces of the Ox, Seeing the Ox, and Catching the Ox), ox (mind) and oxherd (man) are not yet completely united into one. Therefore, these stages should be called ordinary ranks. But the sixth stage, at which only the ox is forgotten in its integration with the oxherd, may be regarded as a superior rank. Even at this sacred stage, however, one is not allowed to linger, for it means a kind of attachment to the ordinary human predilection for sacredness. One must go beyond it. At the eighth stage, the man, holy as he is in rank, is negated as well as the ox. This stage is called "Both Man and Ox Completely Forgotten." Suppose this absolute negation of man and object is represented by a circle. In my opinion, the following stages, Return to the Original Life, and Return to the Source, and Entering the City with Bestowing Hands respectively, may be regarded as the two aspects of the concrete content of the circle which stands for the twofold negation.

In Japanese Shintoism, gods and goddesses are said to have descended from their heavenly abodes in Takamagahara to carry out their own missions in conformity to the Whole (principle). As I have written before, I think that true Zen life indeed consists in such downward operation from the Whole. While the opposition between man and ox is already completely dissolved in the sixth chapter (Both Man and Ox Completely Forgotten), I would like to deal with the oxherd and his ox, as I should, in terms of "holiness" rather than with "Both Man and Ox Completely Forgotten" in the literal sense of the words. Regarding this point, I agree with Master Shibayama Zenkei who says, "The meaning of the title of this picture is open to debate."

If we are liberated from our attachment to all kinds of petty feelings, we naturally attain Buddhahood and become invested with "holiness." The stage of "Both Man and Ox Forgotten" pertains to nonattachment to such dualities as being and nonbeing, enlightenment and unenlightenment, or sacred and profane. At this stage, all the previously obtained "holiness" is negated and renounced, and even the evidently sacred "Buddhahood" and the empty ideas of "non-Buddhahood" are both evaded. All the spiritually inflexible things are removed from the mind of the free and nonabiding man of enlightenment who is not attached to anything. It is impossible even for the one-thousand-eyed Kannon to see through his mind.

Master Gozu Hoyu, whose words are quoted in the fifth stage, "Herding the Ox," used to sit in quiet meditation in a cave every day. Seeing this, the villagers were impressed and brought offerings. Even mountain birds brought flowers to him in admiration of his virtues. However, he happened to meet the Fourth Patriarch Doshin (Tao-hsin)[15] later, and through his influence he came to realize the ultimate meaning of Zen. After this, they say, the villagers became indifferent to him and the birds stopped bringing flowers.

Master Gozu had become a mere ordinary man of the world as he used to be before enlightenment. He had transcended his former admirable merits which caused so much respect and adoration in his neighbors. Now that he was back to the state of nothingness, shedding off all his profane feelings and negating all his holiness, birds no longer dedicated flowers to him. Seen from the viewpoint of the truly enlightened eyes, those who obviously look so great as to cause birds to dedicate flowers to them are evidently not yet at the ultimate stage of enlightenment in which all holiness is negated. That means such people are not truly admirable yet.

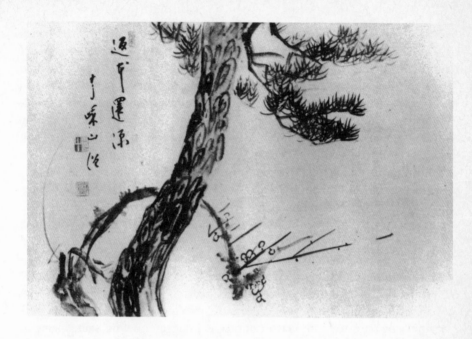

9. RETURN TO THE ORIGINAL LIFE, RETURN TO THE SOURCE

The mountains are just as they originally were,
Showing no trace of Dharma.
Pine needles are green,
And flowers white with dewdrops.
The mountains have turned green
Even though they are not dyed.
Each flower in its own color
Is nonexistent.

He is originally pure, free from any speck of dust. Seeing through
the ups and downs in this world of forms, he acts in the absolute
tranquility. He is not caught by deceptive images around him nor
does he stand in need of further discipline. The waters are blue and
the mountains are green. Changes are perceived in meditation.

"Return to the original life, return to the source" means retracing one's steps to the original abode and regaining the source of life. This is the state of reinstatement in the former world of actuality and discrimination. It is reached through the transcendence of absolute nothingness represented by a circle in the preceding eighth chapter. Priest Takuan[16] compares this state to the musical scale as he writes in his *Fudo Chi shin-myoroku*, "Being very high and being very low are mutually similar." He continues, "At the highest stage of the Buddhist Teachings, an enlightened man is like an ordinary man ignorant of anything about Buddha and Dharma." Ordinarily, the destination of religious discipline is the land of God, the absoluteness of being. But, if human beings linger there forever, it is as if they were forced to remain in hospitals after recovery from their illness. Admission to hospitals is for the sake of their prospective recovery. Therefore, as soon as they are recovered they should return to the societies to work again as hard as they can.

Zarathustra said to the Sun, "As you set below the horizon of the twilight sea in order to illuminate the world again, . . . I must descend, too." So saying, he descended to the world. He ran down the mountain of his enlightenment to be reunited with masses of people in negation of his sacred state of mind so assiduously earned, crying, "God is dead!" Likewise, the gods and goddesses of Takamagahara descended to the chaotic world in order to "repair and consolidate the basis of the drifting country."

Just like Zarathustra and the gods and goddesses of Takamagahara, those of us who have once attained the state of sacredness by negating ourselves, are obligated to negate even our attainment of sacredness in order to return from this world of absolute nothingness to that of actuality, where mountains are high and rivers long as they naturally are. In the world of ordinary men, mountains are mountains and waters are waters. In the state of sacredness, mountains are not mountains and waters are not waters. Now that we are reinstated in our former world of ordinary men, we again perceive mountains as mountains and waters as waters together with the unenlightened.

However ordinary an enlightened man may look externally, he is completely different internally from the men of the world who are at the mercy of desires and delusions, for he has now attained his primal unity in which he is "originally pure, free from any speck of dust." That is why he is said to be in "the absolute tranquility of non-action" and free from any artificiality and agitation in all his actions while he lives in this dream-like world of changes, in the transmigratory rounds of prosperity and decline, birth and extinction. He is in the state of tranquil concentration where he is always flowing and turning together with myriads of things around him without even knowing his own flowing and turning.

Even when we are enlightened, we have a body so we still have sickness and death; we have suffering and joy. But, even though we exist within such circumstances, we truly understand that everything is emptiness and so we are not controlled by circumstances. We do not lose ourselves in suffering or in joy. While all of these conditions are originally activities of the True Self, they do not occur at this stage because of discrimination or because we try to experience them.

We say that this state of being is not cultivated through Zen discipline because in reality you have it originally. "The waters are blue and the mountains are green"—that is the original world. In that world of everyday life (suffering and joy), the absolute eternal light is shining.

10. Entering the City with Bliss-Bestowing Hands

Oh, the manly mountain, with bliss-bestowing hands,
And with feet flung up to the void sky,
Birds must be at ease
Among the withered branches.
The body cherishing the body
Troubles the mind.
The true being is to be
As natural as it should be.

Even one thousand sages do not know his movements. Passing through the brushwood gate all alone, with his natural beauty concealed and without following the good examples set by his wise predecessors, he visits the city with his wine container in his hand and returns home, supported by his walking stick. He thus turns even wine dealers and fishmongers into Buddhas.

The *Ten Oxherding Pictures* have at last toiled onto their final stage. "Entering the City with Bliss Bestowing Hands" pertains to the enlightened man entering the city and offering his helpful hands to the people living there, upon his descent to this world in enlightenment. In other words, it corresponds to the altruistic conduct of the enlightened man in his freedom of

conduct and choice upon his reunion with masses of people and the "drifting country," as I have mentioned before. Just like the invalid who leaves his hospital and returns to his community to resume his work upon his recovery from his illness, the students of Zen are obligated to share their blessings of enlightenment with others as soon as they are enlightened. Such terms as "a head of ashes and a face of mud" and "harmony with light and integration with dust" pertains to this altruistic mission of universal salvation.

But at this stage of enlightenment, there is no longer any trace of endeavor on our part to save other human beings or to think of being men of religion, motivated by the universal compassion of Buddha. There is nonabiding freedom, with everything left to the care of Heaven. He does nothing outside the bounds of propriety even when he spontaneously follows the dictates of his desire. The term "playing in samadhi" is more suitable for this stage of enlightenment than the stiff expression of "salvation of human beings."

"Passing through the brushwood gate all alone," the oxherd has at last come home and is well settled now. At this ultimate stage of enlightenment, nobody, "even one thousand sages," can tell any longer whether he is a fool or a clever man, and whether he is sacred or profane. To such an extent has he lost his own identity, whether he is enlightened or unenlightened, good or bad, male or female. In addition, he has completely deprived himself of his beauty gained at any cost. It does not matter to him at all now, if others call him a lunatic or a traitor. He is, therefore, no longer bound to external laws in his freedom, and no longer arrested by any moral codes in his self-liberation. He is capable of acting freely at will in accordance with his varying opportunities and circumstances without necessarily restricting himself to the "good examples set by his wise predecessors."

He never hesitates to visit the shops of wine-dealers and fishmongers with his wine container in his hand when he goes to the city. But this is far from meaning that he is drowned in rice-wine and passions like ordinary men of the world. In this way, he prompts the enlightenment of the other people who are agonized in the darkness of this world. When he is through with his work, he returns home, supported by his walking stick, as traceless and nonattached as a clear running stream.

There is a poem about the person who is returning home surrounded by falling blossoms after having left home for the fragrant grasses of delusions. This poem seems to be in perfect keeping with the man at this ultimate stage of enlightenment, as if it were specially composed in his honor. It goes without saying that this is due to the operation of the power of Zen enlightenment, that is, the self-receptive and self-effective power of samadhi, which seeks nothing outside the mind, "passing through the brushwood gate all alone."

Thus, if we are capable of becoming horses to visit the house in the east and becoming oxen to play in the house in the west in our absolute freedom, with everything left to the care of Heaven, we are also capable of acting freely, playing in samadhi. We will then be one with all our surroundings in harmonious unity with light and integration with dust, completely transformed into things around us. And yet, we spontaneously turn "even wine-dealers and fishmongers into Buddhas" in spite of ourselves. What makes it possible for us to do all these things must indeed be the tremendously great power of concentration nurtured in samadhi. I must say in conclusion that it is truly the life of Zen Mind to make it possible for us to live in the state of freedom and serenity, leaving everything unforeseen to the benevolent provision of destiny as it really is, wherever we may be in this world of actuality.

Budo Dojo, Daihonzan Chozen-ji, Honolulu.

Epilogue

Recently a number of Europeans and Americans, fearing that their modern civilization is at stake, have visited Japan to be trained in Zen. Among them are those who eagerly seek to be disciplined in the traditional Zen monasteries, wearing the Buddhist robes and having their hair shaven.

What do such people think of Zen Buddhism?

Judging from my own personal experiences, these people do not always treat Zen as one of the Buddhist sects. A few years ago, or, to be exact, in the spring of 1968, I was visited by Dora Kalff, a Swiss psychoanalyst and distinguished disciple of the famous Dr. Jung. In the course of her visit she called Zen "education as experience."

"Education in Europe has been based on the acquisition of knowledge. It has already been developed to its limits and is now on the point of collapsing. There is nothing but the traditional Eastern method of education as experience which may possibly save our education from its present crisis." So saying, this psychoanalyst asked me several questions about Zen.

Some time after her visit, a Fritz Buri came to visit me and asked me about Zen. He was on his way back to Switzerland after having taught theology and philosophy at the International Christian University in Tokyo as an exchange professor. Toward the end of his visit with me, he summarized the dialogue that took place in the course of our interview, "As far as I understand, Zen is something most essential to us, forming the basis of World Culture, rather than one sect of Buddhism. Is this idea of Zen wrong?"

Again, I was visited twice by Trevor Leggett from England. The first visit was in the fall of the year before last (1970), and the second in the spring of this year (1972). He is Director of the Department of Japanese Culture in the British Broadcasting Corporation. He is also known for his book titled *A First Zen Reader*.[1] He said to me,

> European culture is characterized by its proclivity for duality and opposition within itself. In its individual fields it has developed highly, but it has no unifying principle to fundamentally unite these individual fields. For this reason, European culture is now confronted with a crisis and the creation of a new kind of culture is crucial. In order to create a new culture, there must be a unifying principle such as Zen that can be shared by all those mutually opposing and conflicting fields of contemporary culture.

It is in this way that we anticipate the contribution of Japanese culture to ours. I think that Japan owes her present prosperity to European culture. To return thanks to our culture, shouldn't Japanese culture in turn contribute to the liberation of ours from its present crisis?

These are but three examples of remarks I have directly heard from Western visitors. Needless to say, conclusions on the whole cannot be based on them, but, just as we can tell the concentration of salt in the ocean by analyzing one drop of seawater, I can safely say that these few instances suggest, even in part, how Zen is viewed by informed people abroad.

I am now going to discuss this point further in terms of an essay, "Zen and Western People" by Professor Phillips, an American philosopher. This paper is presented in Master Tsuji Somei's *Zen Shukyo ni Tsuite no Jugo Sho*.[2]

To begin with, Professor Phillips asks himself, "What has caused the tremendous interest in Zen in the Western world these days?" He answers his own question by writing about Suzuki Daisetz and his success in almost single-handedly making the Western world recognize the huge spiritual heritage called Zen.

The professor continues that, "notwithstanding the tremendous indebtedness of the West to Suzuki's lifelong efforts, he has, in fact, only played his role as a mediator between Zen and the demand for it which already exists in the Western world."

Well, what does "the demand for it which already exists in the Western world" mean?

For the period of at least four hundred years, people in the West have been suffering from spiritual hunger and thirst. Their hunger and thirst are becoming increasingly intensified as it is getting clearer and clearer that they will never be cured by the religious resources intrinsic to the Western culture. The ultimate demands of human spirit are directed toward the absolute basis of human life.

In spite of this fact, however, "most of the above-mentioned demands exist as insatiable demands due to the erosive influences of modern learning and mode of life on the traditional religions of the West." According to the analysis carried out by Professor Phillips, "Zen seems to offer a key to the possibility for many Westerners to tide over their present spiritual crises." This opinion of Professor Phillips is shared by all of the three European scholars introduced above.

In what respect does Professor Phillips write that "Zen seems to offer the possibility" for them "to tide over their present spiritual crises"? He writes,

> When human races are making rapid progress from their former state of segregation to the unified state of the "One World," their religions must likewise emerge out of their present provincialism to join forces with the 'One World.' There is no true cosmopolitan religion except Zen.

It is from this viewpoint that Professor Phillips praises the absolute universality of Zen which is free from any conceptualized creed. Further, it is for this reason that Zen "can transcend the collision of science and religion" and is thought to have the power to integrate the dualities of all things in their mutual conflicts.

In conclusion, Professor Phillips contends that the limitations of all religions in both the East and the West lie in their supernaturalism or belief in the world to come, and that, in these religions, our actual life in this reality is deemed to be "inferior to the Ultimate Existence" which transcends it. But Zen is an exception, for, in his opinion, "Zen seeks to sublimate life as such in an absolute way."

According to him, it is the great characteristic of Zen "to lead human beings to the appreciation of the actuality of life, or speaking more precisely, the life of actuality, instead of guiding us toward the existence beyond our actual life here and now."

As you must have noticed in Chapter 5 and in Chapter 7, I would not hesitate to say that Professor Phillips' opinion of Zen conforms to mine in general. I have the impression that Professor Phillips is a little different from the other Western scholars who visited me, for he deems Zen to be the true "cosmopolitan religion," whereas Kalff, Buri, and Leggett refrain from using the word "religion."[3]

As I have introduced above, Professor Phillips writes, on the one hand, "There is no true cosmopolitan religion except Zen." On the other hand, however, he writes elsewhere, "What Zen seeks is the wholehearted and wholespirited mode of life stemming from the 'true self' which is the very thing discovered and advocated by Zen. This is one reason why the power of Zen is so appealing to Westerners." Professor Phillips' viewpoint coincides with mine. As I wrote at the beginning of this book, I contend that Zen is to "know one's True Self." I wonder, however, if this brief definition of Zen does in fact conform with Professor Phillips' idea of Zen as a "religion."

It is beyond my knowledge to define Zen in terms of religion. But I can say at least that Zen seems to be different from what is called "religion." If Zen has to be defined as a religion at all, it should be called a meditation type of religion.

Few people today are aware of the fact that during the Sung Dynasty of China, more than nine hundred years ago, the word "religion" (Jpn. *shukyo*; Chin. *tsung-chiao*) was already in use. In the fifth article titled *Suiji* (Ch'ui-shih) in *Hekigan Roku* (Pi-yen Lu) we read, "In order to believe in religion at all, it is essential for us to become men of superior spirituality." Also, at the beginning of the tenth article titled *Hyosho* (P'ing-ch'ang), we read, "In order to believe in religion at all, it is essential for us to have the eyes of the teacher to see into the Origin." "Tsung" of "*Tsung-chiao*" signifies "meaning" and "honorable." Probably people in those days used this character "tsung" in the sense of the essence of various teachings or the honorable teachings of Shakyamuni. If so, religion must indeed be the ultimate and fundamental teaching of what human beings should be. It is also the same as what Professor Phillips calls the "wholehearted and whole-spirited mode of life stemming from one's True Self."

I wonder if the word "religion," in its original sense, pertains only to the union of the descendants of Adam and Eve (accused of the original sin) with the omniscient and omnipotent God, the Creator, through the intermediary Jesus, and not to the "wholehearted and whole-spirited mode of life stemming from one's True Self." Religion has recently come to be defined as the "determinant factor of man's ultimate attitude." It seems to me that the latest tendency of religion to lead us to the "One World" has begun to be revealed here, too.

Well, contrary to our expectation that the epoch-making development of science and technology would bring about the most supreme blessings to human beings, the modern world has begun to reveal itself as the most disturbed period unprecedented in the history of the human race.

The sense of self-alienation, the sense of futility, and the sense of frustration, with which we are possessed, are becoming more and more prevalent in our modern life, causing us to lose sight of how to live rewarding lives. This is the proof of our loss of "the ultimate center or the ultimate foundation of life," as Professor Phillips points out above. Why have we thus come to be alienated from the ultimate foundation of life? It is because we have come to find it difficult to adapt our human nature to the rapidly changing external conditions of human life due to the remarkable development of science and industrial technology, as already pointed out by Arnold Toynbee if my memory is correct.

At this turn of our era, we must go beyond the age of science in order to ask anew what human beings are and to inquire into our True Selves. And by so doing, we must try to ground our True Selves and make efforts to restore humanity.

Zen, which has its origin in India, was introduced to Japan through China on its gradual eastward journey. As I have already mentioned, Zen is now ardently sought by some European and American people out of their need to solve the problems of their lives and societies. Zen will have to continue its long eastward journey to America, and still further to Europe in order to establish a new mode of life as an expression of the True Self, and also to offer "the ultimate center or the ultimate foundation of life" to the people living there.

Only with this possible contribution of Zen as the pivot will world history be able to take a remarkable turn from the age of science to that of human beings. I join Professor Phillips in thinking that "it is essential for Zen to create a new 'vehicle' as the medium of self-expression" for the salvation of contemporary civilization from its crisis.

Appendices

Notes

Preface

1 Shakyamuni. (Skt.) Literally "Sage of the Shakya Clan," the founder of Buddhism.

2 Zazen. (Jpn.) Zen meditation.

3 Kawajiri Hogin, *Zazen no Shokei* (The Shortcut to *Zazen*) (Tokyo: Sumiya-sho-ten, 1909).

4 Harada Sogaku, *Sanzen no Hiketsu* (The Essence of Zen Discipline) (Tokyo: Do-ai Kai, 1936).

5 Seki Seisetsu. Japanese Zen master. 1877–1945. Former Archbishop of Tenryu-ji, Kyoto.

6 Seki Bukuo. Japanese Zen master. 1903–1991. Former Archbishop of Tenryu-ji, Kyoto.

Chapter 1   Why Do Zazen

1 Imazu Kogaku, *Shishi Sojo Ron* (A Treatise on the Transmission of the Teaching from the Master to the Student) (Publisher and Date unknown).

2 *Samadhi*. (Skt.) A state of complete concentration and relaxation.

3 Lin-chi I-hsuan. Chinese Zen Master. d. 867. (Jpn., Rinzai Gigen). The phrase comes from his work, *Lin-chi Lu* (Jpn. Rinzai Roku) (Record of the Words of Lin-chi) (Publisher and Date Unknown).

4 Tariki (Other Power) Buddhism calls for reliance on the saving grace of Amida Buddha.

5 Ching-ch'ing Tao-fu. Chinese Zen Master. 868–937. (Jpn., Kyosho Dofu).

6 Hsuan-sha Shih-pei. Chinese Zen Master. 835–908. (Jpn., Gensha Shibi).

Chapter 2   The Aim of Zazen

1 Bodhidharma. (Skt.) (Chin. P'u-ti-ta-mo). (Jpn. Bodaidaruma or Daruma). 470–543. The first patriarch of Chinese Zen.

2 *Prajna*. (Skt.) Transcendental Wisdom.

3 *Zazen-gi* is the Japanese title of the 12th century Chinese text, *Tso-ch'an I* (How to Practice *Zazen*). Because this text is so widely quoted by Omori Roshi throughout this book, we will continue to use the title of the Japanese edition: Choro Sosaku, trans., *Tso-ch'an I* (Jpn. Zazen-gi) (How to Practice *Zazen*) (Kyoto: Institute of Zen Studies, date unknown).

4 Harada, *Sanzen no Hiketsu*.

5 Nanin Zengu. Japanese Zen Master. 1835–1904. Former head priest of Ryu-un-in, Tokyo.

6 Kuei-feng Tsung-mi. Chinese Zen Master. 780–841. (Jpn. Keiho Shumitsu). The following classification comes from his book, *Ch'an-yuan Chu Ch'uan-chi Tu Hsu* (Jpn. Zengon Sho Senshu Tsujo) (Preface to the Selected Collection of Various Zen Sources) (Publisher and

date unknown).

7 *Dharma.* (Skt.) The Ultimate Truth.

8 Daikaku. Japanese Zen Master. 1213–1278. Also known as Rankei Doryu. The following quotations came from his work, *Zazen Ron* (A Treatise on *Zazen*) (Publisher and date unknown).

9 *Satori* (Jpn.) Enlightenment.

10 The inscription was four Chinese characters: *ha* means wave and can also be read as *nami*; *hei* means calm or flat and can be read as *taira* or *hira*; *gyo* means discipline and can be read as *yuku* or *yuki*; and *an* means easy and can be read as *yasushi* or *yasu*.

11 *Tathagata.* (Skt.) (Jpn. Nyorai). Literally, "the-thus-gone-one." Refers to one who on the way of truth has attained supreme enlightment.

12 *Kensho.* (Jpn.) Seeing your true nature, or enlightenment.

13 Ma-tsu Tao-i. Chinese Zen Master. 707–786. (Jpn., Baso Doitsu).

14 Nan-yueh Huai-jang. Chinese Zen Priest. 677–744. (Jpn., Nangaku Ejo).

15 Tao-hsuan, comp., *Ching-te ch'uan-teng-lu* (Jpn. Keitoku Dento-roku) (The Record of the Transmission of Light) (1004).

16 Dogen Zenji. Japanese Zen master, 1200–1253, who brought the tradition of the Soto School from China to Japan. The reference is from his work, *Shobo-genzo* (Treasure Chamber of the Eye of True *Dharma*) (Publisher and date unknown).

17 Tao-hsuan, *Ching-te Ch'uan Teng Lu.*

18 Hirai Tomio, *Zen Meditation and Psychotherapy* (Tokyo: Japan Publications, Inc., 1989). Although Omori Roshi's original source is unknown, this research has been published in English.

19 Kanbe Tadao, "*Zenjo to Noha* (Zen Concentration and Brain Waves)," *Shinri Zen*, Volume unknown (Date unknown).

20 Suzuki Shosan. Japanese Soto Zen Master. 1579–1655. Advocate of a vigorous form of Zen that he called Nio Zen after the two Nio, or deities, that guard the entrance to Buddhist temples.

21 Jizo. (Jpn.) A small statue, sculpted in stone, of a bodhisattva who vowed to deliver all people from this suffering world.

22 Suzuki Shosan, *Roankyo* (Donkey-Saddle Bridge) (Collected by Echu, 1660).

23 Hakuin Ekaku, Japanese Rinzai Zen Master. 1689–1769. One of the most important Japanese Rinzai Zen Masters. He is often referred to as the father of modern Rinzai Zen.

24 Dokyo Etan. Japanese Rinzai Zen Master. 1642–1721.

25 Daito Kokushi. Japanese Rinzai Zen Master. 1282–1338. The founder of Daitoku-ji in Kyoto. Also referred to as Shuho Myocho.

26 Kawajiri, *Zazen no Shokei.*

27 Hata Shinji, *Makoto no Michi* (The Way of Truth) (Publisher and date unknown).

28 *Rohatsu sesshin.* (Jpn.) The intense training period held in commemoration of the training that led to Shakyamuni's enlightenment on the eighth of December.

[29] The story comes from Hakuin's essay, *Rohatsu Jishu*, that appears in Torei Enji's compilation *Goke Sansho Yoro Mon* (The Gate to the Details of the Essence to the Way of the Patriarchs of the Five Branches of Zen) (1827).

[30] Hui-neng Ta-chien. 638–713. (Jpn., Eno Daikan). The quotation comes from his work, *Liu-tsu-ta-shih fa-pao-t'an-ching* (Jpn. Rokuso daishi hobodan-gyo) (The Platform Sutra of the Sixth Patriarch) (Publisher and date unknown). Also known by its short title, *T'an-ching* (Jpn. Dan-gyo).

[31] Machimoto Donku, *Kanchu Jubu Roku* (Head Notes to Ten Zen Texts) (Kyoto: Baiyo-shoten, 1913).

[32] Hannya Shingyo. (Jpn.) Abbreviation of the full Japanese title, *Maka hannyaharamita shingyo*, translated from the original Sanskrit *Mahaprajnaparamita-hridaya-sutra*. A sutra presenting the essence of the transcendental wisdom of the Emptiness. Shortest of the four sutras that constitute the *Prajnaparamita-sutra*, also referred to as the Heart Sutra.

[33] Hui-neng Ta-chien, *Liu-tsu-ta-shih fa-pao-t'an-ching*.

[34] Dogen Zenji, *Shobo-genzo*, *Genjo Koan* volume.

[35] Iida Toin. Japanese Soto Zen Master. 1863–1937. The comment comes from his book, *Sanzen Manroku* (A Random Record of Sanzen Interviews With the Zen Master) (Tokyo: Chu-o Bu'kyo-sha, 1934).

[36] Imazeki Tenpo, trans., *Shina Zengaku no Hensen* (The Transformation of the Study of Zen in China) (Tokyo: Toho-gakugei-shoin, 1936). This is a translation of Hu Shih's book; the original Chinese title is unknown.

[37] Iida, *Sanzen Manroku*.

[38] Naval engagement in the Shimonoseki Straits on April 25, 1185. The conclusive battle of the Heike-Genji War, ending in the destruction of the Heike and the rise of the Genji for political control.

[39] *Shikantaza*. (Jpn.) Nothing but precisely sitting. A form of the practice of *zazen*. This term is frequently used in Soto Zen.

[40] Iida, *Sanzen Manroku*.

[41] Ashikaga Takauji. 1305–1358. Warrior chieftain; head of the Ashikaga family and founder of the Muromachi Shogunate (1338–1573).

[42] *Hara*. (Jpn.) Literally, *hara* refers to the lower abdomen, but it has a much broader pschological and spiritual connotation as well.

[43] Dogen, *Shobo-genzo*.

Chapter 3   How to Sit in Zen Meditation

[1] Otsuki Fumihiko, *Daigenkai* (Dictionary of Chinese Characters) (Publisher and date unknown).

[2] Choro, *Zazen-gi*.

[3] Dogen Zenji, *Shobo-genzo*, *Bendowa* volume.

[4] Right View. One of the precepts of the Eightfold Noble Path, so called because it leads to nirvana (perfect liberation). The eight divisions are: 1) *Shoken* (right view), 2) *Shoshiyui* (right thinking), 3) *Shogo* (right speech), 4) *Shogyo* (right action), 5) *Shomyo* (right livelihood), 6) *Shoshojin* (right endeavor), 7) *Shonen* (right memory), 8) *Shojyo* (right meditation).

[5] T'ien-t'ai. 538–598. The third patriarch of the T'ien-t'ai (Tendai) sect of Buddhism, he is also referred to as Master Chih'i (Jpn. Chisha). His writings are collected in a work known as *Makashikan* (Chn. Mo-ho Chih-kuan) (Discourse on Mahayana Meditation and Contemplation). There is also an abridged form of this work called *Shoshikan* (Hsiao Chih-kuan).

[6] *Sesshin*. (Jpn.) Literally "Collecting (*Setsu*) the Mind (*Shin*)." Several day period of especially intensive, strict practice of *zazen* as carried out in Zen Monasteries at regular intervals.

[7] *Stupa*. (Skt.) Originally stupas were memorial monuments built over the mortal remains of the historical Buddha and other saints. They are the characteristic expression of Buddhist architecture.

[8] Daruma. (Jpn.) Refers to the common Japanese depiction of Bodhidharma without arms or legs.

[9] *Saika tanden*. (Jpn.) The point of strength in the lower abdomen, the center of tension.

[10] Sato Tsuji, *Shisei no Tetsuri* (The Philosophical Principle of Postures) (Publisher and date unknown).

[11] Itsuzan Sojin. Japanese Rinzai Zen Master. (18th century). Master Itsuzan was the religious successor of Zen Master Bankei. The passage is from his book, *Keiko Kakun* (Family Precepts of Keiko) (Publisher and date unknown).

[12] Dogen Zenji, *Shobo-genzo*, *Shin-shin Gakudo* volume.

[13] Dogen Zenji, *Fukan Zazen-gi* (Manual of *Zazen*) (Publisher and date unknown). This is a general presentation of the principles of *zazen*.

[14] T'ien-t'ai, *Mo ho Chih-kuan*.

[15] T'ien-t'ai, *Hsiao Chih-kuan*.

[16] Takeuchi Daishin. Japanese Physician. Dates unknown.

[17] No citation provided for this book.

[18] *Kendo*. (Jpn.) Japanese Fencing; swordsmanship. Literally "The Way (*Do*) of the Sword (*Ken*)."

[19] Omori Sogen, *Ken to Zen* (Swordsmanship and Zen) (Tokyo: Shun-jusha, 1966).

[20] Yamamoto Genpo. Japanese Rinzai Zen Master. The comment is from his book, *Mumonkan Teisho* (Lectures on *Mumonkan*) (Tokyo: Dai-horin-kaku Co. Ltd., 1960).

[21] *Koan*. (Jpn.) A kind of paradox presented by the Zen teacher to his disciple.

Kufu. (Jpn.) The work needed to achieve a solution.

[22] Ito Nobujiro, trans., *Shoshikan* (Chin. Hsiao Chih-kuan) (Publisher and date unknown).

[23] Jinbo Nyoten and Ando Bunei, eds., *Zengaku Jiten* (A Dictionary of Zen Studies) (Tokyo: Mugasan-bo, 1915).

[24] Muso Soseki. 1275–1351. Also known as Muso Kokushi (National Teacher). A Japanese Rinzai Zen Master who made a major contribution to the spread of Zen in Japan. He was the founder of Tenryu-ji, one of the great *daihonzan* (headquarters temple) in Kyoto. The following passage comes from his book, *Muchu Mondo* (The Dialogue in Dream) (Privately published by Otaka Shigenari in 1344).

[25] Kawajiri, *Zazen no Shokei*.

[26] The *koan* of Mu. (Jpn.) One of the most famous Zen *koan*, it is the first *koan* in *Mumonkan* (Wu-men-kuan), the collection made by Mumon Ekai (Wu-men Hui-k'ai).

[27] Chu Hsi. Chinese Neo-Confucianist philosopher. 1130–1200. (Jpn. Shushi).

[28] Torei Enji. 1721–1792. Japanese Rinzai Zen Master, the successor of Zen Master Hakuin. The following passage comes from his work, *Shumon Mujinto Ron* (A Treatise on the Inexhaustible Light of the Religious Gate) (Publisher and date unknown).

[29] Wu-men Hui-k'ai. Chinese Zen Master. 1183–1260. (Jpn. Mumon Ekai). The following commentary is from his compilation, *Wu-men-kuan* (Jpn. Mumonkan) (The Gateless Gate), one of the most important *koan* collections in Zen literature.

[30] Pai-chang Huai-hai. Chinese Zen Master. 720–814. (Jpn. Hyakujo Ekai).

[31] Miyamoto Musashi. 1584–1645. Master swordsman and painter of the Edo period.

[32] *Go*. (Jpn.) A game of strategy that uses black and white stones on a square board.

[33] Yamaoka Tesshu. 1836–1888. Famous Japanese Sword Master of the Muto School, the Master Calligrapher of Jyuboku School and also known as a Lay Zen Master.

Chapter 4   Things to Pay Attention to during Meditation

[1] Hida Haramitsu, *Nikon no Shimei* (Mission of Japan) (Publisher and date unknown).

[2] Suzuki, *Roankyo*.

[3] Hakuin Ekaku, *Neboke no Mezamashi* (Waking Up From Dreaming) (Publisher and date unknown).

[4] Bankei Eitaku, Japanese Rinzai Zen Master. 1622–1693. He is famous for his teaching of *Fu-sho Zen* (Unborn Mind Zen). The following is from his work, *Bucchi Kozai Zenji Hogo* (The Religious Sayings of Master Bucchi Kosai) (Publisher and date unknown).

[5] Bankei Eitaku, *Gojimon Sho* (Notes on *Dharma* Instructions)

[6] Priest Honen. 1133–1212. The founder of Japanese Jodo (Pure Land) School.

[7] *Amida Buddha*. (Jpn.) (Skt. Amita). The Buddha in the Western Pure Land.

[8] *Huai-nan-tzu*. (Jpn. Enanji). A Chinese Classic written in the Former Han Dynasty (140–1) by guests attached to the Court of Liu An, Prince of Huai-nan.

[9] Ta-hui Tsung-kao. Chinese Zen Master. 1089–1163. (Jpn. Daie Soko). The source for the following quotation in unknown.

[10] Kawajiri, *Zazen no Shokei*.

[11] Takeda Mokurai. Japanese Rinzai Zen Master. 1854–1930. Former Archbishop of Kenni-ji in Kyoto. The quote is from his book, *Zen no Katsatsu* (Zen Enlivening and Zen Killing) (Tokyo: Chu-o-shu'pan-sha, 1931).

[12] This is similar to trying to get to San Francisco but arriving in Chicago instead.

[13] Kawajiri, *Zazen no Shokei*.

[14] If the answers are merely words, they do not fulfill the purpose of *koan* which is to demonstrate the state of being of the answer.

[15] Myo-gen Anshu, *Koan Kaito Shu* (The Collection of Answers to Koan) (Tokyo: Daiyu-sha, 1922)

[16] Chung-feng Ming-pan. Chinese Rinzai Zen master. 1263–1323. (Jpn., Chuho Myohon). The following is from his work, *The Night Talk in the Mount T'ien-mu* (Publisher and date unknown). The original Chinese title is unknown.

[17] Ta-hui Tsung-kao, *Fa Lun* (Jpn. Hogo) (A Book of Religious Teachings) (Publisher and date unknown).

[18] See Chapter 7 for a discussion of the *Ten Oxherding Pictures*.

[19] Tokugawa Ieyasu. 1543–1616. The warrior chieftain who emerged as the successful survivor of Japan's late 16th century wars of unification and went on to set up the Tokugawa Shogunate.

[20] Mino. (Jpn.) Japanese rice paper, approximately 10" by 14".

[21] Early 20th Century.

[22] *Judo*. (Jpn.) Japanese martial art. Literally "The Gentle (*Ju*) Way (*Do*)."

[23] *Dojo*. (Jpn.) Literally "The Hall (*Jo*) of the Way (*Do*)." A hall or room in which one of the Japanese "Ways" (*Do*) of spiritual-practical training if practiced. In its original Sanskrit meaning, it is the "place of enlightenment."

[24] Harada, *Sanzen no Hiketsu*.

[25] Dogen, *Gakudo Yojinshu* (A Collection of Precautions in Zen Discipline) (Publisher and date unknown).

[26] Torei, *Shumon Mujinto Ron*.

[27] Hsuan-ts'e (Jpn. Gensaku). Chinese Zen Master. Dates Unknown. The successor of the Sixth Patriarch.

[28] Yung-chia Hsuan-chueh (Yoka Genkaku). Chinese Zen Master. 665–713.

[29] *Bodhi*. (Skt.) Enlightenment.

[30] Dogen, *Shobo-genzo*, *Reihai Tokuzui* volume.

[31] Kawajiri Hogin, *Zazen no Shokei*.

[32] Torei Enji, *Shumon Mujinto Ron*.

[33] Ryogon Kyo. (Jpn.) (Skt., Shurangama) The "Sutra of the Heroic One."

[34] *Gakudo Jasei Meikan* (The Book of the Right and the Wrong Ways of Learning) (Tokyo: Rosho-Kai, 1926).

[35] *Vijnapti-matrata*. (Skt.) (Chin. Wei-shih Lun). (Jpn. Yuishiki).The "consciousness-only"

doctrine, which explains all phenomena as manifestation of one's consciousness, of which the eighth, called *Alaya*, is the basic one. Hisao Inagaki, *A Dictionary of Japanese Buddhist Terms* (Kyoto: Nagata Bunshodo, 1984).

[36] Ch'ang-sha Ching-ts'en. Chinese Zen Master. d. 868. (Jpn. Chosha Keijin). The source of the following quotation is unknown.

[37] Hakuin Ekaku, *Kaian Kokugo* (Tales from the Land of Locust-tree Tranquility) (1750).

[38] T'ien-t'ai (Jpn. Tendai), *Hsiao Chih-kuan* (Jpn. Shoshikan).

[39] Ch'eng-yuan. Chinese Zen Master. 908–987.

[40] Harada Sogaku, *Sanzen no Hiketsu*.

[41] The "five desires" which arise in connection with the five senses of form, sound, smell, taste and touch. Also, the desire for wealth, sex, food and drink, fame, and sleep. Hisao Inagaki, *A Dictionary of Japanese Buddhist Terms*.

[42] The "seven emotions" are joy, anger, sadness, pleasure, love, hate, and greed.

[43] Yamada Mumon. Japanese Rinzai Zen master. 1900–1988. Former Archbiship of Myoshin-ji. The source for the following story is unknown.

[44] Tung-kao Hsin-yueh. Chinese Zen Master. (1642–1696).

[45] Tokugawa Mitsukuni. 1607–1678. The second Lord of the Mito domain, now part of Ibaraki Prefecture, Japan.

[46] Iida, *Sanzen Manroku*.

[47] Bassui Tokusho. Japanese Zen Master. 1327–1387. The following quote comes from his work, *Kana Hogo* (The Buddhist Teachings Written in Kana) (Publisher and date unknown).

[48] Hakuin, *Oniazami* (Thistle) (1751).

[49] Myocho Shuho. Japanese Zen Master. 1282–1338. Daito Kokushi is the honorific title awarded to Myocho posthumously. Founder of Daitoku-ji in Kyoto. The source of the poem is unknown.

[50] Ikkyu Sojun. Rinzai Zen Master. 1394–1481. The source of the verse is from, *Hogo* (The Buddhist Teachings) (Publisher and date unknown).

[51] Shido Bunan. Japanese Rinzai Zen master. 1602–1676. The source of the quotation is his *Soku-shin Ki* (a collection of Bunan's teachings).

[52] Tokugawa Hidetada. 1579–1632. Second Shogun of the Tokugawa Shogunate (1603–1867), the third son of its founder, Tokugawa Ieyasu.

[53] Suzuki Daisetz Teitaro. 1870–1966. A Japanese Buddhist scholar and practitioner, one of the best known modern interpreters of Zen in the West.

[54] Noh. (Jpn.) The oldest extant professional theater; a form of musical dance-drama originating in the 14th century.

[55] Suzuki, *Roankyo*.

[56] Suzuki, *Roankyo*.

[57] Wang Yang-ming. Chinese Philosopher of the Ming Era (1368–1661). 1473–1529. (Jpn.

O Yomei). The story is from his work, *Ch'uan-hsi Lu* (Denshu Roku) (Record of Instructions) (Publisher and date unknown).

58 Yuan-wu K'o-ch'in, *Pi-Yen Lu* (Jpn. Hekigan Roku) (The Blue Cliff Record) (12th century). This famous Chinese Zen text is composed of a series of one hundred lectures given by Yuan-we K'o-ch'in (1063–1135), a famous master in the 4th generation of the Yang-Ch'i line of Lin-Chi (Rinzai) Zen.

59 O Yomei (Wang Yang-ming). The source for this quotation is unknown.

60 Chu-hung, comp., *Ch'an-Kuan Ts'e-chin* (Jpn. Zenkan Sakushin) (How to Go Through the Barriers to Zen Enlightenment) (1600).

61 Ui Hakujyu, *Daini Zenshu Shi Kenkyu* (The Second Study of the History of Buddhism) (Tokyo: Iwanami-shoten, 1935).

62 Hui-neng Ta-chien, *Liu-tsu-ta-shih fa-pao-t'an-ching* (The Platform Sutra of the Sixth Patriarch).

63 "This sutra expounds the profound principle of Mahayana and refutes Hinayana through the mouth of the layman bodhisattva Vimalakirti." Hisao, *Japanese Buddhist Terms*.

64 The irony of Sariputra's explanation becomes more clear as you continue reading. Sariputra thought he was sitting in serene repose but he was scolded by Vimalakirti for sitting in "vain silence," meaning Vimalakirti still saw duality in Sariputra's condition.

65 Nirvana. (Jpn.) Literally, extinction. The state of perfect liberation.

66 Hui-yen Chih-chao, comp., *Jen-t'ien Yen-mu* (Jpn. Ninden Ganmoku) (The Essence of Man and Heaven) (1188).

67 Torei Enji, *Goke Sansho Yoro Mon*.

68 Shen-hsiu. Chinese Zen Master. 605–706. (Jpn. Jinshu). One of the principal students of Hung-jen, the Fifth Patriarch of Zen.

69 Hung-jen. The Fifth Patriarch of Zen in China. 601–674. (Jpn. Gunin).

70 Nampo Shomyo (1235–1309, also known as Daio Kokushi), Shuho Myocho (1282–1338, also known as Daito Kokushi), and Kanzan Egen (1277–1360, also known as Muso Daishi).

71 Imakita Kosen. Japanese Rinzai Zen Master. 1816–1892. Former Archbishop of Engaku-ji, Kamakura. Known as the first Zen teacher of D. T. Suzuki.

72 Shibayama Zenkei. Japanese Zen Master. 1894–1975. Former Archbishop of Nanzen-ji. The following reference is to his book, *Rinzai Zen no Seikaku* (The Characteristics of Rinzai Zen) (Tokyo: Rokuya-on, 1951).

73 Author unknown, *Ta-ch'eng-ch'i-hsin-lun* (Jpn. Daijo Kishin Ron) (Treatise on the Awakening of Faith in Mahayana Buddhism) (Publisher and date unknown). One of the basic texts of Mahayana Buddhism, used by most of its major schools.

74 Takamagahara. (Jpn.) Literally, High Celestial Plain. Standard term for the abode of the heavenly divinities in Japanese mythology.

75 The Ten Oxherding Pictures. (Chin., Shih-niu-t'u) (Jpn., Jugyu-zu). Illustrations of ten

stages of Zen discipline. The best known series comes from the Chinese Zen Master K'uo-an Chih-yuan.

[76] Hakuin Zenji, *Zazen Wasan* (Song of Zazen) (Publisher, date and volume unknown).

[77] *Shiku Seigan Mon.* (Jpn.) The Four Great Vows:

However innumerable beings are, I vow to save them;

However inexhaustible the passions are, I vow to extinguish them;

However immeasurable the Dharmas are, I vow to master them;

However incomparable the Buddha-truth is, I vow to attain it.

Suzuki, Daisetz Teitaro. *A Manual of Zen Buddhism* (New York: Causeway, 1974)

[78] Tekisui Giboku. Japanese Rinzai Zen Master. 1822–1899. Former Archbishop of Tenryu-ji, Kyoto. Also referred to as Yuri Giboku.

Chapter 5   Physiological Effects

[1] Chao-chou Ts'ung-shen, Chinese Zen Master. 778–897. (Jpn. Joshu). One of the most important Zen Masters of China, but more commonly known by the Japanese reading of his name.

[2] The source of this quotation is noted as an article from the *Tokyo Asashi* newspaper from "some years ago."

[3] Hasegawa Usaburo, *Igaku Zen* (Medical Zen) (Osaka: Sogen-sha, 1958).

[4] Takeuchi Daishin, *Itsu made no Wakaku Nagaku Kenko de Ikiru Okugi Sho* (A Book of Initiation into the Way of Living Forever Young and Healthy) (Publisher and date unknown).

[5] Hirata Kurakichi, *Suwari no Kenkyu* (A Study of Meditation) (Tokyo: Sanga-bo, 1939).

[6] Sato Tsuji, *Shintai Ron* (A Treatise on the Human Body) (Publisher and date unknown).

[7] Ueno Yoichi, *Za no Seiri Shinriteki Kenkyu* (A Physiological and Psychological Study of Meditation) (Tokyo: Shoshin-doai-kai, 1938).

[8] Takahashi Deishu. 1835–1903. Master of *Yari* (Japanese Spear Fighting). Yamaoka Tesshu's brother-in-law.

Katsu Kaishu. 1823–1899. Statesman active during transition from the Tokugawa Shogunate (1603–1867) to the new Meiji government.

Yamaoka Tesshu. 1836–1888. Swordsman and retainer of the Tokugawa Shogunate active during the Meiji Restoration (1868).

[9] Kobosawa Kan, *Nigemuzu* (Mirage) (Tokyo: Chuo-koron-sha, 1961).

[10] Yoshimoto Noboru, ed., *Hikawa Seiwa* (The Collection of Kaishu's Talk) (1898).

[11] *Goi-Kenchuto.* (Jpn.) The Fifth Rank of the Five Ranks of Zen teaching, which pertains to the middle road between simultaneously affirmed and negated discrimination and indiscrimination.

[12] Roughly translated, Itto Shoden Muto Ryu means "the School of One Sword transformed into the Swordless Sword."

[13] Yamada Ittokusai. 1863–1931. Master of Japanese Swordsmanship. 15th headmaster of Jikishinkage Ryu. Also referred to as Yamada Jirokichi.

[14] Harigaya Sekiun. Died 1662. A Master Swordsman.

[15] This story is told in the *Zensho-an Kiroku Bassui* (The Excerpts from the Record of Zensho-an) (Publisher and date unknown).

[16] *Shogi*. (Jpn.) Board game based on strategy.

[17] *Daihorin* (The Great Wheels of *Dharma*). A Buddhist monthly magazine published in Japan.

[18] Takagi Ryoen. Japanese Zen Master. 1842–1918.

[19] Priest Tekisui was not a man of letters, though he excelled in spiritual power. In addition, his sharp wit often bred stubbornness in him. Priest Ryoen, on the contrary, was well-learned. Consequently, he supported Priest Tekisui behind his back, contributing to his distinction in the religious world to a great extent.

[20] *Suramgama-sutra*. (Skt.) (Chin. Leng Yen Ching) (Jpn. Ryogon Kyo) (Sutra of the Heroic One).

[21] Bodhisattva Manjusri. (Skt). (Jpn. Monju Bosatsu).The Bodhisattva of Wisdom.

[22] Takagi Tagaku. Japanese Rinzai Zen Master. 1842–1918. Former Archbishop of Tenryu-ji, Kyoto. Also referred to as Takagi Ryoen.

[23] Yun-men Wen-yen. Chinese Zen Master. 864–949. (Jpn. Unmon Bunen). The founder of Yun-man School, one of the Five Schools of Chinese Zen.

[24] Sugawara Jiho. Japanese Rinzai Zen Master. 19th/20th Century. Archbishop of Kencho-ji, Kamakura.

[25] Hsueh-tou Ch'ung-hsien. Chinese Zen Master. 980–1052. (Jpn. Setcho Juken). The reference to the poem is unknown.

[26] Takeyama Michio, trans., *Japanese title unknown* (Germ. Also Sprach Zarathustra) (Publisher and date unknown).

[27] Tomonaga Sanjyuro, *Kinsei ni Okeru Ware no Jijaku-Shi* (A History of Self-Awareness in the Modern World) (Tokyo: Hobun-kan, 1916).

[28] Chin-niu. Chinese Zen Master. Dates unknown. (Jpn. Kingyu). This story appears in the *Hekigan Roku*.

[29] *Kojiki*. (Jpn.) Records of Ancient Matters. Japan's oldest extant chronicle, recording events from the mythical age of the gods up to the time of Empress Suiko (593–628).

[30] *Kagura*. (Jpn.) Sacred music and dances.

[31] Pai-chang Huai-hai. Chinese Zen Master. 720–814. (Jpn. Hyakujo Ekai). Pai-chang founded the Zen monastic tradition by establishing precise rules for the life and daily routine of a Zen monastery. The rules referred to are found in his work, *Pai-chang ch'ing-kuei* (The Pure Rules Specified by Pai-chang) (Publisher and date unknown).

[32] Omori, *Ken to Zen*.

[33] Wakayama Bokusui. Famous Japanese Poet. 1885–1928. The reference to the poem is

unknown.

34 Futabayama. 1912–1968. 35th *Yokozuna Sumo* (Grand Champion of *Sumo*). The following reference is from his book, *Sumo Kyudo Roku* (The Record of Religious Discipline in
Wrestling) (Publisher and date unknown).

35 Hui-chung (Jpn. Echu). Chinese Zen Master. d. 775.

36 Date Masamune. 1567–1636. Warrior of the Azuchi-Momoyama (1568–1600) and early
Edo (1600–1868) periods.

37 Author unknown, *Chung Yung* (Jpn. Chuyo) (The Doctrine of the Mean) (Publisher and
date unknown). A Classic Chinese text of the Confucian School.

38 Uesugi Kenshin. 1530–1578. Lord during the Sengoku (1467–1568) and Azuchi -
Momoyama (1568–1600) periods.

39 Takeda Shingen. 1521–1573. Lord during the Sengoku (1467–1568) and Azuchi -
Momoyama (1568–1600) periods.

40 Soken. Japanese Soto Zen Master. Died 1570. The teacher of Uesugi Kenshin.

41 Kaisen. Japanese Rinzai Zen Master. Died 1582. Held the title of National Teacher.
Archbishop of Myoshin-ji.

42 Satake Yoshioki. Dates unknown. Lord of Akita domain (now Akita Prefecture, Japan).

43 *Myokonin.* (Jpn.) A simple, uneducated, and enlightened person, usually of the Pure Land
Sect of Buddhism.

44 Bankei, *Gojimon Sho.*

45 The translation comes from Miura and Sasaki's *Zen Dust* (Kyoto: The First Zen Institute
of America, 1966). The original reads as follows:
Tokuun no kankosui
Ikutabi ka myobucho o kudaru
Ta no chiseijin o yatote
Yuki o ninatte tomo ni sei o uzumu.

Chapter 6   Zazen Wasan

1 Ninomiya Sontoku. 1787–1856. Farm technologist and the leading agricultural philosopher of the late Edo period (1600–1868). The following reference is from his work, *Yawa*
(Night Tales) (Publisher and date unknown).

2 Yung-chia Hsuan-chueh (Jpn. Yoka Genkaku). Early Chinese Zen Master (665–713). The
phrase quoted is from *Cheng Tao Ko* (Jpn. Shodoka) (A Song of Enlightenment).

3 Dogen, *Shobo-genzo*, *Genjo Koan* volume.

4 *Saddharmapundarika-sutra.* (Skt.) (Chin. Maio-fa-lien-hua-ching). (Jpn. Myoho Renge
Kyo). The Lotus Sutra.

5 Avolokitesvara. (Skt.) (Jpn. Kannon). One of the most significant bodhisattvas of
Mahayana Buddhism, the embodiment of compassion.

6 Matsuura Seizan. Early 19th century. Lord of Hizen Hirado, now Hirado-city, Nagasaki

Prefecture, Japan. Famous as the Master swordsman of "Shin Kei To Ryu" school of swordsmanship. The following reference comes from his book, *Ken Dan* (Talks on Swordsmanship) (19th Century).

[7] Imakita Kosen, *Zenkai Ichiran* (One Large Wave in the Sea of Zen) (1876).

[8] Ayusmat Nagarjuna. 2nd and 3rd century. (Jpn. Ryuju Sonja). One of the most important philosophers of Buddhism and the founder of Madhyamika School. The following reference comes from his work, *Madhyamikasastra* (Jpn. Churon) (Treatise of the Middle Way) (Publisher and date unknown).

[9] Source unknown.

Chapter 7   The Ten Oxherding Pictures

[1] Tz'u-yuan. Chinese Zen Priest. Dates Unknown. (Jpn. Jion).

[2] K'uo-an Chih-yuan. Chinese Zen Priest. Dates Unknown. (Jpn. Kakuan).

[3] Kukai. Japanese Shingon Priest. 774–835. Founder of the Shingon school of Japanese Buddhism. More commonly referred to as Kobo Daishi.

[4] Saicho. Japanese Tendai Priest. 767–822. Founder of the monastic center on Mount Hiei and of the Japanese Tendai School of Buddhism. Also referred to as Dengyo Daishi.

[5] Tenkai. Japanese Tendai Priest. 1536–1643. Also referred to as Jigen Daishi.

[6] Johann Gottlieb Fichte. 1762–1814. German idealist philosopher.

[7] Friedrich Wilhelm Joseph von Schelling. 1775–1854. German philosopher.

[8] *Karma.* (Skt.) Literally, "Deed." "*Karma* is understood as 1) a mental or physical action; 2) the consequence of a mental or physical action; 3) the sum of all consequences of the actions of an individual in this or some previous life; 4) the chain of cause and effect in the world of morality." Schuhmacher and Woerner, *The Encyclopedia of Eastern Philosophy and Religion.*

[9] *Hamsa-raja.* (Skt.) (Jpn. Gao) Goose-King. An epithet of the Buddha.

[10] *Vajrachchedika-prajnaparamita-sutra.* (Skt.) (Jpn. Kongo Kyo). (Diamond Sutra). "Sutra of the Diamond-cutter of Supreme Wisdom."

[11] According to Omori Rotaishi, for most serious Zen students, it is possible to achieve either stage 2 or stage 3 in this sequence of 10 stages of enlightenment. Almost no one attains stage 4 (Catching the Ox), however. It is only possible with totally committed training and discipline.

[12] Shibayama Zenkei, *Jugyu-zu* (The Ten Oxherding Pictures) (Kyoto: Kobundo-shoten, 1941).

[13] Niu-t'ou Fa-jung. Chinese Zen Master. 594–657. (Jpn. Gozu Hoyu).

[14] Lu Xin-wu. Chinese Scholar. 16th century. (Jpn. Ro Shingo). The following quote comes from his work, *Chinese title unknown* (Jpn. Shingin Go) (Words Sung and Recited) (Publisher and date unknown).

[15] Tao-hsin. Chinese Zen Master. 580–651. (Jpn. Doshin).

[16] Takuan. Japanese Zen Master. 1573–1645. Also referred to as Takuan Soho. The following quote comes from his work, *Fudo Chishin-myoroku* (Immovable Wisdom) (Publisher and date unknown).

Epilogue

[1] Trevor Leggett, *A First Zen Reader* (Rutland, Vermont: Charles E. Tuttle, 1960).

[2] Tsuji Somei. Japanese Rinzai Zen Master. 1903–1991. The following quotations are from Professor Phillip's essay entitled, *Zen and Western People* (Jpn. Zen to Seiyo no Ningen), which is found in Master Tsuji's book, *Zen Shukyo ni Tsuite no Jugo Sho* (Fifteen Chapters on Zen and Religion) (Tokyo: Shunjyu-sha, 1960).

[3] Professor Phillips' words quoted above are not his original words, but the words retranslated from the Japanese translation of his original words in English. The word "religion" used here, of course, would not mean the meditation type but the prayer type of religion.

Lineage

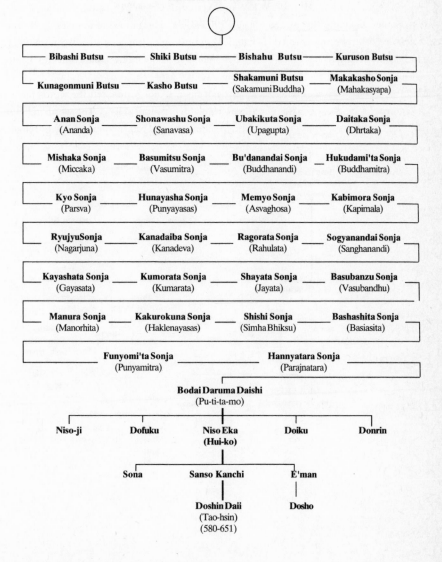

RINZAI ZEN LINEAGE

Bibashi Butsu ——— Shiki Butsu ——— Bishahu Butsu ——— Kuruson Butsu

Kunagonmuni Butsu ——— Kasho Butsu ——— **Shakamuni Butsu** (Sakamuni Buddha) ——— **Makakasho Sonja** (Mahakasyapa)

Anan Sonja (Ananda) ——— **Shonawashu Sonja** (Sanavasa) ——— **Ubakikuta Sonja** (Upagupta) ——— **Daitaka Sonja** (Dhrtaka)

Mishaka Sonja (Miccaka) ——— **Basumitsu Sonja** (Vasumitra) ——— **Bu'danandai Sonja** (Buddhanandi) ——— **Hukudami'ta Sonja** (Buddhamitra)

Kyo Sonja (Parsva) ——— **Hunayasha Sonja** (Punyayasas) ——— **Memyo Sonja** (Asvaghosa) ——— **Kabimora Sonja** (Kapimala)

Ryujyu Sonja (Nagarjuna) ——— **Kanadaiba Sonja** (Kanadeva) ——— **Ragorata Sonja** (Rahulata) ——— **Sogyanandai Sonja** (Sanghanandi)

Kayashata Sonja (Gayasata) ——— **Kumorata Sonja** (Kumarata) ——— **Shayata Sonja** (Jayata) ——— **Basubanzu Sonja** (Vasubandhu)

Manura Sonja (Manorhita) ——— **Kakurokuna Sonja** (Haklenayasas) ——— **Shishi Sonja** (Simha Bhiksu) ——— **Bashashita Sonja** (Basiasita)

Funyomi'ta Sonja (Punyamitra) ——— **Hannyatara Sonja** (Parajnatara)

Bodai Daruma Daishi (Pu-ti-ta-mo)

Niso-ji ——— **Dofuku** ——— **Niso Eka (Hui-ko)** ——— **Doiku** ——— **Donrin**

Sona ——— **Sanso Kanchi** ——— **E'man**

Doshin Daii (Tao-hsin) (580-651) ——— **Dosho**

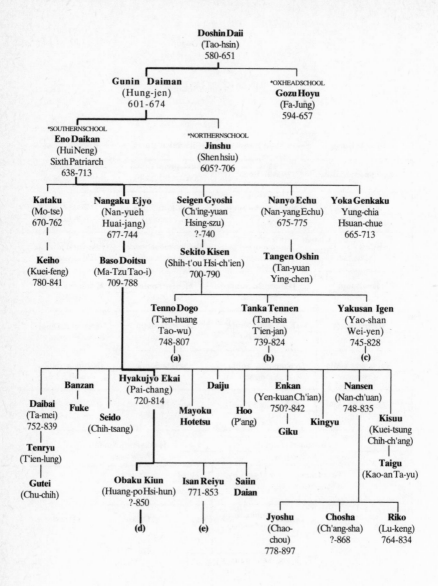

Doshin Daii
(Tao-hsin)
580-651

Gunin Daiman
(Hung-jen)
601-674

*OXHEADSCHOOL
Gozu Hoyu
(Fa-Jung)
594-657

*SOUTHERNSCHOOL
Eno Daikan
(Hui Neng)
Sixth Patriarch
638-713

*NORTHERNSCHOOL
Jinshu
(Shen hsiu)
605?-706

Kataku
(Mo-tse)
670-762

Nangaku Ejyo
(Nan-yueh
Huai-jang)
677-744

Seigen Gyoshi
(Ch'ing-yuan
Hsing-szu)
?-740

Nanyo Echu
(Nan-yang Echu)
675-775

Yoka Genkaku
Yung-chia
Hsuan-chue
665-713

Keiho
(Kuei-feng)
780-841

Baso Doitsu
(Ma-Tzu Tao-i)
709-788

Sekito Kisen
(Shih-t'ou Hsi-ch'ien)
700-790

Tangen Oshin
(Tan-yuan
Ying-chen)

Tenno Dogo
(T'ien-huang
Tao-wu)
748-807
(a)

Tanka Tennen
(Tan-hsia
T'ien-jan)
739-824
(b)

Yakusan Igen
(Yao-shan
Wei-yen)
745-828
(c)

Daibai
(Ta-mei)
752-839

Banzan

Fuke

Seido
(Chih-tsang)

Hyakujyo Ekai
(Pai-chang)
720-814

Daiju

**Mayoku
Hotetsu**

Hoo
(P'ang)

Enkan
(Yen-kuan Ch'ian)
750?-842

Giku

Kingyu

Nansen
(Nan-ch'uan)
748-835

Kisuu
(Kuei-tsung
Chih-ch'ang)

Tenryu
(T'ien-lung)

Taigu
(Kao-an Ta-yu)

Gutei
(Chu-chih)

Obaku Kiun
(Huang-po Hsi-hun)
?-850
(d)

Isan Reiyu
771-853
(e)

**Saiin
Daian**

Jyoshu
(Chao-
chou)
778-897

Chosha
(Ch'ang-sha)
?-868

Riko
(Lu-keng)
764-834

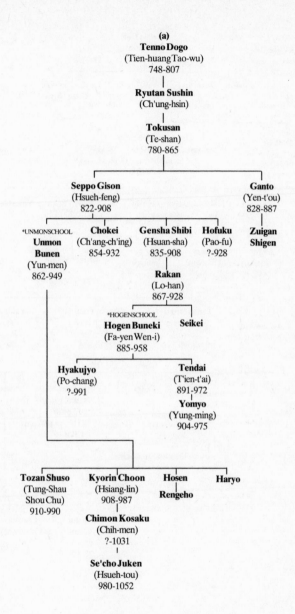

(a)
Tenno Dogo
(Tien-huang Tao-wu)
748-807

Ryutan Sushin
(Ch'ung-hsin)

Tokusan
(Te-shan)
780-865

Seppo Gison
(Hsueh-feng)
822-908

Ganto
(Yen-t'ou)
828-887

*UNMON SCHOOL
Unmon Bunen
(Yun-men)
862-949

Chokei
(Ch'ang-ch'ing)
854-932

Gensha Shibi
(Hsuan-sha)
835-908

Hofuku
(Pao-fu)
?-928

Zuigan Shigen

Rakan
(Lo-han)
867-928

*HOGEN SCHOOL
Hogen Buneki
(Fa-yen Wen-i)
885-958

Seikei

Hyakujyo
(Po-chang)
?-991

Tendai
(T'ien-t'ai)
891-972

Yomyo
(Yung-ming)
904-975

Tozan Shuso
(Tung-Shau Shou Chu)
910-990

Kyorin Choon
(Hsiang-lin)
908-987

Hosen

Rengeho

Haryo

Chimon Kosaku
(Chih-men)
?-1031

Se'cho Juken
(Hsueh-tou)
980-1052

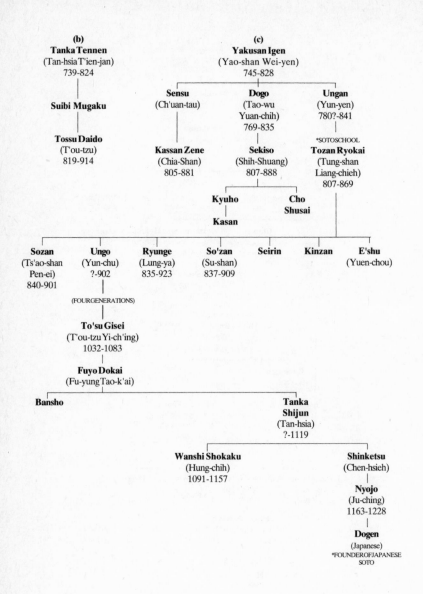

(b)
Tanka Tennen
(Tan-hsia T'ien-jan)
739-824

Suibi Mugaku

Tossu Daido
(T'ou-tzu)
819-914

(c)
Yakusan Igen
(Yao-shan Wei-yen)
745-828

Sensu
(Ch'uan-tau)

Kassan Zene
(Chia-Shan)
805-881

Dogo
(Tao-wu
Yuan-chih)
769-835

Sekiso
(Shih-Shuang)
807-888

Ungan
(Yun-yen)
780?-841

*SOTO SCHOOL
Tozan Ryokai
(Tung-shan
Liang-chieh)
807-869

Kyuho

Kasan

**Cho
Shusai**

Sozan
(Ts'ao-shan
Pen-ei)
840-901

Ungo
(Yun-chu)
?-902

Ryunge
(Lung-ya)
835-923

So'zan
(Su-shan)
837-909

Seirin

Kinzan

E'shu
(Yuen-chou)

(FOUR GENERATIONS)

To'su Gisei
(T'ou-tzu Yi-ch'ing)
1032-1083

Fuyo Dokai
(Fu-yung Tao-k'ai)

Bansho

**Tanka
Shijun**
(Tan-hsia)
?-1119

Wanshi Shokaku
(Hung-chih)
1091-1157

Shinketsu
(Chen-hsieh)

Nyojo
(Ju-ching)
1163-1228

Dogen
(Japanese)
*FOUNDER OF JAPANESE
SOTO

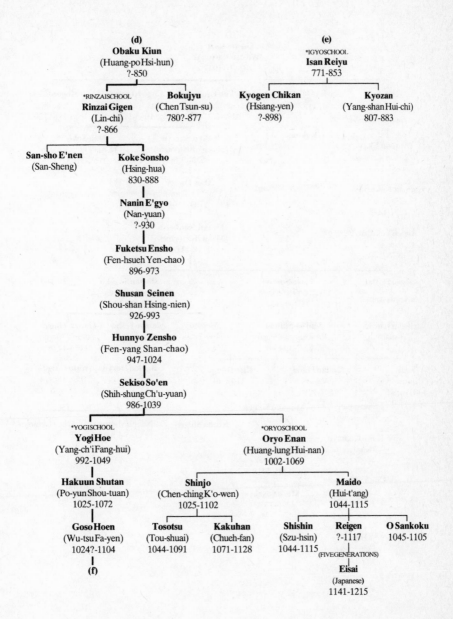

(d)
Obaku Kiun
(Huang-po Hsi-hun)
?-850

*RINZAI SCHOOL.
Rinzai Gigen
(Lin-chi)
?-866

Bokujyu
(Chen Tsun-su)
780?-877

(e)
*IGYO SCHOOL.
Isan Reiyu
771-853

Kyogen Chikan
(Hsiang-yen)
?-898)

Kyozan
(Yang-shan Hui-chi)
807-883

San-sho E'nen
(San-Sheng)

Koke Sonsho
(Hsing-hua)
830-888

Nanin E'gyo
(Nan-yuan)
?-930

Fuketsu Ensho
(Fen-hsueh Yen-chao)
896-973

Shusan Seinen
(Shou-shan Hsing-nien)
926-993

Hunnyo Zensho
(Fen-yang Shan-chao)
947-1024

Sekiso So'en
(Shih-shung Ch'u-yuan)
986-1039

*YOGI SCHOOL
Yogi Hoe
(Yang-ch'i Fang-hui)
992-1049

Hakuun Shutan
(Po-yun Shou-tuan)
1025-1072

Goso Hoen
(Wu-tsu Fa-yen)
1024?-1104

(f)

*ORYO SCHOOL
Oryo Enan
(Huang-lung Hui-nan)
1002-1069

Shinjo
(Chen-ching K'o-wen)
1025-1102

Tosotsu
(Tou-shuai)
1044-1091

Kakuhan
(Chueh-fan)
1071-1128

Maido
(Hui-t'ang)
1044-1115

Shishin
(Szu-hsin)
1044-1115

Reigen
?-1117
(FIVE GENERATIONS)

O Sankoku
1045-1105

Eisai
(Japanese)
1141-1215

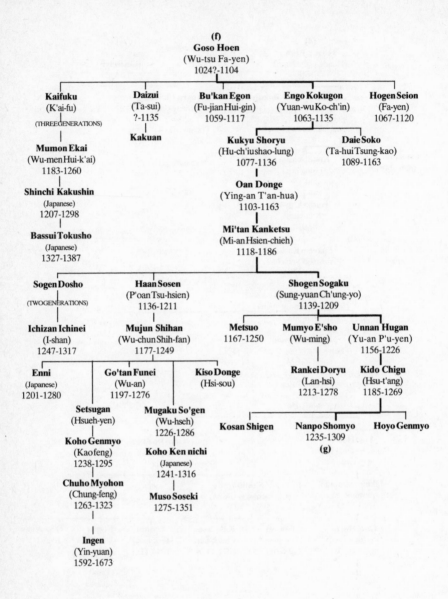

(f)
Goso Hoen
(Wu-tsu Fa-yen)
1024?-1104

Kaifuku
(K'ai-fu)
(THREE GENERATIONS)

Mumon Ekai
(Wu-men Hui-k'ai)
1183-1260

Shinchi Kakushin
(Japanese)
1207-1298

Bassui Tokusho
(Japanese)
1327-1387

Daizui
(Ta-sui)
?-1135

Kakuan

Bu'kan Egon
(Fu-jian Hui-gin)
1059-1117

Engo Kokugon
(Yuan-wu Ko-ch'in)
1063-1135

Hogen Seion
(Fa-yen)
1067-1120

Kukyu Shoryu
(Hu-ch'iu shao-lung)
1077-1136

Daie Soko
(Ta-hui Tsung-kao)
1089-1163

Oan Donge
(Ying-an T'an-hua)
1103-1163

Mi'tan Kanketsu
(Mi-an Hsien-chieh)
1118-1186

Sogen Dosho
(TWO GENERATIONS)

Ichizan Ichinei
(I-shan)
1247-1317

Haan Sosen
(P'oan Tsu-hsien)
1136-1211

Mujun Shihan
(Wu-chun Shih-fan)
1177-1249

Shogen Sogaku
(Sung-yuan Ch'ung-yo)
1139-1209

Metsuo
1167-1250

Mumyo E'sho
(Wu-ming)

Unnan Hugan
(Yu-an P'u-yen)
1156-1226

Enni
(Japanese)
1201-1280

Go'tan Funei
(Wu-an)
1197-1276

Kiso Donge
(Hsi-sou)

Rankei Doryu
(Lan-hsi)
1213-1278

Kido Chigu
(Hsu-t'ang)
1185-1269

Setsugan
(Hsueh-yen)

Koho Genmyo
(Kao feng)
1238-1295

Chuho Myohon
(Chung-feng)
1263-1323

Mugaku So'gen
(Wu-hseh)
1226-1286

Koho Ken nichi
(Japanese)
1241-1316

Muso Soseki
1275-1351

Kosan Shigen

Nanpo Shomyo
1235-1309
(g)

Hoyo Genmyo

Ingen
(Yin-yuan)
1592-1673

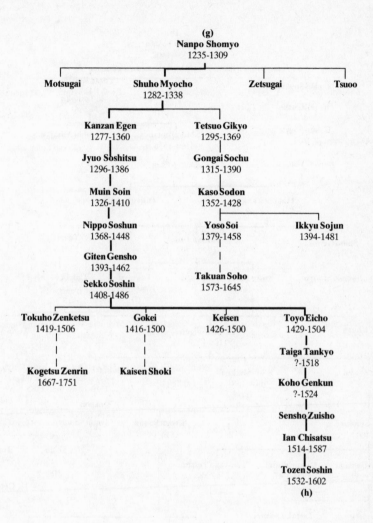

(g)
Nanpo Shomyo
1235-1309

Motsugai   **Shuho Myocho**   **Zetsugai**   **Tsuoo**
1282-1338

Kanzan Egen   **Tetsuo Gikyo**
1277-1360   1295-1369

Jyuo Soshitsu   **Gongai Sochu**
1296-1386   1315-1390

Muin Soin   **Kaso Sodon**
1326-1410   1352-1428

Nippo Soshun   **Yoso Soi**   **Ikkyu Sojun**
1368-1448   1379-1458   1394-1481

Giten Gensho
1393-1462

Sekko Soshin   **Takuan Soho**
1408-1486   1573-1645

Tokuho Zenketsu   **Gokei**   **Keisen**   **Toyo Eicho**
1419-1506   1416-1500   1426-1500   1429-1504

Taiga Tankyo
?-1518

Kogetsu Zenrin   **Kaisen Shoki**   **Koho Genkun**
1667-1751   ?-1524

Sensho Zuisho

Ian Chisatsu
1514-1587

Tozen Soshin
1532-1602
(h)

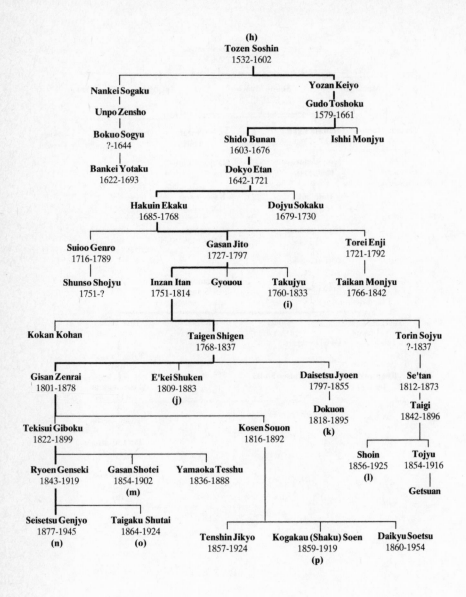

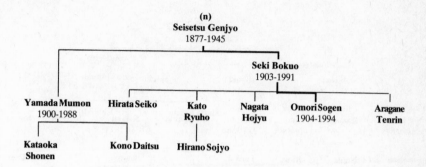

(n)
Seisetsu Genjyo
1877-1945

Seki Bokuo
1903-1991

Yamada Mumon
1900-1988

Hirata Seiko

Kato Ryuho

Nagata Hojyu

Omori Sogen
1904-1994

Aragane Tenrin

Kataoka Shonen

Kono Daitsu

Hirano Sojyo

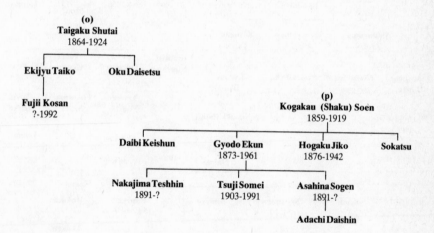

(o)
Taigaku Shutai
1864-1924

Ekijyu Taiko

Oku Daisetsu

Fujii Kosan
?-1992

(p)
Kogakau (Shaku) Soen
1859-1919

Daibi Keishun

Gyodo Ekun
1873-1961

Hogaku Jiko
1876-1942

Sokatsu

Nakajima Teshhin
1891-?

Tsuji Somei
1903-1991

Asahina Sogen
1891-?

Adachi Daishin

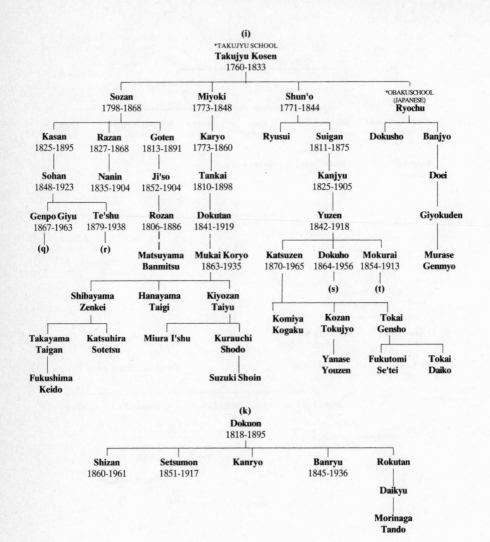

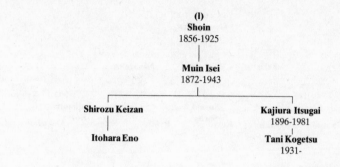

(l)
Shoin
1856-1925

Muin Isei
1872-1943

Shirozu Keizan

Itohara Eno

Kajiura Itsugai
1896-1981

Tani Kogetsu
1931-

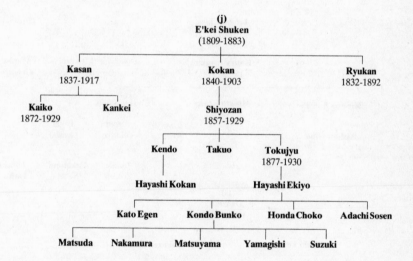

(j)
E'kei Shuken
(1809-1883)

Kasan
1837-1917

Kokan
1840-1903

Ryukan
1832-1892

Kaiko
1872-1929

Kankei

Shiyozan
1857-1929

Kendo   **Takuo**   **Tokujyu**
1877-1930

Hayashi Kokan   **Hayashi Ekiyo**

Kato Egen   **Kondo Bunko**   **Honda Choko**   **Adachi Sosen**

Matsuda   **Nakamura**   **Matsuyama**   **Yamagishi**   **Suzuki**

(q)
Genpo Giyu
1867-1963

Sokaku

Nakagawa
Soen

Suzuki
Sochu

Fujimori
Kozen

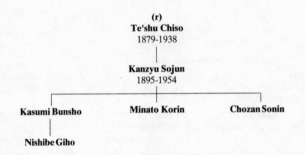

(r)
Te'shu Chiso
1879-1938

Kanzyu Sojun
1895-1954

Kasumi Bunsho

Minato Korin

Chozan Sonin

Nishibe Giho

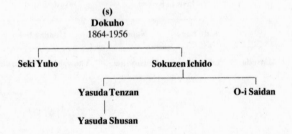

(s)
Dokuho
1864-1956

Seki Yuho

Sokuzen Ichido

Yasuda Tenzan

O-i Saidan

Yasuda Shusan

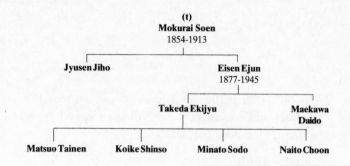

(t)
Mokurai Soen
1854-1913

Jyusen Jiho

Eisen Ejun
1877-1945

Takeda Ekijyu

Maekawa Daido

Matsuo Tainen   Koike Shinso   Minato Sodo   Naito Choon

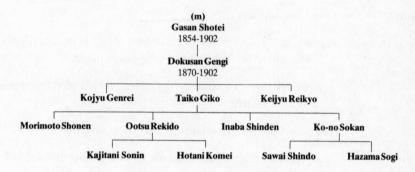

(m)
Gasan Shotei
1854-1902

Dokusan Gengi
1870-1902

Kojyu Genrei   Taiko Giko   Keijyu Reikyo

Morimoto Shonen   Ootsu Rekido   Inaba Shinden   Ko-no Sokan

Kajitani Sonin   Hotani Komei   Sawai Shindo   Hazama Sogi

Glossary

Bodhidharma	470–543. (Skt.) (Jpn., Bodaidaruma or Daruma) The first patriarch of Chinese Zen. According to legend, he was a red-bearded, blue-eyed barbarian.
dharma	Ultimate Truth.
dhyana	(Skt.) Meditation.
dojo	A place in which one of the Japanese Ways is practiced; also a *Zendo* where formal Zen training takes place.
go	A Japanese game of strategy that uses black and white stones on a square board.
hara	The word physically relates to the lower abdomen.
Hojo	A patterned series of movements from a traditional school of swordsmanship.
inkin	Small metal bell.
jikijitsu	The leader in charge of the meditation hall during zazen.
Jizo	A small statue of a bodhisattva who vowed to deliver all people from suffering before entering nirvana himself.
joriki	Physical/spiritual energy generated by strong concentration.
judo	A Japanese martial art.
kan	True intuitive seeing or perception.
karma	(Skt.) The consequence of a mental or physical action; the sum of all consequences of the actions of an individual in this or some previous life; the chain of cause and effect in the world of morality.
kendo	Literally "The Way of the Sword"; Japanese swordsmanship.

kensho	Seeing one's true self-nature, or enlightenment.
ki	Intrinsic energy.
kiai	Concentrated spiritual energy.
kinhin	Walking meditation.
koan	Zen training method based on incidents or cases in which the Buddhist patriarchs attained enlightenment, providing an opportunity for questions and answers between teacher and student.
koshi	Lower back.
ku	(Skt. Shunyata) Emptiness.
kufu	Working with intense concentration.
majime	Seriousness, straightforwardness, honesty, and truthfulness.
makyo	Phenomena, ranging from visual hallucinations or sleepiness to boredom, which sometimes occur during meditation.
mu	Nothingness.
nembutsu	Repetition of Amida Buddha's name.
nirvana	(Skt.) literally, extinction, the state of perfect liberation.
prajna	(Skt.) Transcendental Wisdom.
rohatsu sesshin	The intense training period held in commemoration of the training that led to Shakyamuni's enlightenment on the eighth of December.
samadhi	A state of complete concentration and relaxation.
sanzen	Personal interview where the student presents his Master with an account of his realization in terms of his koan.
satori	Seeing one's true self-nature, enlightenment.
sesshin	Literally "Collecting the Mind"; several days of intensive, strict practice of zazen as carried out in Zen Monasteries at regular intervals.

Shakyamuni   (Skt.) literally "Sage of the Shakya Clan," the founder of Buddhism.

shikan   Perception in concentration.

shikantaza   "Just sitting," a form of the practice of zazen; this term is used frequently in Soto Zen.

soku   Breath; also a particular method of breathing in and out with out any break in between.

susoku   Counting the cycles of respiration.

sutra   Discourses from the Buddhas in prose text.

suwaru   To sit; to be settled and unmoving; well suited.

tanden   The point of strength in the lower abdomen, the center of tension; traditionally said to be two-and-a-half or three inches below the navel.

teisho   A Zen Master's lecture on a classic text by one of the great Zen Masters to demonstrate the ultimate meaning of the Zen teachings.

zabuton   Cushion used for zazen; a zabu is a smaller pillow used to help position the hips on the zabuton.

zazen   Zen meditation.

zenjo   The power of concentration attained in samadhi.

Index